# Contributions to Management Science

The series *Contributions to Management Science* contains research publications in all fields of business and management science. These publications are primarily monographs and multiple author works containing new research results, and also feature selected conference-based publications are also considered. The focus of the series lies in presenting the development of latest theoretical and empirical research across different viewpoints.

This book series is indexed in Scopus.

Rossen Kazakov • Penka Petrova
Yavora Kazakova

# Understanding and Managing Socioeconomic Systems Behaviour

## Applications of Qualitative and Quantitative System Dynamics and Agent-Based Modelling in Healthcare and Pharmaceuticals, Finance, Arts and Culture, Sociology and Education Systems

Springer

Rossen Kazakov
Edinburgh Business School
Heriot Watt University
Edinburgh, UK

Penka Petrova
Strateggo Ltd
Sofia, Bulgaria

Yavora Kazakova
Scenario Simulation Laboratory
Sofia, Bulgaria

ISSN 1431-1941 ISSN 2197-716X (electronic)
Contributions to Management Science
ISBN 978-3-031-57056-8 ISBN 978-3-031-57057-5 (eBook)
https://doi.org/10.1007/978-3-031-57057-5



This Springer imprint is published by the registered company Springer Nature Switzerland AG
The registered company address is: Gewerbestrasse 11, 6330 Cham, Switzerland

# Contents

# About the Authors

**Rossen Kazakov** is a Management Science expert with more than ten years of experience in qualitative and quantitative system dynamics and agent-based simulation modelling, affiliated at present with the Edinburgh Business School, Heriot Watt University, UK, where he continues to develop scenario simulators for exploring global socioeconomic issues. He has worked on consulting and research projects in healthcare and pharmaceuticals, agrifood value chains, sustainability transitions and sustainable development goals across EU countries, the UK and Australia. Rossen is a member of the System Dynamics Society (including various society groups), UK OR Society and the EURO Society group on OR and Ethics for Public Good, and he participates frequently in their conferences as a paper author and working groups member.

**Penka Petrova** is a Finance, Law and System Dynamics expert, experienced in practical system dynamics applications in finance and economics, in risk management and in business intelligence and data analytics. She has worked in the last ten years in consulting and research projects at Strateggo in the fields of finance, economics and sustainable development and is a recipient of the EURO Award in OR and Ethics. Penka is a member of the Switzerland Society of Operational Research (SVOR), EURO Society group on Ethics and Public Good and the System Dynamics Society (including groups on Psychology, Education and Economics).

**Yavora Kazakova** is a Researcher at Scenariosim.eu in the areas of psychology and society, sociology, arts and culture, marketing and consumer behaviour and in sustainable development goals, applying systems approaches to solving societal issues. She specializes in cognitive and behavioural psychology, neuroscience and neuromarketing, people and data analytics, leadership effectiveness and environmental, social and governance (ESG) perspectives and systems research applications. Yavora is a member of the System Dynamics Society, including groups on Psychology, Education and Sustainable Development, and the EURO Society group on Ethics and Public Good and participates in their annual conferences, in working groups meetings and as a conference paper author.

# Chapter 1
# Socio-Economic Systems as Complex Adaptive Systems

**Abstract** This chapter provides an introduction to the theoretical lenses and methodological framework applied consistently throughout the practical examples included in the book, centred around the key concepts of resources and agents, and modelling and simulation of their interactions.

This approach is supported by the resource-dependence theory and resource-based theory, the behavioural decision theory and the anticipatory systems theory, and by qualitative and quantitative system dynamics and agent-based modelling and simulation apparatus.

Also, the chapter highlights the key complex adaptive features of the socioeconomic systems and gives an overview of their characteristics within the context of important spheres of society like healthcare and pharmaceuticals, financial markets, art, culture and sociology, public education and social networks.

## 1.1 Introduction

The aim of this research is to apply multimethodological approach in qualitative and quantitative modelling and simulation for the exploration and understanding of the behaviour of socio-economic systems through designing an interactive modelling and simulation learning environment by applying a multimethodology (Mingers, 2001; Howick & Ackermann, 2011; Kazakov & Kunc, 2016; Kazakov et al., 2021) approach integrating system dynamics (SD) and agent-based (AB) qualitative and quantitative modelling and simulation in one framework.

A hybrid SD and AB modelling and simulation approach is capable of revealing socio-economic systems dynamics and their hidden dialectical interrelations, coming out of resources and agents complex adaptive behaviour. This approach can help for the exploration of what-if scenarios and their effects on agents competitive and adaptive behaviour for available resources and supply and demand dynamics in socio-economic systems. Socio-economic systems are



R. Kazakov et al., *Understanding and Managing Socioeconomic Systems Behaviour*, Contributions to Management Science,
https://doi.org/10.1007/978-3-031-57057-5_1

complex adaptive systems that are characterized by the interactions and feedback loops between different resources and agents, as well as the institutions and rules that govern their behaviour (Holland, 2006; Buckley, 2017). In a socio-economic system, agents can be individuals, organizations, or even countries, and they are typically heterogeneous in their goals, beliefs, and behaviours. These agents interact with each other in various ways, such as through trade, competition, cooperation, or conflict, and their interactions can give rise to emergent patterns of behaviour and outcomes that cannot be easily predicted from the individual actions of each agent.

Moreover, socio-economic systems are also influenced by the institutional and organizational resources and normative frameworks that shape the behaviour of agents, such as natural resources, production resources, financial resources and information resources, laws, regulations, cultural norms, and social expectations. These factors can create flows and feedback loops that reinforce or modify the behaviour of agents and the level of resources, as well as enable or constrain the emergence of new patterns of behaviour and outcomes.

The complex adaptive systems perspective emphasizes the dynamic and emergent nature of socio-economic systems, as well as the interplay between agents and resources, and interrelated feedback loops in shaping their behaviour and outcomes.

In their book 'Complex Adaptive Systems: An Introduction to Computational Models of Social Life', Miller and Page (2009) provide a comprehensive overview of the complex adaptive systems perspective in the social sciences, including the study of socio-economic systems. It covers various topics, such as agent-based modelling, emergence, path dependence, and evolutionary dynamics, and applies them to a wide range of social phenomena, from markets and organizations to culture and politics.

Colander and Kupers (2014) also talk about complexity science, which is made possible by modern analytical and computational science. These methods are changing the way we think about social systems and social theory. Traditional economists' policy models have not kept up and are stuck in either a market liberalist or government control perspective. A more flexible policy approach is needed, which envisions society as a complex evolving system that can be influenced.

Another approach to understanding complex socio-economic systems is to explore their networks characteristics (Jackson, 2010). Here the focus is on exploring the coevolution of social and economic networks, and how they influence each other in a complex adaptive system. Humans are fundamentally a social species with interaction patterns that shape their behaviours. The full network of relationships affects how information spreads and how people behave. Using complex systems simulation modelling approach can also help understanding networks and socio-economic behaviour.

The literature on socio-economic systems as complex adaptive systems is vast and multidisciplinary, drawing on insights from economics, sociology, political science, and other fields.

## 1.2 Theoretical Perspectives

This book provides a novel view for an integrative SD and AB modelling framework, which is centred around the key concepts of resources and agents, and is supported by the theoretical perspectives of resource-dependence theory and resource-based view, behavioural decision theory, and anticipatory systems theory.

The attempt to bring together in a unified theoretical prism, theories related to SD and AB modelling and simulation follows the idea that 'alternative theoretical frameworks to provide practical guidance for multimethodology design need to be investigated' (Mingers & Brocklesby, 1997). This idea is relevant to the challenge of 'borrowing and developing theory to further our understanding of problem structuring practice' (Ackermann et al., 2014), and the challenge of 'developing effective procedure for mixing methods' (Ackermann et al., 2014; Howick & Ackermann, 2011).

Research has been recently developed in the direction of the above challenges (Ackermann et al., 2014) but in relation to the integration of SD and AB modelling there has not been any advancement in developing a common unified theoretical frame behind the practice of the hybridization of both methodological approaches, capable to inform a generalized procedure for their effective mixing and integration.

Howick and Ackermann (2011) also have identified the need for a good conceptual perspective and good theory supporting the practice of mixing OR methods by stating a need for '...development of conceptual frameworks and ultimately theory—ensuring that Lewin's (1946) view that "there is nothing as practical as good theory" can be applied to the combination of different OR methodological frameworks' (Bargal, 2006; Connelly, 2003).

The novel view for a joint SD and AB modelling conceptual framework is proposed to be conceptualized through the perspectives of the resource dependence theory (RDT) and the resource-based theory (RBT) (Pfeffer & Salancik, 1978; Hillman et al., 2009; Wernerfeldt, 1984; Barney, 1991; Peteraf, 1993), the behavioural decision theory (BDT) (Kahneman, 2003; Kahneman & Tversky, 1979), and the anticipatory systems theory (AST) (Butz et al., 2007; Pezzulo, 2008; Rosen, 1985; Louie, 2010).

Each of the above theoretical perspectives provides different knowledge and explanations of socioeconomic phenomena and integrating them provides a more holistic view for critically exploring and interpreting market resource and agent interrelated behaviour. Conceptualizing complex adaptive socio-economic systems as emerging out of agents' heuristic rules and forward-looking behaviour, competing for limited resources within an imperfect environment, would further complement the general systems and complex adaptive systems theoretical frameworks, underpinning the practical integration of SD and AB modelling approaches.

The resource-based theory and the resource dependance theory are combined together to enhance the appreciation of resources within the system dynamics modelling and simulation approach. The behavioural decision theory and the anticipatory systems theory are combined to enhance the decision-making perspective within the agent-based modelling and simulation. Applied together they form the theoretical framework, supporting the combination and application of the above two distinctive methods.

## 1.3 Healthcare and Pharmaceutical Systems

Healthcare and pharmaceutical markets are composed of multiple interdependent resources and agents who adapt their behaviours in response to one another and to changing external conditions. In this perspective, the resources of the healthcare and pharmaceutical markets include physical and human resources (such as medicines, medical equipment, and personnel), financial resources (such as funding for research and development and healthcare services), and informational resources (such as medical research, drug-related data, market data, and patient data). The agents in these markets include healthcare providers, pharmaceutical companies, regulators, doctors and pharmacists, patients, and other stakeholders.

Some of the key interactions between these resources and agents in healthcare and pharmaceutical markets include pharmaceutical companies, which invest in research and development for new drugs and therapies, often relying on public funding and partnerships with academic and research institutions. This process is influenced by the availability of financial resources, as well as by regulatory requirements and patient demand.

On the other side, regulators play a key role in the pharmaceutical market by evaluating new drugs for safety and efficacy, and determining whether they should be approved for use. This process can be influenced by a range of factors, including public health considerations, financial pressures, and lobbying efforts from pharmaceutical companies. In parallel, healthcare providers must manage complex supply chains to ensure that drugs, medical devices, and other resources are available to patients when they are needed. This process can be influenced by factors such as pricing, availability of resources, and regulatory requirements.

The healthcare market is also shaped by issues of patient access and equity, with many stakeholders advocating for increased access to healthcare resources and more equitable distribution of these resources across different populations. This can be influenced by a range of factors, including public policy, regulatory requirements, and market forces. Technological resources also play an important role, leading to the development of new therapies and treatment services. These resources are influenced by market demand and regulatory requirements.

A complex adaptive systems perspective highlights the interconnectedness of resources and agents in healthcare and pharmaceutical markets, and emphasizes the importance of understanding how these interactions shape market outcomes and influence the delivery of healthcare services.

## 1.4 Financial Systems

Financial systems can also be explored as complex adaptive systems consisting of resources and agents, where the resources include money, capital, and other financial assets, and the agents include individuals, investors, banks, and other financial institutions. The interactions and feedback loops between these resources and agents can give rise to emergent patterns of behaviour and outcomes that cannot be easily predicted from the individual actions of each agent.

In a financial system, agents can have heterogeneous goals, beliefs, and behaviours, and they can interact with each other in various ways, such as through lending and borrowing, trading, investing, or hedging. These interactions can create feedback loops that reinforce or modify the behaviour of agents and the level of available resources, as well as enable or constrain the emergence of new patterns of behaviour and outcomes. Financial systems are also influenced by institutional and normative frameworks that frame the behaviour of agents, such as laws, regulations, norms, and expectations.

A complex adaptive systems perspective emphasizes the dynamic and emergent nature of financial systems, as well as the interplay between resources, agents, and feedback loops. Some of the key features of financial systems that can be analyzed from this perspective include self-organization, nonlinearity, path dependence, adaptation, and resilience. Financial systems can self-organize through the interactions and feedback loops between agents and resources. They can exhibit nonlinear behaviour, where small changes in one part of the system can lead to large and unexpected changes in other parts of the system. Financial systems can exhibit path dependence, where the history of the system can influence its future behaviour and outcomes, through the creation of feedback loops and the accumulation of institutional and normative factors. In the same time, these systems can adapt to changing conditions and environments, through the evolution of agents' behaviours, the creation of new institutions and norms, and the emergence of new patterns of behaviour. Financial systems can also exhibit resilience, where they are able to withstand and recover from shocks and disturbances, through the creation of redundancies, diversification, and other risk management strategies.

A complex adaptive systems perspective for analyzing financial systems can help inform policy decisions and improve our understanding of the behaviour and outcomes of these systems.

## 1.5 Education Systems and Social Networks Systems

Public education systems can also be viewed as complex adaptive systems consisting of resources and agents. In this context, resources include public financing, educational materials, facilities, curriculum, and technologies that support teaching and learning, while agents include students, teachers, administrators, parents, and policymakers that participate in the educational process.

The same principle of interactions and feedback loops between resources and agents applies here too. Because of these interactions, various patterns of behaviour and outcomes can emerge influenced by internal and external socio-economic and policy factors, which can enable, constrain, reinforce, or modify the behaviour of agents.

In a public education system, agents can have heterogeneous goals, preferences, and behaviours, and they can interact with each other in various ways, such as through instruction, assessment, feedback, and support. Some of the key features of public education systems that can be analyzed from this perspective include diversity, co-evolution and change, diffusion, and adaptation.

Diversity is related to multiple and heterogeneous sources of knowledge, skills, and social and individual values, which can interact and compete with each other. Co-evolution happens where the production, use, and transmission of educational resources can influence the evolution of agents' knowledge, skills, and values, as well as the emergence of new educational methods and perspectives. Public education systems can exhibit educational change, where the historical, social, and institutional factors that shape these systems can change over time, leading to the emergence of new educational resources, goals, and policies. Educational resources, goals, and policies can diffuse and spread across geographic, social, and institutional boundaries, through various forms of communication, migration, and exchange, for example, online learning and social networks. At the same time agents and resources adapt to changing educational conditions and environments.

## 1.6 Art, Culture, and Ideological Systems

Using the same lenses, art, cultural, and ideological systems can be interpreted as being complex adaptive socio-economic systems, consisting of resources and agents, interacting among each other. In this context, resources include artifacts, ideas, beliefs, values, and norms, while agents include individuals, groups, institutions, and organizations that create, hold, and propagate these ideas and beliefs.

In an ideological system, agents can have heterogeneous goals, beliefs, and behaviours, and they can interact with each other through communication, persuasion, socialization, and mobilization. These interactions can create feedback loops that reinforce or modify the behaviour of agents and the level of used resources. Examples for ideological systems can include political campaigns, referendums, public policy consultations, and others, which can influence public opinions and social groups behaviour.

Art- and culture-related systems consist of resources like art, literature, music, language, symbols, and other cultural artifacts that can propagate ideas and beliefs, while agents include individuals, groups, institutions, and organizations that produce and consume these artifacts. Art- and culture-related systems are influenced by social, economic, and institutional factors, and in turn they can also influence socio-economic and institutional environment. This can produce reinforcing or balancing effects, as well as enable or constrain the emergence and evolution of new art and culture structures and interrelations. In such systems, agents can have diverse goals and preferences and they can interact with each other and with available resources through production, consumption, appropriation, and opinion-making activities.

## References

Ackermann, F., Franco, L. A., Rouwette, E., & White, L. (2014). Special issue on problem structuring research and practice. *EURO Journal on Decision Processes, 2*(3–4), 165–172. https://doi.org/10.1007/s40070-014-0037-6

Bargal, D. (2006). Personal and intellectual influences leading to Lewin's paradigm of action research: Towards the 60th anniversary of Lewin's 'action research and minority problems' (1946). *Action Research, 4*(4), 367. https://doi.org/10.1177/1476750306070101

Barney, J. (1991). Firm resources and sustained competitive advantage. *Journal of Management, 17*(1), 99–120.

Buckley, W. (2017). Society as a complex adaptive system. In *Systems research for behavioral science: A sourcebook*. Routledge.

Butz, M. V., Sigaud, O., Pezzulo, G., & Baldassarre, G. (2007). Anticipations, brains, individual and social behavior: An introduction to anticipatory systems. In *Anticipatory behavior in adaptive learning systems: From psychological theories to artificial cognitive systems* (pp. 1–18). Springer. https://doi.org/10.1007/978-3-540-74262-3_1

Colander, D., & Kupers, R. (2014). Complexity and the art of public policy: Solving society's problems from the bottom up. In *Complexity and the art of public policy: Solving society's problems from the bottom up*. Springer. https://doi.org/10.1080/09538259.2015.1010767

Connelly, M. (2003). The Kurt Lewin model of change. *Change Management Model*.

Hillman, A. J., Withers, M. C., & Collins, B. J. (2009). Resource dependence theory: A review. *Journal of Management, 35*(6), 1404–1427. https://doi.org/10.1177/0149206309343469

Holland, J. H. (2006). Studying complex adaptive systems. *Journal of Systems Science and Complexity, 19*(1), 1–8. https://doi.org/10.1007/s11424-006-0001-z

Howick, S., & Ackermann, F. (2011). Mixing or methods in practice: Past, present and future directions. *European Journal of Operational Research, 215*(3), 503–511. https://doi.org/10.1016/j.ejor.2011.03.013

Jackson, M. O. (2010). Social and economic networks. *Social and Economic Networks*. https://doi.org/10.1093/acprof:oso/9780199591756.003.0019

Kahneman, D. (2003). A perspective on judgment and choice: Mapping bounded rationality. *American Psychologist., 58*(9), 697–720. https://doi.org/10.1037/0003-066X.58.9.697

Kahneman, D., & Tversky, A. (1979). Prospect theory: An analysis of decision under risk. *Econometrica, 47*(2), 263–292. https://doi.org/10.1111/j.1536-7150.2011.00774.x

Kazakov, R., & Kunc, M. (2016). Foreseeing the dynamics of strategy: An anticipatory systems perspective. *Systemic Practice and Action Research, 29*(1), 1–25. https://doi.org/10.1007/s11213-015-9349-0

Kazakov, R., Howick, S., & Morton, A. (2021). Managing complex adaptive systems: A resource/agent qualitative modelling perspective. *European Journal of Operational Research, 290*(1), 386. https://doi.org/10.1016/j.ejor.2020.08.007

Louie, A. H. (2010). Robert Rosen's anticipatory systems. *Foresight, 12*(3), 18–29. https://doi.org/10.1108/14636681011049848

Miller, J. H., & Page, S. E. (2009). Complex adaptive systems: An introduction to computational models of social life. In *Complex adaptive systems: An introduction to computational models of social life*. Princeton University Press. https://doi.org/10.1080/01488370802162558

Mingers, J. (2001). Combining IS research methods: Towards a pluralist methodology. *MIS Quarterly, 12*(3), 240–259. https://doi.org/10.1287/isre.12.3.240.9709

Mingers, J., & Brocklesby, J. (1997). Multimethodology: Towards theory and practice for mixing methodologies. *International Journal of Management Science, 25*(5), 489–509. https://doi.org/10.1016/S0305-0483(97)00018-2

Peteraf, M. (1993). The cornerstones of competitive advantage: A resource-based view. *Strategic Management Journal, 14*(April 1992), 179–191. https://doi.org/10.1017/CBO9781107415324.004

Pezzulo, G. (2008). Coordinating with the future: The anticipatory nature of representation. *Minds and Machines, 18*(2), 179–225. https://doi.org/10.1007/s11023-008-9095-5

Pfeffer, J., & Salancik, G. R. (1978). The external control of organizations: A resource dependence perspective. *Academy of Management Review, 4*(814). https://doi.org/10.5465/AMR.1979.4289039

Rosen, R. (1985). *Anticipatory systems: Philosophical, mathematical, and methodological foundations* (IFSR international series on systems science and engineering) (Vol. 1). Springer. https://doi.org/10.1080/03081079.2012.726322

Wernerfeldt, B. (1984). A resource-based view of the firm. *Strategic Management Journal (Pre-1986), 5*(2), 171.

# Chapter 2
# Theoretical Prism

**Abstract** This chapter provides a novel view for an integrative system dynamics (SD) and agent-based (AB) modelling framework, which is centred around the key concepts of resources and agents, and is supported by the theoretical perspectives of resource-dependence theory and resource-based view, behavioural decision theory, and anticipatory systems theory.

Each of the above theoretical perspectives provides different knowledge and explanations of socio-economic phenomena and integrating them provides a more holistic view for critically exploring and interpreting market resource and agent interrelated behaviour. Conceptualizing complex adaptive socio-economic systems as emerging out of agents' heuristic rules and forward-looking behaviour, competing for limited resources within an imperfect environment, would further complement the general systems and complex adaptive systems theoretical frameworks, underpinning the practical integration of SD and AB modelling approaches.

The resource-based theory (RBT) and the Resource dependance theory (RDT) are combined together to enhance the appreciation of resources within the system dynamics modelling and simulation approach. The behavioural decision theory and the anticipatory systems theory are combined to enhance the decision-making perspective within the agent-based modelling and simulation. Applied together they form the theoretical framework, supporting the combination and application of the above two distinctive methods.

## 2.1 System Dynamics Theoretical Enhancement

System dynamics (SD) practice developed following two key concepts of systems theory related to the feedback loops principle, and to the principle that system's stock structure drives system's behaviour.

Forrester (1961a, 1961b), Forrester et al. (1976) pioneered SD practice following two key concepts of systems theory related to the feedback loops principle, and to the principle that system's structure drives system's behaviour. A main view behind



R. Kazakov et al., *Understanding and Managing Socioeconomic Systems Behaviour*, Contributions to Management Science,
https://doi.org/10.1007/978-3-031-57057-5_2

the behaviour of complex dynamic systems identifies hidden endogeneity and feedback effects due to delay in time and bound rationality, leading to non-linear and often counterintuitive behaviour (Sterman, 2000, 2001; Morecroft, 2015). Hence, systems dynamics modelling practice tries to uncover the hidden mechanisms underlying the observed non-linear effects in the economic systems and as opposed to only treating their symptoms (Forrester, 1961a).

Main building blocks in SD modelling are stocks or resources (Richardson & Pugh, 1981; Forrester, 1961a; Wolstenholme, 1999; Sterman, 1991), flows and auxiliary variables. The more complex a model becomes the harder it is for the modeller to maintain accurate representation of the modelled environment and to manage the model behaviour and outcome adequacy to the issue under exploration.

Understanding the endogenous and exogenous characteristics of organizational and market complexity, being a source of causal ambiguity, emergent behaviour and self-organizational dynamics (Morel & Ramanujam, 1999) is well advanced by general systems theory (Von Bertalanffy, 1968; Andrew, 2003) and the system dynamics field of research (Forrester, 1961a, 1987, 1998; Radzicki & Sterman, 1994; Richardson & Pugh, 1981; Randers, 1980). Systems complexity comes from dynamic components and their non-linear interactions which cause emergent behaviour, the reasons for which are hardly obvious. The more complex interrelations are among the systems internal and external components, the more ambiguous are the causes of the system behaviour and its self-organizational dynamics.

## 2.2 The Resource-Based Theory (RBT)

The 'resource-based theory' (RBT) of the firm (Barney, 1991; Helfat & Peteraf, 2003; Peteraf, 1993; Wernerfeldt, 1984) focused its analyses on the internal or introvert perspective to posit that firms' performance differences are based on a certain set of internal capabilities or unique organizational assets (Dierickx & Cool, 1989), or resources which should lead to sustainable competitive advantage only if they are 'valuable, rare, imperfectly imitable, and non-substitutable' (Barney, 1991, pp. 105–111).

RBT also posits that firms can be conceptualized as bundles of resources, which are heterogeneously distributed across firms (Amit & Schoemaker, 1993; Pitelis, 2004) are dynamic and need to be managed by (Helfat, 2011; Helfat & Peteraf, 2003, 2015; Sirmon & Hitt, 2009) dynamic capabilities which align, coordinate, reconfigure, and renew the firms' resource base (Teece et al., 1997).

The RBT is recognized to fit the SD theory and practice (Gary et al., 2007) by the use of similar central concepts like resources, stocks, and accumulation. Also, the RBV has supported theoretically the application of resource maps (RM) qualitative modelling technique by the use of SD stock and flows, and causal loops analytical instrumentarium (Kunc & Morecroft, 2010).

## 2.3 Resource Dependence Theory (RDT)

The RBV gives an internalized resource management perspective to the competitive behaviour of the industrial organizations. However, an externalized perspective can bring further clarity and unity in relation to the conceptualization of market resources and how the organizations and market systems are dependent on them.

The external resource dependence perspective of RDT (Pfeffer & Salancik, 1978; Hillman et al., 2009) can complement the internal perspective of resource management of RBV and can further develop more round understanding of the intra- and inter-organizational resource structure in pharmaceutical market systems.

RDT views the organization as being open system, dependent on contextual contingencies in the external market and regulatory environment. External micro- and macroeconomic context influences organizational behaviour and a key goal of market agents would be reducing environmental uncertainty and dependence on valuable resources through control over vital resources (Ulrich & Barney, 1984) by reducing competitors' and institutions power over them, attempting to increase their own power over the others.

RDT can provide a vital knowledge frame of what are the resource depending forces of organizational behaviour on the market and how organizations take actions to manage external interdependencies in order to reduce uncertainty and interdependence on the larger socio-economic system including market regulation. Further to the above, integrating RDT with the resource-based view of the firm can provide a complementary focus on resources, and may offer new insights into the organizational resource depending behaviour, including controlling valuable, rare, nonsubstitutable, and limited resources from the external environment (Hillman et al., 2009). Learning from the RBV and RDT allows for a richer consideration of how organizations develop routine to control resource needs internally and externally.

In the above perspective, the authors have extended the RM by gaining broader insight from the RDT regarding the dependence of organizations on the limited resources in the socio-economic and regulatory environment and their competitive behaviour related to maintaining control over them. Since any market including the pharmaceutical one needs to be conceptualized as a structurally coupled complex adaptive system of agents and resources with imperfect information, internal firm perspective, explained by the RBV as well as external perspective, explained by the RDT would be needed for a more round and comprehensive application of the RM technique.

## 2.4 Agent-Based (AB) Modelling Theoretical Enhancement

AB modelling and simulation practice and applications are traditionally supported by CAS theory to explain agent behaviour. According to Axtell (2000) and Axtell et al. (2001), agent-based modelling compared to traditional approaches to modelling economic systems could be a more viable approach when there are reasons to think in terms of agents. For example, when the problem or the research question we need to explore is naturally represented by a large number of agents which decisions and behaviours which can be well-defined, exhibit adaptation and change, learning and engaging in dynamic strategic interactions, and relationships with other agents can have a spatial component to their behaviours and interactions. A very important feature of Axtell's AB modelling criteria is linked to the structure of the system which has endogenously emerging mechanisms governing its future evolution and is not dependent only on the past (Axtell et al., 1996).

Macal and North (2015) acknowledge that AB modelling could be linked to complex systems (Deffuant et al., 2000; Weisbuch, 2006) and complex adaptive systems (Kauffman, 1992, 1995, Holland, 1975, 1992) theory and exploration. They understand ABM as a set of 'ideas, techniques, and tools for implementing computational models of complex adaptive systems' with the aim to reveal origin of self-organization, emergent phenomenon, and adaptation (Macal & North, 2009, 2010).

The behavioural rules, emergence, and adaptation effect of agent behaviour are tightly connected with the theory of complex adaptive systems (CAS) which do not have a controlling centre and a fixed structure. Rather they are structurally coupled with their environment and exhibit a co-evolutionary emerging feature, that is, as the result of decentralized bottom-up decisions and behaviour of individual entities or agents over time (Guerrero et al., 2016; Macal, 2010; Macal et al., 2002), agents' decisions and behaviour 'shape and change the state and structure of the system and react to the dynamic changes in the system, which can potentially alter their decision rules' (Guerrero et al., 2016).

Agents have decision rules and autonomous actions, and interact with their environment forming non-linear and feedback effect (Axtell et al., 1996; Bonabeau, 2002; Phelan, 1999). Agents' decision rules which govern agents' behaviour are linked to a goal-oriented behaviour related to achieving a certain individual benefit, guided by the behavioural decision theory (BDT) principle of satisficing/criteria of accessibility, risk aversion, and anchoring and adjustment/rather than maximizing a utility function (Kahneman & Tversky, 1979) due to their bounded rationality, and incomplete knowledge (Fiori, 2009; Simon, 1972a; Jennings, 2000) and unequal distribution of information (Akerlof, 1970; Stiglitz, 2016). Interestingly, according to Phelan (1999) when agents coordinate their decisions to achieve common goals, a 'collective intelligence' phenomenon may emerge. According to Schieritz (2002) and Schieritz and Milling (2003) the building blocks of AB modelling are the individual agent, agent behavioural rule, inner- and intra-agent feedback connection, adaption of agent behaviour, inductive inference from individual agents' behaviour to system behaviour and discrete or continuous time frame. The agent pattern of behaviour or schema is 'a cognitive structure that determines what action the agent takes at time t, given its perception of the environment' (Anderson, 1999), and can change or evolve in order to adapt to the agent environment.

However, modelling agent behaviour routine or schema should account for the agent 'cognitive structure' and a relevant theory for the agent behavioural decision-making and cognition principles is needed. Behavioural decision and anticipation theory can enhance the practical understanding and explanation of agent behaviour and condition/action decision making.

## 2.5 Behaviour Decision Theory (BDT)

Behavioural decision theory (BDT) is a field of study that examines how people make decisions under conditions of uncertainty, and how psychological biases can influence the decision-making process. This literature review will summarize some of the key findings and theories in BDT.

One of the most influential theories in BDT is prospect theory, developed by psychologists Daniel Kahneman and Amos Tversky in the 1970s. Prospect theory posits that people do not evaluate outcomes in an objective or rational manner, but rather their decisions are influenced by subjective factors such as the reference point for the decision, the perceived likelihood of outcomes, and the emotional impact of gains and losses.

Simon (1972a, 1972b, 2007), Kahneman (2003a, 2003b), and Kahneman and Tversky (1979, 1982) can provide fruitful theoretical underpinning in support of AB modelling practice in a complex adaptive socio-economic paradigm. Market agents being they individual or organizational follow certain behavioural pattern informed by their cognition (perception of the environment) and decision making which are rationally bounded due to incomplete information and imperfect cognition.

People behave following heuristics principle in order to reduce judgement and choice complexity (Tversky & Kahneman, 1974) like the principle of 'availability', 'anchoring and adjustment', 'representativeness', 'loss aversion' (Kahneman & Tversky, 1979; Tversky & Kahneman, 1991). According to Simon, people tend to make decisions by 'satisficing' heuristic rather than optimizing a utility. Heuristics can also lead to cognitive biases. 'Recognition' is another heuristic which simplifies decision making and makes best use of the limited information available to individuals (Gigerenzer & Goldstein, 2011).

The BDT can inform the modelling of agents' decision making and their behaviour providing a scientific explanation of agents' decision and behavioural protocol. Socio-economic systems agents make decisions which are rule based and also follow heuristic principles rather than utility maximization. BDT can help a better and more realistic modelling of their behaviour including agents reactive or prospective activities.

## 2.6 Anticipatory Systems Theory

Anticipatory systems theory posits that 'anticipation is the process which enables a living system to contain a predictive model of itself and its environment. This allows it to adapt by changing its state in accordance with the model's predictions' (Louie, 2010; Rosen & Kineman, 2005; Rosen, 1978, 1985) and to base its course of actions on their anticipated effects. In cognitive science, anticipation is a core cognitive process responsible for the mental simulation of the would-be effects of human interaction with the external environment (Butz et al., 2007, 2008; Pezzulo, 2007, 2008; Pezzulo & Castelfranchi, 2009).

The cognitive process of anticipation is connected to building mental models of the external environment and simulating alternative actions and outcomes, where actions are triggered by the anticipated (mentally simulated) effect associated with their outcome (Pezzulo, 2008).

Butz and Pezzulo (2008) expand the definition of anticipatory systems with their ability to exhibit apart from 'sensory' anticipations, 'pay-off' anticipations, and 'state' anticipations. Pay-off anticipations are pertinent to systems that 'have knowledge of behaviourally dependent payoff and can base action selection on that representation', that is, 'different payoff may be predicted for alternative actions, which allows the selection of the current best action'. State anticipation is based on anticipatory processes which enhance behavioural decision making by future anticipatory representations of not only the goal but of the whole system.

In relation to drug pricing regulation, regulatory authorities apply pricing control policy anticipating that prices would become more affordable and that the public interest/return would be optimized. However, pharmaceutical companies anticipating the behaviour of the pricing regulators react proactively in order to optimize their private interest/return and apply international pricing strategies in order to offset any unwanted effect. Meyer and Szirbik (2007) stress the importance of state anticipation ability of organizations, which leads to emergent behaviour of the whole system 'as predictions about future states directly influence current behavioural decision making'.

Anticipatory systems perspective posits that agents and organizations build 'forward models' of themselves (Pezzulo, 2008), thus simulating different paths ahead with different outcomes. Applying an anticipatory theoretical perspective to mapping agent behaviour can complement the complexity and behavioural perspectives to agent decision-making analysis.

## 2.7 Application of the Resource Agent Conceptual Framework for the Analysis of Socio-Economic Complex Adaptive Systems

Figure 2.1 represents socio-economic complex systems through the resource agent theoretical framework described so far, which are considered as main components of a novel resource agent methodological framework. For example, healthcare and pharmaceutical markets (Marshall et al., 2015a, 2015b; Roberts, 2015) are complex adaptive socio-economic systems and agents and resources are key part of their complexity. All agents behave in parallel competing for control over firm and market resources in an adaptive manner, subject to a condition action rule pattern (Forrest & Mitchell, 2016) and heuristic protocol of decision making (Kahneman & Tversky, 1979; Koumakhov, 2009) following a forward-looking pay-off or state anticipation behaviour.

Agent and resource configurations produce feedback, nonlinearity, and emergent properties of the systems where information is imperfect and not equally available. Agents can adapt/alter their pattern of behaviour by deliberate action in order to fit to an observation or can take action to adapt an observation to their existing schema.

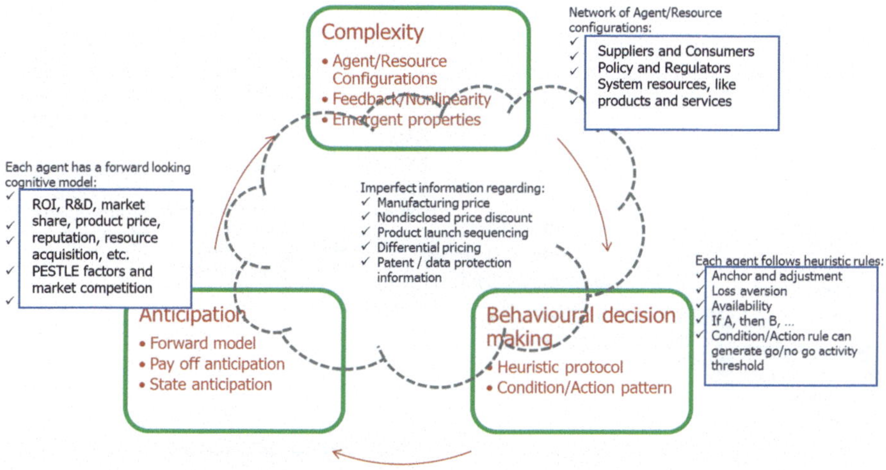


**Fig. 2.1** Agents competing for resources, and imperfect system information as main features of socio-economic complex adaptive systems (CAS)

Schema can change purposefully or randomly or by combination with other schema in order to adapt to the environment. Agents communicate/interact through exchanging information and or resources, which can have multiplier effects due to the interconnectedness in the system with flows that may be non-linear.

Resources and agent interactions form complex systemic behaviour emerging out of resource agent configurations with feedback and non-linear inter- and intra-configurational dynamics. These configurations in turn can also form further higher-order configurations by interacting further between themselves and forming higher-order feedback loops.

Apart from the large number of interactive elements, complex systems have also emergent properties, that is, causal relations and feedback loops lead to the appearance of patterns or emergent structures (or constellations) of tightly coupled components. Managerial decisions are more or less concerned with discovering courses of action that satisfy a whole set of constraints, rather than maximizing a fitness function, which is consistent with the bounded rationality property of individuals and organizational systems (Simon, 1955; Bendor & Neil, 2001; Morel & Ramanujam, 1999). Such behaviour is known as 'satisficing' as opposed to the maximizing rational behaviour, and is subject to certain behavioural decision rules (Kahneman & Tversky, 1979; Kahneman, 2003a, 2003b).

## 2.8 Methodological Approach

The methodological approach used in this book is summarized in Fig. 2.2, which presents the main stages (qualitative and quantitative) and their related steps in the method's practical application.

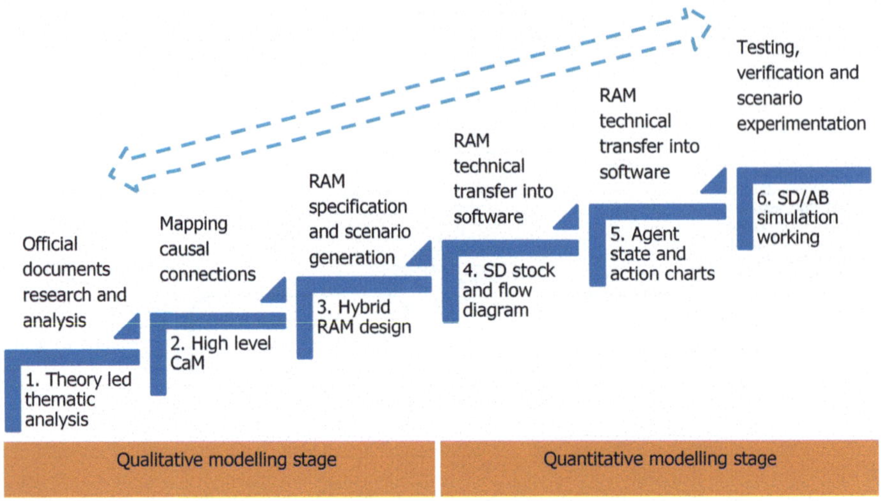


**Fig. 2.2** Design procedure for the resource agent simulation modelling approach

Collecting and analyzing qualitative information for the building of a conceptual qualitative model of the socio-economic system regarding systems behaviour and context can be collected through written documentation output such as stakeholders' position papers, observation and participation in working group meetings and meetings with regulatory authorities. The goal is to use the data collected from document analysis (Barr et al., 1992), official positions (Huff, 1990, 1997), conversations and interviews with experts, researcher notes and reflection (Ackermann & Alexander, 2016; Ackermann & Eden, 2010; Eden & Ackermann, 1998, 2004), for the mapping of mental models (Doyle & Ford, 1998; Carley, 1997; Schreiber et al., 2006; Jones et al., 2011) of key stakeholders in the explored complex system. These are pharmaceutical industry representatives, doctors, pharmacists, patients and healthcare regulators, financial industry representatives and financial regulators, including investors, managers and employees, artists and galleries including art customers and art experts, sociologists and social behaviour experts, public education system representatives like school administrators, teachers and students, and educational authorities.

To extract relevant information, the authors used a theory led thematic analysis (Hayes, 1997) protocol, consisting of looking for, and elucidating, meaning connected to the following themes:

- Key resources and key agents in the relevant system:
  - Textual analysis for the identification and categorization of main resources and actors in the system.
- Influencing factors and their effects on the system, including regulation and public policies:
  - Textual analysis for identification of main assertions regarding systemic effects

- Key agent resources and agent–agent interrelations, including the main influencing factors affecting resource levels and flow rates and agent behavioural routines:
  - Textual analysis regarding agents' behavioural routines and how these influence on main resources levels and vice versa
  - Textual analysis regarding main actors' interrelations influencing their behavioural routines
- Agents' behavioural routines (agents IF THEN condition action rules), in relation to the system's components:
  - What are agents' decision and action patterns in relation to their interactions with endogenous and exogenous system components (agents, resources, and influencing factors)

Creating cause maps to highlight the key conceptual interrelations among the main systems components following (Howick et al., 2008; Howick & Ackermann, 2011; Roberts et al., 1997; Kim & Andersen, 2012) relates to creating causal maps connected to the thematic purposive textual analysis performed in the first step. Their purpose is to support the transfer of the textual analysis of the system's resources and agents, and their interdependence into a resource agent map (RAM). Designing of the maps must ensure that the content of each map (resources, agents, agents' rules and interconnections) represents how the 'world' works (Howick et al., 2008). Further, conversations with experts would provide helpful feedback to ensure a correct and trustful representation of the real functioning of the system.

The quantitative simulation phase includes using the validated RAM as a hybrid simulation modelling procedure to transfer the qualitative representation of the resource agent system into a quantitative one. Transferring the elements of the RAM into a chosen software environment must ensure keeping their resource and agents' behaviour characteristics conceptually consistent with the RAM. The first step of the quantitative stage consisted of transferring the resources and related components into a coded stock and flow charts and associated variables, while the second step included transfer of the agents and related components into coded agents state charts and behaviour algorithms, matching the conceptualized system through the RAM.

Throughout the above procedure the quantitative simulation model must be continuously tested to ensure methodological consistency and robustness in performance outcomes. After a simulation model is built, it is tested with including real data where available (Gilbert et al., 2018) or compared to a real system behaviour (Ghaffarzadegan et al., 2011) with the purpose to ensure confidence in the simulation model correct structural and operational configuration (related to resource and agent structures and behaviours). Parameter variation and policy scenarios experiments can be conducted in order to increase confidence in the simulation performance and explore their effects in connection to the research question.

## References


Ackermann, F., & Alexander, J. (2016). Researching complex projects: Using causal mapping to take a systems perspective. *International Journal of Project Management, 34*, 891. https://doi.org/10.1016/j.ijproman.2016.04.001

Ackermann, F., & Eden, C. (2010). Strategic options development and analysis. In *Systems approaches to managing change: A practical guide* (pp. 135–190). Springer. https://doi.org/10.1007/978-1-84882-809-4_4

Akerlof, G. A. (1970). The market for lemons: Qualitative uncertainty and the market mechanism. *Quarterly Journal of Economics, 84*(3), 488–500. https://doi.org/10.2307/1879431

Amit, R., & Schoemaker, P. J. (1993). Strategic assets and organisational rent. *Strategic Management Journal, 14*, 33–46. https://doi.org/10.1002/smj.4250140105

Anderson, P. (1999). Complexity theory and organization science. *Organization Science, 10*(3), 216–232. https://doi.org/10.2307/2640328

Andrew, A. M. (2003). General systems theory: Ideas and applications. *Kybernetes, 32*(3/4), 571–574. https://doi.org/10.1017/CBO9781107415324.004

Axtell, R. (2000). *Why agents? On the varied motivations for agent computing in the social sciences* (Vol. 17, pp. 1–23). Center on Social and Economics Dynamics - The Brookings Institution. https://doi.org/10.1016/j.cep.2007.02.029

Axtell, R., Axelrod, R., Epstein, J. M., & Cohen, M. D. (1996). Aligning simulation models: A case study and results. *Computational & Mathematical Organization Theory, 1*(2), 123–141. https://doi.org/10.1007/BF01299065

Axtell, R., Epstein, J. M., & Young, H. P. (2001). The emergence of classes in a multi agent bargaining model. *Social Dynamics, 9*, 191–213.

Barney, J. (1991). Firm resources and sustained competitive advantage. *Journal of Management, 17*(1), 99–120.

Barr, P. S., Stimpert, J. L., Huff, A. S., Wiley, J., & Barr, S. (1992). Action, and change, strategic cognitive renewal. *Strategic Management Journal, 13*(S1), 15–36. https://doi.org/10.1016/0024-6301(93)90335-D

Bendor, J., & Neil, J. S. (2001). Bounded rationality. *Policy Studies Journal, 30*(3), 1303–1307. https://doi.org/10.3989/ris.2011.10.20

Bonabeau, E. (2002). Agent-based modeling: Methods and techniques for simulating human systems. *Proceedings of the National Academy of Sciences, 99*(suppl. 3), 7280–7287. https://doi.org/10.1073/pnas.082080899

Butz, M. V., & Pezzulo, G. (2008). Benefits of anticipations in cognitive agents. In *The challenge of anticipation: A unifying framework for the analysis and design of artificial cognitive systems* (pp. 45–62). Springer Berlin Heidelberg.

Butz, M. V., Sigaud, O., Pezzulo, G., & Baldassarre, G. (2007). Anticipations, brains, individual and social behavior: An introduction to anticipatory systems. In *Anticipatory behavior in adaptive learning systems: From psychological theories to artificial cognitive systems* (pp. 1–18). Springer. https://doi.org/10.1007/978-3-540-74262-3_1

Carley, K. M. (1997). Extracting team mental models through textual analysis. *Journal of Organizational Behavior, 18*, 533–558. https://doi.org/10.2307/3100264

Deffuant, G., Neau, D., Amblard, F., & Weisbuch, G. (2000). Mixing beliefs among interacting agents. *Advances in Complex Systems, 03*(01n04), 87. https://doi.org/10.1142/s0219525900000078

Dierickx, I., & Cool, K. (1989). Asset stock accumulation and sustainability of competitive advantage. *Management Science, 35*(12), 1504–1511.

Doyle, J. K., & Ford, D. N. (1998). Mental models concepts for system dynamics research. *System Dynamics Review, 14*(1), 3–29. https://doi.org/10.1002/(SICI)1099-1727(199821)14:1<3::AID-SDR140>3.0.CO;2-K

Eden, C., & Ackermann, F. (1998). Analysing and comparing idiographic causal maps. In *Managerial and organizational cognition. Theory, methods and research* (pp. 192–209). Sage.

Eden, C., & Ackermann, F. (2004). Cognitive mapping expert views for policy analysis in the public sector. *European Journal of Operational Research, 152*(3), 615–630. https://doi.org/10.1016/S0377-2217(03)00061-4

Fiori, S. (2009). Herbert A. Simon and contemporary theories of bounded rationality. In *SSRN eLibrary*. Accessed from http://ssrn.com/paper=1367091

Forrest, S., & Mitchell, M. (2016). Adaptive computation: The multidisciplinary legacy of John H. Holland. *Communications of the ACM, 59*(8), 58. https://doi.org/10.1145/2964342

Forrester, J. (1961a). *Origin of system dynamics*. System Dynamics Society. Accessed from http://www.systemdynamics.org/DL-IntroSysDyn/start.htm

Forrester, J. W. (1961b). *Industrial dynamics*. MIT Press.

Forrester, J. W. (1987). Lessons from system dynamics modeling. *System Dynamics Review, 3*(2), 136–149. https://doi.org/10.1002/sdr.4260030205

Forrester, J. W. (1998). System dynamics, alternative futures, and scenarios. In *16th international conference of the system dynamics society*. Accessed from http://www.systemdynamics.org/conferences/1998/PROCEED/00095.PDF

Forrester, J. W., Mass, N. J., & Ryan, C. J. (1976). The system dynamics national model: Understanding socio-economic behavior and policy alternatives. *Technological Forecasting and Social Change, 9*(1–2), 51–68. https://doi.org/10.1016/0040-1625(76)90044-5

Gary, S., Kunc, M., Morecroft, J., & Rockart, S. (2007). System dynamics and strategy: Accomplishments and future opportunities. In *Proceedings of the 2007 International Conference of the System Dynamics Society*.

Ghaffarzadegan, N., Lyneis, J., & Richardson, G. P. (2011). How small system dynamics models can help the public policy process. *System Dynamics Review, 27*(1), 22–44. https://doi.org/10.1002/sdr.442

Gigerenzer, G., & Goldstein, D. G. (2011). Reasoning the fast and frugal way: Models of bounded rationality. In *Heuristics: The foundations of adaptive behavior*. Oxford University Press. https://doi.org/10.1093/acprof:oso/9780199744282.003.0002

Gilbert, N., Ahrweiler, P., Barbrook-Johnson, P., Narasimhan, K. P., & Wilkinson, H. (2018). Computational modelling of public policy: Reflections on practice. *JASSS, 21*(1), 10.18564/jasss.3669.

Guerrero, C. N., Schwarz, P., & Slinger, J. H. (2016). A recent overview of the integration of system dynamics and agent-based modelling and simulation. In: *34th international conference of the system dynamics society*.

Hayes, N. (1997). Theory-led thematic analysis: Social identification in small companies. In *Doing qualitative analysis in psychology* (pp. 93–114). Psychology Press.

Helfat, C. E. (2011). Dynamic capabilities and strategic management: Organizing for innovation and growth. *R&D Management, 41*, 217–218. https://doi.org/10.1111/j.1467-9310.2011.00638.x

Helfat, C., & Peteraf, M. (2003). The dynamic resource based view: Capability lifecycles. *Strategic Management Journal, 24*(10), 997–1010.

Helfat, C. E., & Peteraf, M. A. (2015). Managerial cognitive capabilities and the microfoundations of dynamic capabilities. *Strategic Management Journal, 36*(February), 831–850. https://doi.org/10.1002/smj.2247

Hillman, A. J., Withers, M. C., & Collins, B. J. (2009). Resource dependence theory: A review. *Journal of Management, 35*(6), 1404–1427. https://doi.org/10.1177/0149206309343469

Holland, J. H. (1975). *Adaptation in natural and artificial systems* (Vol. 1). University of Michigan Press.

Holland, J. H. (1992). Complex adaptive systems. *Daedalus, 121*(1), 17–30. https://doi.org/10.2307/20025416

Howick, S., & Ackermann, F. (2011). Mixing or methods in practice: Past, present and future directions. *European Journal of Operational Research, 215*(3), 503–511. https://doi.org/10.1016/j.ejor.2011.03.013

Howick, S., Eden, C., Ackermann, F., & Williams, T. (2008). Building confidence in models for multiple audiences: The modelling cascade. *European Journal of Operational Research, 186*(3), 1068–1083. https://doi.org/10.1016/j.ejor.2007.02.027

Huff, A. S. (1990). *Mapping strategic thought* (pp. 11–49). Goodreads. https://doi.org/10.5465/AMR.1992.4279590

Huff, A. S. (1997). A current and future agenda for cognitive research in organizations. *Journal of Management Studies, 34*(6), 947–952. https://doi.org/10.1111/1467-6486.00079

Jennings, N. R. (2000). On agent-based software engineering. *Artificial Intelligence, 117*(2), 277–296. https://doi.org/10.1016/S0004-3702(99)00107-1

Jones, N. A., Ross, H., Lynam, T., Perez, P., & Leitch, A. (2011). Mental model an interdisciplinary synthesis of theory and methods. *Ecology and Society, 16*(1), 46–46. 46.

Kahneman, D. (2003a). A perspective on judgment and choice: Mapping bounded rationality. *American Psychologist, 58*(9), 697–720. https://doi.org/10.1037/0003-066X.58.9.697

Kahneman, D. (2003b). Maps of bounded rationality: Psychology for behavioral economics. *American Economic Review, 93*(5), 1449–1475. https://doi.org/10.1257/000282803322655392

Kahneman, D., & Tversky, A. (1979). Prospect theory: An analysis of decision under risk. *Econometrica, 47*(2), 263–292. https://doi.org/10.1111/j.1536-7150.2011.00774.x

Kahneman, D., & Tversky, A. (1982). The simulation heuristic. In *Judgment under uncertainty: Heuristics and biases* (pp. 201–208). Springer. https://doi.org/10.1093/oxfordhb/9780195376746.013.0038

Kauffman, S. A. (1992). The origins of order: Self-organization and selection in evolution. In *Understanding origins*. Oxford University Press. https://doi.org/10.1126/science.260.5113.1531

Kauffman, S. (1995). *At home in the universe: The search for the laws of self-organization and complexity*. Oxford University Press. https://doi.org/10.1017/S0016672300033772

Kim, H., & Andersen, D. F. (2012). Building confidence in causal maps generated from purposive text data: Mapping transcripts of the Federal Reserve. *System Dynamics Review, 28*(4), 311. https://doi.org/10.1002/sdr.1480

Koumakhov, R. (2009). Conventions in Herbert Simon's theory of bounded rationality. *Journal of Economic Psychology, 30*(3), 293–306. https://doi.org/10.1016/j.joep.2009.03.001

Kunc, M., & Morecroft, J. (2010). Managerial decision making and firm performance under a resource based paradigm. *Strategic Management Journal, 1182*(March), 1164–1182. https://doi.org/10.1002/smj.858

Louie, A. H. (2010). Robert Rosen's anticipatory systems. *Foresight, 12*(3), 18–29. https://doi.org/10.1108/14636681011049848

Macal, C. M. (2010). To agent-based simulation from system dynamics. *Simulation, 2001*, 135–150. https://doi.org/10.1109/WSC.2010.5679148

Macal, C. M., & North, M. J. (2009). Agent-based modeling and simulation. In *Proceedings of the 2009 winter simulation conference (WSC)*, pp. 86–98. https://doi.org/10.1109/WSC.2009.5429318

Macal, C., & North, M. (2010). Tutorial on agent-based modelling and simulation. *Journal of Simulation, 4*, 151–162. https://doi.org/10.1057/jos.2010.3

Macal, C., & North, M. (2015). Introductory tutorial: Agent-based modeling and simulation. *Proceedings of the Winter simulation conference, 2015-January*, pp. 6–20. https://doi.org/10.1109/WSC.2014.7019874

Macal, C. M., Carson, J. S. J. S., Macal, C. M., & Carson, J. S. J. S. (2002). Concepts of model verification and validation. *Proceedings of the Winter Simulation Conference, 1*, 52–58. https://doi.org/10.1109/WSC.2002.1172868

Marshall, D. A., Burgos-Liz, L., IJzerman, M. J., Crown, W., Padula, W. V., Wong, P. K., Pasupathy, K. S., Higashi, M. K., & Osgood, N. D. (2015a). Selecting a dynamic simulation modeling method for health care delivery research-part 2: Report of the ISPOR dynamic simulation modeling emerging good practices task force. *Value in Health: The Journal of the International Society for Pharmacoeconomics and Outcomes Research, 18*(2), 147–160. https://doi.org/10.1016/j.jval.2015.01.006

Marshall, D. A., Burgos-Liz, L., IJzerman, M. J., Osgood, N. D., Padula, W. V., Higashi, M. K., Wong, P. K., Pasupathy, K. S., & Crown, W. (2015b). Applying dynamic simulation modeling methods in health care delivery research—The SIMULATE checklist: Report of the ISPOR simulation modeling emerging good practices task force. *Value in Health, 18*, 5. https://doi.org/10.1016/j.jval.2014.12.001

Meyer, G. G., & Szirbik, N. B. (2007, September). Agent behavior alignment: A mechanism to overcome problems in agent interactions during runtime. In *International workshop on cooperative information agents* (pp. 270–284). Springer Berlin Heidelberg.

Morecroft, J. D. W. (2015). *Strategic modelling and business dynamics: A feedback systems approach* (2nd ed.). Wiley. https://doi.org/10.1002/9781119176831

Morel, B., & Ramanujam, R. (1999). Through the dynamics the of looking glass of complexity: Adaptive organizations as systems and evolving. *Organization Science, 10*(3), 278–293.

Peteraf, M. (1993). The cornerstones of competitive advantage: A resource-based view. *Strategic Management Journal, 14*(April 1992), 179–191. https://doi.org/10.1017/CBO9781107415324.004

Pezzulo, G. (2007). Anticipation and future-oriented capabilities in natural and artificial cognition. In *Years of Artificial Intelligence* (Vol. 50, pp. 257–270). Springer. https://doi.org/10.1007/978-3-540-77296-5_24

Pezzulo, G. (2008). Coordinating with the future: The anticipatory nature of representation. *Minds and Machines, 18*(2), 179–225. https://doi.org/10.1007/s11023-008-9095-5

Pezzulo, G., & Castelfranchi, C. (2009). Intentional action: From anticipation to goal-directed behavior. *Psychological Research, 73*(4), 437–440. https://doi.org/10.1007/s00426-009-0241-3

Pfeffer, J., & Salancik, G. R. (1978). The external control of organizations: A resource dependence perspective. In *The sociology of organization* (pp. 233–242).

Phelan, S. E. (1999). A note on the correspondence between complexity and systems theory. *Systemic Practice and Action Research, 12*(3), 237–246. https://doi.org/10.1023/A:1022495500485

Pitelis, C. N. (2004). Edith Penrose and the resource-based view of (international) business strategy. *International Business Review, 13*(4), 523. https://doi.org/10.1016/j.ibusrev.2004.04.002

Radzicki, M. J., & Sterman, J. D. (1994). Evolutionary economics and system dynamics. In *Evolutionary concepts in contemporary economics* (pp. 61–89). Accessed from https://www.press.umich.edu/14207/evolutionary_concepts_in_contemporary_economics

Randers, J. (1980). Guidelines for model conceptualization. In *Elements of the system dynamics method.* MIT Press. https://doi.org/10.1057/palgrave.jors.2600456

Richardson, G. P., & Pugh, A. L. I. (1981). Introduction to system dynamics modeling with DYNAMO. *Journal of the Operational Research Society, 48*(11). https://doi.org/10.1038/sj.jors.2600961

Roberts, M. S. (2015). Dynamic simulation in health care comes of age. *Value in Health, 18*(2), 143–144. https://doi.org/10.1016/j.jval.2015.02.006

Roberts, N., Anderson, D., Deal, R., Garet, M., & Shaffer, W. (1997). Introduction to computer simulation—A system dynamics modeling approach. *Journal of the Operational Research Society, 48*(11), 1145–1145.

Rosen, R. (1978). On anticipatory systems: I. When can a system contain a predictive model of another? *Journal of Social and Biological Systems, 1*(2), 155–162. https://doi.org/10.1016/S0140-1750(78)80003-7

Rosen, R. (1985). *Anticipatory systems: Philosophical, mathematical, and methodological foundations* (IFSR international series on systems science and engineering) (Vol. 1). Springer. https://doi.org/10.1080/03081079.2012.726322

Rosen, J., & Kineman, J. J. (2005). Anticipatory systems and time: A new look at Rosennean complexity. *Systems Research and Behavioral Science, 22*(5), 399–412. https://doi.org/10.1002/sres.715

Schieritz, N. (2002). Integrating system dynamics and agent-based modeling. In *System dynamics* (pp. 1–3). Springer. https://doi.org/10.1007/s10841-010-9333-z

Schieritz, N., & Milling, P. (2003). Modeling the forest or modeling the trees: A comparison of system dynamics and agent-based simulation. In *Proceedings of the 21st international system dynamics society, Phelan 1999*, pp. 1–15. Accessed from http://www.systemdynamics.org/conferences/2003/proceed/PAPERS/140.pdf

Schreiber, C., Marion, R., Uhl-Bien, M., & Carley, K. (2006). Multi-agent based simulation of a model of complexity leadership. In *International Conference on Complex Systems.*

Simon, H. A. (1955). A behavioral model of rational choice. *The Quarterly Journal of Economics, 69*(1), 99–118. https://doi.org/10.2307/1884852

Simon, H. (1972a). Theories of bounded rationality. In *Decision and organization* (pp. 161–176). Accessed from http://innovbfa.viabloga.com/files/Herbert_Simon___theories_of_bounded_rationality___1972.pdf

Simon, H. (1972b). Theories of bounded rationality. In *Decision and organization* (pp. 161–176).

Simon, H. (2007). Administrative behavior. In *Bloomsbury business library - Management library* (Vol. 2). A & C Black Publishers. https://doi.org/10.1177/019263658206645522

Sirmon, D. G., & Hitt, M. A. (2009). Contingencies within dynamic managerial capabilities: Interdependent effects of resource investment and deployment on firm performance. *Strategic Management Journal, 30*(13), 1375–1394. https://doi.org/10.1002/smj.791

Sterman, J. D. (1991). A skeptic's guide to computer models. In *Managing a nation: The microcomputer software catalog* (pp. 209–229). Routledge. Accessed from http://web.mit.edu/jsterman/www/Skeptic's_Guide.pdf

Sterman, J. D. (2000). *Business dynamics: Systems thinking and modeling for a complex world* (p. 928). Irwin/McGraw-Hill.

Sterman, J. (2001). System dynamics modeling. *California Management Review, 3*, 163. https://doi.org/10.1007/978-1-4419-9416-5

Stiglitz, J. (2016, June). *The revolution of information economics: The past and the future.*

Teece, D. J., Pisano, G., & Shuen, A. (1997). Dynamic capabilities and strategic management. *Strategic Management Journal, 18*, 509–533. https://doi.org/10.1142/9789812834478_0002. Accessed from http://www.jstor.org/stable/3088148

Tversky, A., & Kahneman, D. (1974). Judgment under uncertainty: Heuristics and biases. *Science, 185*(4157), 1124–1131. https://doi.org/10.1126/science.185.4157.1124

Tversky, A., & Kahneman, D. (1991). Loss aversion in riskless choice: A reference-dependent model. *The Quarterly Journal of Economics, 106*(4), 1039–1061. Accessed from http://www.jstor.org/stable/2937956?seq=1#page_scan_tab_contents%5Cnhttp://qje.oxfordjournals.org/content/106/4/1039.full.pdf+html

Ulrich, D., & Barney, J. B. (1984). Perspectives in organizations: Resource dependence, efficiency, and population. *Academy of Management Review, 9*(3), 471–481. https://doi.org/10.5465/AMR.1984.4279680

Von Bertalanffy, L. (1968). *General system theory* (Vol. 1, p. 289). George Braziller.

Weisbuch, G. (2006). Modeling complex systems: Do it! *Complexity, 11*(3), 25. https://doi.org/10.1002/cplx.20113

Wernerfeldt, B. (1984). A resource-based view of the firm. *Strategic Management Journal (Pre-1986), 5*(2), 171.

Wolstenholme, E. F. (1999). Qualitative vs quantitative modelling: The evolving balance. *Journal of the Operational Research Society, 50*(4), 422–428. https://doi.org/10.1057/palgrave.jors.2600700

# Chapter 3
# Methodological Framework

**Abstract** This chapter introduces the resource agent maps (RAM) method and its application to qualitative and quantitative analyses and management of complex adaptive systems. These systems are characterized by socio-economic dynamics where agents compete for control over available resources, operating under condition-action rule patterns and dealing with incomplete or biased information. These systems and their evolution emerge through the interactions between resources and agents.

The RAM method includes first, the development of a resource map, which maps key internal and external resources, their structure, influencing factors, and feedback interrelations. Second is the development of an agent map, containing both an agent interaction map (AiM), which maps key agents, their interrelations, influencing factors, and identifying the agents' main behavioural rules, and agent behavioural map (AbM), which maps agents' behavioural decision action pattern in more detail, revealing each agent's cognitive structure.

The RAM represents an integration of the above maps. It aims to analyze the interactive behaviour of resources and agents while identifying scenarios that emerge due to variations in resource structure, agent behavioural rules, and contextual factors. Using RAM method can help decision makers achieve comprehensive evaluation of the effects of system interventions, including generating management scenarios for system improvement.

## 3.1 Introduction

In the study conducted by Kazakov et al. (2021), the authors introduced the resource agent maps (RAM) method and its application to qualitatively analyze and manage complex adaptive systems. These systems are characterized by socio-economic dynamics where agents compete for control over available resources, operating under condition-action rule patterns (Holland, 1992), and dealing with incomplete and/or biased information (Fiori, 2009; Simon, 1955, 1972). The behaviour of



R. Kazakov et al., *Understanding and Managing Socioeconomic Systems Behaviour*, Contributions to Management Science,
https://doi.org/10.1007/978-3-031-57057-5_3

agents in these systems is subject to adaptation as they interact with their environment, exchanging information and resources.

Complex socio-economic systems consist of interconnected agents, resource structures, and processes. An example for healthcare systems include doctors, patients, drugs and drug suppliers, hospitals, regulators, and various other multi-level interrelations that evolve and undergo change together (Roberts, 2015; Begun et al., 2003). Another instance of such complexity can be observed in financial markets, which involve suppliers, intermediaries, and consumers of financial services and products, operating within a highly regulated and competitive environment (LeBaron & Tesfatsion, 2008; Block et al., 2013).

These complex socio-economic systems and their evolution emerge through the dialectical interactions between resources and agents. Even minor changes at any level can result in unexpected imbalances, as exemplified by the global financial crisis (Crotty, 2009; Joseph, 2010; Stiglitz, 2000; Farmer et al., 2012). In the healthcare sector, both local and global inefficiencies can arise due to disparities in access to affordable healthcare and medicinal therapies (Council of the European Union, 2016; Haas-Wilson, 2001; Plsek, 2001).

Understanding the behaviour of complex socio-economic systems is facilitated through the utilization of problem structuring methods (PSMs) (Mingers & Rosenhead, 2004; Rosenhead & Mingers, 2001; Rosenhead, 2006). These methods involve mapping and modelling the various components of the system, including their causal interrelations, influencing factors, flows, feedback loops, and emerging properties. Such an approach provides valuable insights into the dynamics and management of these intricate systems (Ackermann et al., 2014).

In practice, there are different modelling techniques used within various methodologies, along with the corresponding theoretical framework supporting each method. Soft systems methodology (SSM) utilizes rich pictures and is grounded in systems theory (Checkland & Scholes, 1990; Von Bertalanffy, 1972; Forrester, 1989). Strategic options development and analysis (SODA) employs cognitive mapping and is underpinned by personal construct theory (Ackermann & Eden, 2010; Eden & Ackermann, 2001; Walker & Winter, 2007; Winter, 2017).

Strategic choice utilizes decision graphs and is influenced by the Ackoff design approach (Friend, 1995, 2011; Ackoff, 1979). Resource maps involve resource mapping and draw upon system dynamics and systems theory (Kunc & Morecroft, 2010; Forrester, 1961). Resource agent maps, developed by Kazakov et al. (2021), incorporate various theories, including RBV (Barney, 1986, 1991; Wernerfeldt, 1984; Peteraf, 1993), RDT (Pfeffer & Salancik, 1978), BDT (Kahneman & Tversky, 1979), and AST (Rosen, 1985).

Strategic management of stakeholders employs stakeholder mapping and is supported by stakeholders theory (Ackermann & Eden, 2010; Agle et al., 2008; Magness, 2008). Robustness analysis involves assessing future system configurations and is grounded in systems theory (Rosenhead, 1980, 1996; Von Bertalanffy, 1972). Drama theory utilizes role 'hyper game' playing to analyze conflict and cooperation, drawing from game theory (Bryant, 2007; Howard, 1998; Von Neumann & Morgenstern, 1944). Decision conferencing focuses on analyzing decision alternatives and is informed by decision theory and requisite modelling (Phillips & Phillips, 1993; Phillips, 1984; Simon, 1965). Lastly, the viable systems model incorporates cybernetic principles for viable organization and is grounded in systems theory (Beer, 1986; Bertalanffy, 1968; von Foerster, 1972, 1979).

## 3.2 Resource Maps

Resource maps (RM) have been used in relation to system dynamics modelling and simulation practice (Kunc & Morecroft, 2006, 2009, 2010) to provide a systems approach to the exploration of the concept of 'Resource' and 'Resource' accumulation and dynamic management (Teece et al., 1997, 2008; Helfat and Peteraf (2015); Helfat and Martin (2015); Sirmon & Hitt, 2009). RM is a qualitative mapping technique tightly linked to cognitive mapping (Eden, 2004; Bryson et al., 2007; Eden et al., 1992; Ackermann & Eden, 2010), employing stock-and-flow and influence diagrams, with the aim of mapping managers' cognitive models focusing on key/strategic resources and resource-building decision-making processes (Kunc & Morecroft, 2009).

Resource maps have been applied mainly for the representation of systems of firms/agents' asset stocks believed to be key for building competitive advantage and superior business performance and, informed by resource-based theory (RBT) (Barney, 1986, 1991; Wernerfeldt, 1984; Peteraf, 1993), present an internalized perspective of resource management. However, existing research that uses resource mapping does not consider the external perspective of resource dependence related to RDT. Extending resource maps through the external perspective taken by RDT (Pfeffer & Salancik, 1978) can therefore complement and extend the RM theoretical frame and its analytical capacity.

RDT (Pfeffer & Salancik, 1978; Hillman et al., 2009) view the organization as being an open system, dependent on contextual contingencies in the external market and regulatory environment. External micro- and macro-economic context influence organizational behaviour and a key goal of market agents would be reducing environmental uncertainty and dependence on valuable resources through control over vital resources (Ulrich & Barney, 1984) by reducing competitors' and institutions' power over them, attempting to increase their own power over their competitors. RDT can provide an awareness of the resource depending forces of organizational behaviour on the market environment and how organizations take actions to manage external interdependencies in order to reduce uncertainty and interdependence on the larger social-economic system including market regulation. In addition, integrating RDT with the resource-based theory of the firm (Barney, 1986, 1991; Wernerfeldt, 1984) can provide a complementary focus on resources, and may offer new insights into the organizational resource depending behaviour, including controlling valuable, rare, nonsubstitutable, and limited resources from the external environment (Hillman et al., 2009) where each agent group interacts and contributes to the overall complexity of the market socio-economic system.

## 3.3 Agent Behaviour Maps

A limitation of RM is its inability to account for market agents' behavioural decision making due to its theoretical connection to the RBT only having a focus on internal resources. This limitation is confirmed by Phelan (1999) and Schieritz and Milling (2003), who have argued that a stock and flow diagram, that is, a system's resource structure, is static and focused on the quantity rather than the quality of resource interrelations, and that an agent perspective is needed to enable quality to be modelled. In this case, quality relates to the agents' behaviour in changing the level of a system's resource through flows of action in response to anticipated environmental change. Further, Scholl (2001a) and Schieritz and Milling (2003) argue that integrating both a system dynamic and agent-based perspective could provide a means for capturing both the macro and the micro level, and that joint application may deliver superior results.

Agents have a predefined goal and follow a 'schema' or a rule/pattern of behaviour, which are 'mental templates that define how reality is interpreted and what are appropriate response for a given stimuli' (Dooley, 1996). They are rationally bounded due to incomplete and/or biased information (Fiori, 2009; Simon, 1978, 1991, 2000) and could have multitude of rules which are formed through a 'selection-enactment-retention process' (Gell-Mann, 1997; Holland, 1992; Jantsch, 1980; Mingers, 1991, 2001; Maturana, 2002; Prigogine & Stengers, 1984). Agents' pattern of behaviour can change purposefully or randomly or by combination with other schema in order to adapt to the environment and can involve exchange of information and or resources producing multiplier effects based on the nature of interconnectedness in the system with flows that may be non-linear.

Two frameworks that can be helpful for thinking about agent mapping are behavioural decision theory (BDT) and anticipatory systems theory (AST). In terms of BDT research, Simon (1972), Kahneman and Tverzky (1982), and Kahneman (2011) provide a theoretical underpinning for the development of AB mapping technique for complex adaptive systems market agents, whether they are individual or organizational, which follow certain behavioural patterns informed by their perception of the environment and decision making and which are rationally bounded due to incomplete information and imperfect cognition (Kahneman & Tversky, 1982; Kahneman, 2011). For that reason, agents behave according to heuristic principles in order to reduce judgement and choice complexity (Tversky & Kahneman, 1974; Kahneman & Tversky, 1982). These principles include 'availability', 'anchoring and adjustment', 'representativeness', and 'loss aversion' (Kahneman & Tversky, 1972, 1979). Heuristics can also lead to cognitive biases (Kahneman, 2003) and decision making is simplified through a 'recognition' heuristic which makes best use of the limited information available to individuals (Gigerenzer, 2000; Gigerenzer & Goldstein, 2011).

A second framework that can be useful for thinking about agent mapping is AST. AST posits that 'anticipation is the process which enables a living system to contain a predictive model of itself and its environment, which allows it to adapt by changing its state in accordance with the model's predictions' (Louie, 2010; Rosen, 1985; Pezzulo, 2007) and to base its course of actions on their anticipated effects. Anticipatory systems have the ability to exhibit 'pay-off' anticipations and 'state' anticipations (Butz & Pezzulo, 2008). Pay-off anticipations are pertinent to systems that 'have knowledge of behaviourally dependent payoff and can base action selection on that representation', that is, 'different payoff may be predicted for alternative actions, which allows the selection of the current best action'. State anticipation is based on anticipatory processes which enhance behavioural decision making by future anticipatory representations of not only the goal but of the whole system. The next section will describe a resource/agent map that has been designed to provide qualitative mapping and analysis of resource/agent behaviour.

## 3.4 Resource Agent Map (RAM)

Kazakov et al. (2021) introduced resource agent maps method (RAM) which include first, the development of a resource map, enhanced by RDT which maps key internal and external resources, their structure, influencing factors, and feedback interrelations; and second, the development of an agent map, containing both an Agent interaction map (AiM), which maps key agents, their interrelations, influencing factors, and identifying the agents' main behavioural rules, and agent behavioural map (AbM), which maps agents' behavioural decision action pattern in more detail, revealing each agent's cognitive structure informed by BDT and AST; finally, the enhanced RM and AM are integrated to produce a hybrid RAM.

The enhanced resource map extends the RM approach initially proposed by Kunc and Morecroft (2009). Building upon the resource-based view (RBV) of the firm, it incorporates elements from the resource dependence theory (RDT). The primary aim of this technique is to map key internal and external market resources, along with their influencing factors and variables, while elucidating feedback interrelations. Through this approach, it facilitates a thorough analysis of the resource structure and feedback dynamics.

The agent interaction map (AiM) builds upon the concept of stakeholders management mapping, as introduced by Ackermann and Eden (2011). It focuses on mapping agent interactions and incorporates feedback mechanisms. Specifically, it identifies each agent's key behavioural decision rules and key influencing factors. This technique enables an analysis of the structural aspects of agents and the dynamics of their influences.

The agent behaviour map (AbM) focuses onto the behavioural aspects of individual agents by creating a detailed agent behavioural IF THEN condition action map. It provides a comprehensive understanding of each agent's behavioural decision rules and their behaviour within the system. This technique is supported by the behavioural decision theory (BDT) and in anticipatory systems theory (AST).

The resource agent map (RAM) represents an integration of the enhanced RM and the agent maps into a hybrid one. It aims to analyze the interactive behaviour of resources and agents while identifying scenarios that emerge due to variations in resource and structure, agent behavioural rules, and contextual factors. Using RAM method can help decision makers achieve comprehensive evaluation of the effect of complex system interventions, including generating management scenarios for system improvement.

## 3.5 System Dynamics Modelling (SD)

Forrester (1958) pioneered SD practice following two key concepts of systems theory related to the feedback loops principle, and to the principle that system's structure drives system's behaviour. A main view behind the behaviour of complex dynamic systems identifies hidden endogeneity and feedback effects due to delay in time and bound rationality, leading to non-linear and often counterintuitive behaviour (John, 2000; Morecroft, 2015). Hence, systems dynamics modelling practice tries to uncover the hidden mechanisms underlying the observed non-linear effects in the economic systems 'instead of only treating their symptoms' (Forrester, 1958).

Main building blocks in SD modelling are stocks or resources (Richardson & Pugh, 1981; Forrester 1976; Wolstenholme, 1999; John, 2000), flows and auxiliary variables which can involve a quite large number of differential/integration and algebraic equations in only one model, depending on model boundary and complexity.

Understanding the endogenous and exogenous characteristics of organizational and market complexity, being a source of causal ambiguity, emergent behaviour and self-organizational dynamics (Morel & Ramanujam, 1999) are well advanced by general systems theory (Bertalanffy, 1968) and the system dynamics field of research (Forrester, 1961, 1995; Radzicki & Sterman, 1994; Richardson & Pugh, 1981; Randers, 1976, 1980; Morecroft, 1999, 2015; John, 2000). Systems complexity comes from dynamic components and their non-linear interactions which cause emergent behaviour, the reasons for which are hardly obvious. The more complex interrelations are among the systems internal and external components, the more ambiguous are the causes of the system behaviour and its self-organizational dynamics.

System dynamics research has tackled important questions related to strategy, organizational behaviour, policy and operations, and purposive managerial decision making as a primary source of market dynamics and performance heterogeneity. Research also has shown that system dynamics modelling and simulation is able to account for the real-world information feedbacks, delays, non-linearities caused by organization and market complexity, and can explain organizational and market behaviour. For example, health-care and pharmaceutical systems are dynamical complex systems and exhibit non-linear behaviour which can be better explained by dynamic modelling approaches like system dynamics rather than traditional linear modelling (Roberts, 2015; Marshall et al., 2015). In that regard, system dynamics approach can be appropriate to explore the healthcare regulation effects on the pharmaceutical market system behaviour.

System dynamics methodological framework follows a complex non-linear and feedback view of the world with accumulation and depletion of resources and time delays. In order to model complex non-linear systems, modellers apply qualitative modelling technique capable to capture their complexity in order to support quantitative model building or use them on their own, like influence and causal loop diagrams (Randers, 1976; Morecroft, 1982; Wolstenholme, 1982; Coyle, 2000), cognitive mapping (Eden, 1988, 2004; Eden & Ackermann, 2001; Ackermann et al., 1992; Ackermann & Eden, 2010; Huff, 1990; Ackermann, 2012); for example, combing qualitative with quantitative modelling approaches (Howick & Ackermann, 2011) like the modelling cascade (Howick et al., 2008) shows how they can support each other and enhance confidence among modellers and users. CLD are standard approach to SD model conceptualization regarded as qualitative modelling used on their own and to support the building of a quantitative SD simulation model. An example of mixed modelling approach like the modelling cascade (Howick et al., 2008) consisting of a cognitive and causal mapping framework of influence maps, formal system dynamics influence diagrams/causal loop diagrams is a specific application of mixed modelling designed with the aim to facilitate group model building and gather multiple perspectives in practice, that is, to support the elicitation of the managers' mental model when working with clients and build confidence in the modelling process and output.

The qualitative tools and quantitative tools applied in the system dynamics modelling, like causal mapping and numerical simulation have the purpose to help the modeler to capture feedback loop processes endogenous to the system, how they are dependent on the stock and flow structure of the system, and how they produce emerging complexity and system's behaviour (Sterman, 2001). Conceptualizing and building a system dynamics model involve four key stages: CLD, stock and flow diagram, equation coding, and Simulation. The modelling process need to be iterative following five general steps (John, 2000): problem articulation (boundary selection), dynamic hypothesis, simulation model formulation, model testing, and policy evaluation. Following Randers' (1980) guide to model conceptualization, modelers need to follow a conceptualization, formulation, testing, and implementation stage. Richardson and Pugh (1981) and Roberts (1981) view the model building stages as problem definition, system conceptualization, model formulation/representation, model behaviour and analysis, evaluation and policy analysis, and use. All the above three perspectives provide a similar, if not the same, logical sequence of steps for conceptualizing, building, validating and use of SD simulation models, but utilizing different terms for each stage.

Following Randers (1980) classification, the first 'conceptualization' stage needs to account for the modeler conceptual understanding of the system components and how they are influencing each other's behaviour. To this aim come the qualitative techniques like influence/causal loop diagrams which help the modeler also to explore model boundary and generate dynamic hypothesis for simulation testing. The next 'formulation' stage is linked to the quantitative model building, meaning that normally a stock and flow formal diagram need to account for the system structure and for the proper mathematical interrelations among the model variables, including coding in the model. The next 'testing' stage is about model calibration and verification having the purpose to prove the proper quantification of the simulation model. The 'implementation' stage is associated with the simulation application to policy evaluation by doing what if scenario simulations in order to test previously identified hypotheses and find how variation in key input variables influences the behaviour of the whole system.

A typology of common behaviour emerging within dynamic systems and exhibited by system dynamic simulations can be related to exponential growth, goal seeking, and oscillation (John, 2000; Morecroft, 2015; Howick & Whalley, 2007; Ghaffarzadegan et al., 2011; Luke & Stamatakis, 2012). Any of that behaviour is generated by a simple feedback structure, for example, related to positive/reinforcing feedback in respect to exponential growth, or negative/balancing feedback in respect to goal seeking, or a combination of negative feedback with time delays in respect to oscillation. Non-linear interactions between feedback structures can further produce S-shaped growth, S-shaped growth with overshoot and oscillation, and overshoot and collapse (John, 2000).

Feedback loops are identified to be inherent endogenous circular interrelations among system variables responsible for the above described non-linear behaviour. The scientific concept of feedback loops can be associated with system control theory or cybernetics (Umpleby & Dent, 1999; Von Foerster, 1979; Von Bertalanffy, 1972), to become a key endogenous mechanism in system dynamic approach and system dynamic modelling and simulation (Forrester, 1961; Morecroft, 1982; Wolstenholme, 1999, 2004; Randers, 1980). Feedback is considered to be a key principle in understanding system behaviour and in doing qualitative and quantitative modelling by SD methodological apparatus.

## 3.6 Agent-Based Modelling and Simulation (ABMS)

According to Axtell (2000), agent-based modelling compared to traditional approaches to modelling economic systems could be a more viable approach when there are reasons to think in terms of agents. For example, when the problem we need to explore is naturally represented by a large number of agents which decisions and behaviours which can be well-defined, exhibit adaptation and change, learning and engaging in dynamic strategic interactions, and relationships with other agents, can have a spatial component to their behaviours and interactions. A very important feature of Axtell's AB modelling criteria is linked to the structure of the system which has endogenously emerging mechanisms governing its future evolution and is not dependent only on the past (Axtell, 2000).

Macal and North (2015) acknowledge that ABMS could be linked to complex systems (Weisbuch, 2006) and complex adaptive systems (Kauffman, 1995; Holland, 1992) theory and exploration. They understand ABM as a set of 'ideas, techniques, and tools for implementing computational models of complex adaptive systems' with the aim to reveal origin of self-organization, emergent phenomenon, and adaptation (Macal & North, 2010).

The behavioural rules, emergence, and adaptation effect of agent behaviour are tightly connected with the theory of complex adaptive systems (CAS) which do not have a controlling centre and a fixed structure, rather they are structurally coupled with their environment and exhibit a co-evolutionary emerging feature, that is, as the result of decentralized bottom-up decisions and behaviour of individual entities or agents over time (Guerrero et al., 2016; Macal, 2010; Macal & North, 2006). Agents' decisions and behaviour 'shape and change the state and structure of the system and react to the dynamic changes in the system, which can potentially alter their decision rules' (Guerrero et al., 2016).

Agents have decision rules and autonomous actions, and interact with their environment forming non-linear and feedback effect (Axtell et al., 1996; Bonabeau, 2002; Phelan, 1999). Agents' decision rules which govern agents' behaviour are linked to a goal-oriented behaviour related to achieving a certain individual benefit, guided by the BDT principle of satisficing criteria of accessibility, risk aversion, and anchoring and adjustment, rather than maximizing a utility function due to their bound rationality and incomplete knowledge (Newell & Simon, 1959; Jennings, 2000) and unequal distribution of information (George, 1970; Stiglitz, 2000). Interestingly, according to Phelan (1999) when agents coordinate their decisions to achieve common goals, a 'collective intelligence' phenomenon may emerge. According to Schieritz (2002), the building blocks of AB modelling are the individual agent, agent behavioural rule, inner and intra agent feedback connection, adaption of agent behaviour, inductive inference from individual agents' behaviour to system behaviour, and discrete or continuous time frame. The agent pattern of behaviour or schema is 'a cognitive structure that determines what action the agent takes at time t, given its perception of the environment' (Anderson, 1999) and can change or evolve in order to adapt to the agent environment.

North and Macal (2007), Macal and North (2010, 2014) give the relevant structure of an agent-based model, which a modeler needs to account for when identifying, modelling, and programming to create an ABM: '(1) A set of agents, their attributes and behaviours; (2) A set of agent relationships and methods of interaction: An underlying topology of connectedness defines how and with whom agents interact; (3) The agents' environment: Agents interact with their environment in addition to other agents'.

From a practical modelling standpoint, they consider agents to have the following essential characteristics:

- An agent is a self-contained, modular, and uniquely identifiable. Agents have attributes that allow the agents to be distinguished from and recognized by other agents.
- An agent is autonomous and self-directed. An agent can function independently in its environment and in its interactions with other agents.

- An agent has behaviours that relate information sensed by the agent to its decisions and actions. An agent's information comes through interactions with other agents and with the environment. An agent's behaviour can be specified by anything from simple rules to abstract models relating agent inputs to outputs through adaptive mechanisms.
- An agent has a state that varies over time. Just as a system has a state consisting of the collection of its state variables, an agent also has a state that represents the essential variables associated with its current situation.
- An agent is social having dynamic interactions with other agents that influence its behaviour.
- An agent may be adaptive, for example, by having rules or more abstract mechanisms that modify its behaviours. An agent may have the ability to learn and adapt its behaviours based on its accumulated experiences;
- An agent may be goal-directed, having goals to achieve (not necessarily objectives to maximize) with respect to its behaviours. This allows an agent to compare the outcome of its behaviours relative to its goals and adjust its responses and behaviours in future interactions.
- Agents may be heterogeneous. Agents may also be endowed with different amounts of resources or accumulate different levels of resources as a result of agent interactions, further differentiating agents.

According to Macal and North (2010), 'a theory of agent behaviour for the situations or contexts the agent encounters in the model is needed to model agent behaviour'. A modeller may apply a behavioural model if there is available empirical data to support the application, relevant to behavioural framework and empirically based heuristics (Sun, 2009). In that regard behavioural decision theory (Kahneman & Tversky, 1979) and anticipatory systems theory (Rosen, 1985; Butz & Pezzulo, 2008) can greatly enhance ABM application.

Comparing the above two modelling frameworks, a key limitation of the system dynamics approach, is that stocks and flows are related to the quantity rather than to the quality and that SD models have fixed structure and lack of capability to modify structurally and to adapt their levels, rates, and equations in response to environmental change. The latter is one of the distinctive capacities of agent-based models, which by their nature consist of a set of autonomous or semiautonomous agents (Parunak et al., 1998; Macal, 2010; Bonabeau, 2002).

Schieritz and Milling (2003) brought further in the debate of integrating system dynamics and ABM the metaphor of 'modeling the forest or modeling the trees' where they argue that an integrating approach would need to take concern about modelling the whole picture, and not concentrate on micro only or macro only level. Agent-based modelling focuses on agents interacting by following rules and rule routines, discovered by observation or by reverse direction of study, following an inductive approach. While systems dynamics is deductive, having feedback structure which differentiates the level of system analysis in both approaches into looking for leverage points in rules and agents in the former, and in the feedback structure in the latter (Scholl, 2001b).

One way to bring in "quality" and flexibility within the SD models structurally can be achieved by 'letting' agents interact with stocks and flows, that is, by integrating each modelling paradigm with one another. This can allow the agent decision action routine and agent attributes to interact with inflow and outflow rates of stock accumulation and depletion, and can transfer agents' adaptive capability to support structure changes by reordering, inclusion of new or elimination of predefined stocks and flows to account for emerging structural flexibility.

An integrated SD and AB modelling facilitates the definition of appropriate levels of aggregation for each component of the system and can be particularly relevant when the modelled environment contain configurations of agents and resources interactions (Popkov & Garifullin, 2007; Borshchev & Filippov, 2004; Kolominsky-Rabas et al., 2015). Furthermore, for many modelling problems, a combination of SD and AB can provide the strategic overview characteristic of SD, while still capturing relevant elements of the individual heterogeneity and stochasticity of entities and processes (Guerrero et al., 2016). Depending on the modelled environment 'resource' or 'agent' features, one or the other modelling and simulation approach could be regarded as being more appropriate. However, in resource agent systems, natural hybridization of the modelling approach could bring further benefits for the mutual complementarity in both macro and micro treatment of the system elements.

No matter of what classification is followed, the goal of SD and AB combination seems to be related to the creation of more 'accurate' (Ghaffarzadegan et al., 2011) hybrid models (Djanatliev & German, 2016; Lättilä et al., 2010) in respect to capturing different levels of systemic granularity from quality (agent decisions), and quantity (resource flows) perspective. 'Accurate' here means that hybrid method combinations have the capabilities to capture better the behaviour of the simulated systems and their components due to their enhanced technical apparatus and to achieve an 'accurate representation' of simulated real systems, comparing simulated vs real 'pattern' of behaviour of those systems (Ghaffarzadegan et al., 2011, pp. 29 and 30).

## References

Ackermann, F. (2012). Problem structuring methods 'in the Dock': Arguing the case for Soft OR. *European Journal of Operational Research, 219*(3), 652–658.

Ackermann, F., & Eden, C. (2010). Strategic options development and analysis. In *Systems approaches to managing change: A practical guide* (pp. 135–190). Springer. https://doi.org/10.1007/978-1-84882-809-4_4

Ackermann, F., & Eden, C. (2011). Strategic management of stakeholders: Theory and practice. *Long Range Planning, 44*(3), 179–196.

Ackermann, F., Eden, C., & Cropper, S. (1992). *Getting started with cognitive mapping* (p. 1992). Banxia Software.

Ackermann, F., Franco, L. A., Rouwette, E., & White, L. (2014). Special issue on problem structuring research and practice. *EURO Journal on Decision Processes, 2*(3–4), 165–172. https://doi.org/10.1007/s40070-014-0037-6

Ackoff, R. L. (1979). The future of operational research is past. *The Journal of the Operational Research Society, 30*(2), 93–104. https://doi.org/10.2307/3009290

Agle, B. R., Donaldson, T., Freeman, R. E., Jensen, M. C., Mitchell, R. K., & Wood, D. J. (2008). Dialogue: Toward superior stakeholder theory. *Business Ethics Quarterly, 18*(2), 153. https://doi.org/10.5840/beq200818214

Anderson, P. (1999). Complexity theory and organization science. *Organization Science, 10*(3), 216–232. https://doi.org/10.2307/2640328

Axtell, R. (2000). *Why agents? On the varied motivations for agent computing in the social sciences* (Vol. 17, pp. 1–23). Center on Social and Economics Dynamics - The Brookings Institution. https://doi.org/10.1016/j.cep.2007.02.029

Axtell, R., Axelrod, R., Epstein, J. M., & Cohen, M. D. (1996). Aligning simulation models: A case study and results. *Computational & Mathematical Organization Theory, 1*(2), 123–141. https://doi.org/10.1007/BF01299065

Barney, J. B. (1986). Organizational culture: Can it be a source of sustained competitive advantage? *The Academy of Management Review, 11*(3), 656–665. https://doi.org/10.2307/258317

Barney, J. (1991). Firm resources and sustained competitive advantage. *Journal of Management, 17*(1), 99–120.

Beer, S. (1986). Diagnosing the system for organizations. *European Journal of Operational Research, 23*(2), 115. https://doi.org/10.1016/0377-2217(86)90249-3

Begun, J. W., Zimmerman, B., & Dooley, K. (2003). Health care organizations as complex adaptive systems. *Advances in Health Care Organization Theory, 33*(3), 253–288. https://doi.org/10.1177/009430610403300325

Bertalanffy, L. V. (1968). *General system theory: Foundations, development, applications*. G. Braziller.

Block, J., Hu, B., & Pickl, S. (2013). Inclusive growth and sustainable finance - A system dynamics model. In *31st International Conference of the System Dynamics Society, March 2016.*

Bonabeau, E. (2002). Agent-based modeling: Methods and techniques for simulating human systems. *Proceedings of the National Academy of Sciences, 99*(suppl. 3), 7280–7287. https://doi.org/10.1073/pnas.082080899

Borshchev, A., & Filippov, A. (2004). From system dynamics to agent based modeling. *Simulation, 66*(11), 25–29. Accessed from http://www.econ.iastate.edu/tesfatsi/systemdyndiscreteeventabmcompared.borshchevfilippov04.pdf

Bryant, J. (2007). Drama theory: Dispelling the myths. *Journal of the Operational Research Society, 58*(5), 602–613. https://doi.org/10.1057/palgrave.jors.2602239

Bryson, J. M., Ackermann, F., & Eden, C. (2007). Putting the resource-based view of strategy and distinctive competencies to work in public organizations. *Public Administration Review, 67*(4), 702–717. https://doi.org/10.1111/j.1540-6210.2007.00754.x

Butz, M. V., & Pezzulo, G. (2008). Benefits of anticipations in cognitive agents. In *The challenge of anticipation* (pp. 45–62). Springer. https://doi.org/10.1007/978-3-540-87702-8_3

Checkland, P., & Scholes, J. (1990). *Soft systems methodology in action*. Wiley.

Council of the European Union. (2016). Council conclusions on strengthening the balance in the pharmaceutical systems in the EU and its member states. *The Council of the European Union, 17/6.*

Coyle, G. (2000). Qualitative and quantitative modelling in system dynamics: Some research questions. *System Dynamics Review, 16*(3), 225–244. https://doi.org/10.1002/1099-1727(200023)16:3<225::AID-SDR195>3.0.CO;2-D

Crotty, J. (2009). Structural causes of the global financial crisis: A critical assessment of the "new financial architecture". *Cambridge Journal of Economics, 33*(4), 563–580. https://doi.org/10.1093/cje/bep023

Djanatliev, A., & German, R. (2016). Towards a guide to domain-specific hybrid simulation. In *Proceedings - Winter simulation conference, 2016-February*, pp. 1609–1620. https://doi.org/10.1109/WSC.2015.7408281

Dooley, K. (1996). Complex adaptive systems: A nominal definition. *The Chaos Network, 8*(1), 2–3.
Eden, C. (1988). Cognitive mapping. *European Journal of Operational Research, 36*(1), 1–13.
Eden, C. (2004). Analyzing cognitive maps to help structure issues or problems. *European Journal of Operational Research, 159*(3), 673–686.
Eden, C., & Ackermann, F. (2001). SODA - the principles. In *Rational analysis for a problematic world revisited* (pp. 21–41).
Eden, C., Ackermann, F., & Cropper, S. (1992). The analysis of cause maps. *Journal of Management Studies, 29*(3), 309–324.
Farmer, J. D., Gallegati, M., Hommes, C., Kirman, A., Ormerod, P., Cincotti, S., Sanchez, A., & Helbing, D. (2012). A complex systems approach to constructing better models for managing financial markets and the economy. *European Physical Journal Special Topics, 214*, 295–324. https://doi.org/10.1140/epjst/e2012-01696-9
Fiori, S. (2009). Herbert A. Simon and contemporary theories of bounded rationality. In *SSRN eLibrary*. Accessed from http://ssrn.com/paper=1367091
Forrester, J. W. (1958). Industrial dynamics: A major breakthrough for decision makers. *Harvard Business Review, 36*(4), 37–66.
Forrester, J. (1961). *Origin of system dynamics*. System Dynamics Society. Accessed from http://www.systemdynamics.org/DL-IntroSysDyn/start.htm
Forrester, J. W. (1976). Business structure, economic cycles, and national policy. *Futures, 8*(3), 195–214.
Forrester, J. W. (1989). The system dynamics national model: Macrobehavior from microstructure. In *Proceedings of the 1989 international system dynamics conference: Computer-based management of complex systems* (pp. 3–12).
Forrester, J. W. (1995). The beginning of system dynamics. *McKinsey Quarterly*, 4–17.
Friend, J. (1995). Supporting developmental decision processes: The evolution of an OR approach. *International Transactions in Operational Research, 2*(3), 225–232. https://doi.org/10.1016/0969-6016(95)00006-S
Friend, J. (2011). The strategic choice approach. In *Wiley Encyclopedia of operations research and management science* (pp. 1–12). Wiley.
Gell-Mann, M. (1997). *The quark and the jaguar: Adventures in the simple and the complex*. St. Martin's Griffin. https://doi.org/10.1119/1.18607
George, A. (1970). The market for lemons: Quality uncertainty and the market mechanism.
Ghaffarzadegan, N., Lyneis, J., & Richardson, G. P. (2011). How small system dynamics models can help the public policy process. *System Dynamics Review, 27*(1), 22–44. https://doi.org/10.1002/sdr.442
Gigerenzer, G. (2000). Bounded rationality: The adaptive toolbox. In. *International Journal of Psychology, 35*(3–4), 203–204. https://doi.org/10.1002/mar.10060
Gigerenzer, G., & Goldstein, D. G. (2011). Reasoning the fast and frugal way: Models of bounded rationality. In *Heuristics: The foundations of adaptive behavior*. Oxford University Press. https://doi.org/10.1093/acprof:oso/9780199744282.003.0002
Guerrero, C. N., Schwarz, P., & Slinger, J. H. (2016). A recent overview of the integration of system dynamics and agent-based modelling and simulation. In *34th international conference of the system dynamics society*.
Haas-Wilson, D. (2001). Arrow and the information market failure in health care: The changing content and sources of health care information. *Journal of Health Politics, Policy and Law, 26*(5), 1031–1044. https://doi.org/10.1215/03616878-26-5-1031
Helfat, C. E., & Peteraf, M. A. (2015). Managerial cognitive capabilities and the microfoundations of dynamic capabilities. *Strategic Management Journal, 36*(6), 831–850. https://doi.org/10.1002/smj
Helfat, C. E., & Martin, J. A. (2015). Dynamic managerial capabilities: Review and assessment of managerial impact on strategic change. Journal of Management, 41(5), 1281–1312.

Hillman, A. J., Withers, M. C., & Collins, B. J. (2009). Resource dependence theory: A review. *Journal of Management, 35*(6), 1404–1427. https://doi.org/10.1177/0149206309343469
Holland, J. H. (1992). Complex adaptive systems. *Daedalus, 121*(1), 17–30. https://doi.org/10.2307/20025416
Howard, N. (1998). N-person 'soft' games. *Journal of the Operational Research Society, 49*(2), 144–150. https://doi.org/10.1057/palgrave.jors.2600514
Howick, S., & Ackermann, F. (2011). Mixing or methods in practice: Past, present and future directions. *European Journal of Operational Research, 215*(3), 503–511. https://doi.org/10.1016/j.ejor.2011.03.013
Howick, S., & Whalley, J. (2007, August). Broadband adoption: The case of rural and remote Scotland. In *Proceedings of the 25th international conference of the system dynamics society*. System Dynamics Society.
Howick, S., Eden, C., Ackermann, F., & Williams, T. (2008). Building confidence in models for multiple audiences: The modelling cascade. *European Journal of Operational Research, 186*(3), 1068–1083. https://doi.org/10.1016/j.ejor.2007.02.027
Huff, A. S. (1990). *Mapping strategic thought* (pp. 11–49). Goodreads. https://doi.org/10.5465/AMR.1992.4279590
Jantsch, E. (1980). The self-organizing universe: Scientific and human implications of the emerging paradigm of evolution. In *Systems science and world order library Innovations in systems science*. Accessed from http://www.kheper.net/evolution/selforguniv.html.
Jennings, N. R. (2000). On agent-based software engineering. *Artificial Intelligence, 117*(2), 277–296. https://doi.org/10.1016/S0004-3702(99)00107-1
John, S. (2000). *Business dynamics: Systems thinking and modeling for a complex world*. Irwin McGrawHill.
Joseph, E. S. (2010). Government failure vs. market failure: Principles of regulation. In *Government and markets: Toward a new theory of regulation* (pp. 1–27). Sage. https://doi.org/10.1017/CBO9780511657504.002
Kahneman, D. (2003). Maps of bounded rationality: Psychology for behavioral economics. *American Economic Review, 93*(5), 1449–1475.
Kahneman, D. (2011). *Thinking, fast and slow*. Macmillan.
Kahneman, D., & Tversky, A. (1972). Subjective probability: A judgment of representativeness. *Cognitive Psychology, 3*(3), 430–454.
Kahneman, D., & Tversky, A. (1979). Prospect theory: An analysis of decision under risk. *Econometrica, 47*(2), 263–292. https://doi.org/10.1111/j.1536-7150.2011.00774.x
Kahneman, D., & Tversky, A. (1982). The psychology of preferences. *Scientific American, 246*(1), 160–173.
Kauffman, S. (1995). *At home in the universe: The search for the Laws of self-organization and complexity*. Oxford University Press. https://doi.org/10.1017/S0016672300033772
Kazakov, R., Howick, S., & Morton, A. (2021). Managing complex adaptive systems: A resource/agent qualitative modelling perspective. *European Journal of Operational Research, 290*(1), 386. https://doi.org/10.1016/j.ejor.2020.08.007
Kolominsky-Rabas, P. L., Djanatliev, A., Wahlster, P., Gantner-Bär, M., Hofmann, B., German, R., Sedlmayr, M., Reinhardt, E., Schüttler, J., Kriza, C., Niederländer, C., Prokosch, H. U., Lenz, R., Baumgärtel, P., Schäffski, O., Emmert, M., Meier, F., Aisenbrey, A., Voigt, W., et al. (2015). Technology foresight for medical device development through hybrid simulation: The ProHTA project. *Technological Forecasting and Social Change, 97*, 105–114. https://doi.org/10.1016/j.techfore.2013.12.005
Kunc, M., & Morecroft, J. (2006). Business dynamics for strategic development. In *The 24th international conference of the system dynamics society*, pp. 1–24. Accessed from http://www.systemdynamics.org/conferences/2006/proceed/papers/MOREC424.pdf
Kunc, M. H., & Morecroft, J. D. W. (2009). Resource-based strategies and problem structuring: Using resource maps to manage resource systems. *Journal of the Operational Research Society, 60*(2), 191–199. https://doi.org/10.1057/palgrave.jors.2602551

Kunc, M., & Morecroft, J. (2010). Managerial decision making and firm performance under a resource based paradigm. *Strategic Management Journal, 1182*(March), 1164–1182. https://doi.org/10.1002/smj.858

Lättilä, L., Hilletofth, P., & Lin, B. (2010). Hybrid simulation models - When, why, how? *Expert Systems with Applications, 37*(12), 7969–7975. https://doi.org/10.1016/j.eswa.2010.04.039

LeBaron, B., & Tesfatsion, L. (2008). Modeling macroeconomies as open-ended dynamic systems of interacting agents. *American Economic Review, 98*(2), 246–250. https://doi.org/10.1257/aer.98.2.246

Louie, A. H. (2010). Robert Rosen's anticipatory systems. *Foresight, 12*(3), 18–29. https://doi.org/10.1108/14636681011049848

Luke, D. A., & Stamatakis, K. A. (2012). Systems science methods in public health: Dynamics, networks, and agents. *Annual Review of Public Health, 33*, 357–376.

Macal, C. M. (2010, December). To agent-based simulation from system dynamics. In *Proceedings of the 2010 winter simulation conference* (pp. 371–382). IEEE.

Macal, C. M., & North, M. J. (2006, December). Tutorial on agent-based modeling and simulation part 2: How to model with agents. In *Proceedings of the 2006 winter simulation conference* (pp. 73–83). IEEE.

Macal, C. M., & North, M. J. (2010, December). Toward teaching agent-based simulation. In *Proceedings of the 2010 winter simulation conference* (pp. 268–277). IEEE.

Macal, C., & North, M. (2014, December). Introductory tutorial: Agent-based modeling and simulation. In *Proceedings of the winter simulation conference 2014* (pp. 6–20). IEEE.

Macal, C., & North, M. (2015). Introductory tutorial: Agent-based modeling and simulation. In *Proceedings - Winter simulation conference, 2015-January*, pp. 6–20. https://doi.org/10.1109/WSC.2014.7019874

Magness, V. (2008). Who are the stakeholders now? An empirical examination of the Mitchell, Agle, and Wood theory of stakeholder salience. *Journal of Business Ethics, 83*(2), 177. https://doi.org/10.1007/s10551-007-9610-2

Marshall, D. A., Burgos-Liz, L., IJzerman, M. J., Osgood, N. D., Padula, W. V., Higashi, M. K., Wong, P. K., Pasupathy, K. S., & Crown, W. (2015). Applying dynamic simulation modeling methods in health care delivery research—The SIMULATE checklist: Report of the ISPOR simulation modeling emerging good practices task force. *Value in Health, 18*, 5. https://doi.org/10.1016/j.jval.2014.12.001

Maturana, H. R. (2002). Autopoiesis, structural coupling and cognition: A history of these and other notions in the biology of cognition. *Cybernetics & Human Knowing, 9*(3), 5–34. https://doi.org/10.1111/j.1471-1842.2008.00767.x

Morecroft, J. D. (1982). A critical review of diagramming tools for conceptualizing feedback system models. *Dynamica, 8*(1), 20–29.

Morecroft, J. (1999). Visualising and rehearsing strategy. *Business Strategy Review, 10*(3), 17–32.

Morecroft, J. D. (2015). *Strategic modelling and business dynamics: A feedback systems approach*. John Wiley & Sons.

Mingers, J. (1991). The cognitive theories of Maturana and Varela. *Systems Practice, 4*(4), 319–338. https://doi.org/10.1007/BF01062008

Mingers, J. (2001). Combining IS research methods: Towards a pluralist methodology. *MIS Quarterly, 12*(3), 240–259. https://doi.org/10.1287/isre.12.3.240.9709

Mingers, J., & Rosenhead, J. (2004). Problem structuring methods in action. *European Journal of Operational Research, 152*(3), 530–554. https://doi.org/10.1016/S0377-2217(03)00056-0

Morel, B., & Ramanujam, R. (1999). Through the dynamics the of looking glass of complexity : Adaptive organizations as systems and evolving. *Organization Science, 10*(3), 278–293.

Newell, A., & Simon, H. A. (1959). *The simulation of human thought* (p. 1734). Rand Corporation.

North, M. J., & Macal, C. M. (2007). *Managing business complexity: Discovering strategic solutions with agentbased modeling and simulation*. Oxford University Press.

Parunak, H. V. D., Savit, R., Riolo, R. L., & Van Dyke Parunak, H. (1998). Agent-based modeling vs. equation-based modeling: A case study and users' guide. In *Multi-agent systems and agent-based simulation* (pp. 277–283). Springer. Accessed from http://www.springerlink.com/index/1EQYEPY5W8XVJCD3.pdf

Peteraf, M. (1993). The cornerstones of competitive advantage: A resource-based view. *Strategic Management Journal, 14*(April 1992), 179–191. https://doi.org/10.1017/CBO9781107415324.004

Pezzulo, G. (2007). Anticipation and future-oriented capabilities in natural and artificial cognition. *Years of Artificial Intelligence, 50*, 257–270. https://doi.org/10.1007/978-3-540-77296-5_24

Pfeffer, J., & Salancik, G. R. (1978). The external control of organizations: a resource dependence perspective. In *The sociology of organization* (pp. 233–242).

Phelan, S. E. (1999). A note on the correspondence between complexity and systems theory. *Systemic Practice and Action Research, 12*(3), 237–246. https://doi.org/10.1023/A:1022495500485

Phillips, L. D. (1984). A theory of requisite decision models. *Acta Psychologica, 56*(1–3), 29–48. https://doi.org/10.1016/0001-6918(84)90005-2

Phillips, L. D., & Phillips, M. C. (1993). Facilitated work groups: Theory and practice. *Journal of the Operational Research Society, 44*(6), 533–549. https://doi.org/10.1057/jors.1993.96

Plsek, P. (2001). Redesigning health care with insights from the science of complex adaptive systems. In *Crossing the quality chasm: A new health system for the 21st century* (pp. 309–322). Springer. https://doi.org/10.1300/J022v19n03_03

Popkov, T., & Garifullin, M. (2007). Multi-approach simulation modeling: Challenge of the future. In *Systems modeling and simulation* (pp. 103–107).

Prigogine, I., & Stengers, I. (1984). *Order out of chaos: Man's new dialogue with nature*. Fontana.

Radzicki, M. J., & Sterman, J. D. (1994). Evolutionary economics and system dynamics. In *Evolutionary concepts in contemporary economics* (pp. 61–89). Accessed from https://www.press.umich.edu/14207/evolutionary_concepts_in_contemporary_economics

Randers, J. (1976). A framework for discussion of model conceptualization. In *Proceedings of the 1976 International Conference on System Dynamics*.

Randers, J. (1980). Guidelines for model conceptualization. In *Elements of the system dynamics method* (pp. 117–138). MIT Press. https://doi.org/10.1057/palgrave.jors.2600456

Richardson, G. P., & Pugh, A. L. I. (1981). Introduction to system dynamics modeling with DYNAMO. *Journal of the Operational Research Society, 48*(11). https://doi.org/10.1038/sj.jors.2600961

Roberts, N. (1981). Developing an introductory curriculum in system modeling and simulation: The system dynamics approach. *Technological Forecasting and Social Change, 19*(2), 175–186.

Roberts, M. S. (2015). Dynamic simulation in health care comes of age. *Value in Health, 18*(2), 143–144. https://doi.org/10.1016/j.jval.2015.02.006

Rosen, R. (1985). *Anticipatory systems: Philosophical, mathematical, and methodological foundations* (IFSR international series on systems science and engineering) (Vol. 1). Springer. https://doi.org/10.1080/03081079.2012.726322

Rosenhead, J. (1980). Planning under uncertainty: 1. The inflexibility of methodologies. *Journal of the Operational Research Society, 31*(3), 209–216. https://doi.org/10.1057/jors.1980.38

Rosenhead, J. (1996). What's the problem? An introduction to problem structuring methods. *Interfaces, 26*(6), 117–131. https://doi.org/10.1287/inte.26.6.117

Rosenhead, J. (2006). Past, present and future of problem structuring methods. *Journal of the Operational Research Society, 57*(7), 759–765. https://doi.org/10.1057/palgrave.jors.2602206

Rosenhead, J., & Mingers, J. (2001). A new paradigm of analysis. In *Rational analysis for a problematic world revisited: Problem structuring methods for complexity, uncertainty and conflict* (pp. 1–19).

Schieritz, N. (2002, July). Integrating system dynamics and agent-based modeling. In *Proceedings of the XX international conference of the system dynamics society*.

Schieritz, N., & Milling, P. (2003). Modeling the forest or modeling the trees: A comparison of system dynamics and agent-based simulation. In *Proceedings of the 21st international system dynamics society, Phelan 1999*, pp. 1–15. Accessed from http://www.systemdynamics.org/conferences/2003/proceed/PAPERS/140.pdf

Scholl, H. J. (2001a). Agent-based and system dynamics modeling: A call for cross study and joint research. In *Proceedings of the 34th Hawaii international conference on system sciences* (pp. 1–8). IEEE Computer Society. https://doi.org/10.1109/HICSS.2001.926296

Scholl, H. J. (2001b). Agent-based and system dynamics modeling: A call for cross study and joint research. In *Proceedings of the Hawaii International Conference on System Sciences*, p. 62. https://doi.org/10.1109/HICSS.2001.926296

Simon, H. A. (1955). A behavioral model of rational choice. *The Quarterly Journal of Economics, 69*(1), 99–118. https://doi.org/10.2307/1884852

Simon, H. A. (1965). The logic of rational decision. *British Journal for the Philosophy of Science, 16*(63), 169–186. https://doi.org/10.1093/bjps/XVI.63.169

Simon, H. (1972). Theories of bounded rationality. In *Decision and organization* (pp. 161–176). Elsevier.

Simon, H. A. (1978). Rationality as process and as product of thought. *American Economic Association Review, 68*(2), 1–16. https://doi.org/10.2307/1816653

Simon, H. A. (1991). Bounded rationality and organizational learning. *Organization Science, 2*(1), 125–134. https://doi.org/10.1287/orsc.2.1.125

Simon, H. A. (2000). Bounded rationality in social science: Today and tomorrow. *Mind & Society, 1*(1), 25–39. https://doi.org/10.1007/BF02512227

Sirmon, D. G., & Hitt, M. A. (2009). Contingencies within dynamic managerial capabilities: Interdependent effects of resource investment and deployment on firm performance. *Strategic Management Journal, 30*(13), 1375–1394. https://doi.org/10.1002/smj.791

Sterman, J. D. (2001). System dynamics modeling: Tools for learning in a complex world. *California Management Review, 43*(4), 8–25.

Stiglitz, J. (2000). The contributions of the economics of information to twentieth century economics. *The Quarterly Journal of Economics, 115*(4), 1441–1478. https://doi.org/10.1162/003355300555015

Sun, R. (2009). Cognitive architectures and multi-agent social simulation. In *Lecture notes in computer science (including subseries lecture notes in artificial intelligence and lecture notes in bioinformatics), 4078 LNAI* (pp. 7–21). Springer. https://doi.org/10.1007/978-3-642-03339-1_2

Teece, D. J., Teece, D. J., Pisano, G., Pisano, G., Shuen, A., & Shuen, A. (1997). Dynamic capabilities and strategic management. *Strategic Management Journal*, 509–533. Accessed from http://www.jstor.org/stable/3088148

Teece, D. J., Pisano, G., & Shuen, A. (2008). Dynamic capabilities and strategic management. *Strategic Management Journal, 18*(March), 509–533. https://doi.org/10.1142/9789812834478_0002

Tversky, A., & Kahneman, D. (1974). Judgment under uncertainty: Heuristics and Biases: Biases in judgments reveal some heuristics of thinking under uncertainty. *Science, 185*(4157), 1124–1131.

Ulrich, D., & Barney, J. B. (1984). Perspectives in organizations: Resource dependence, efficiency, and population. *Academy of Management Review, 9*(3), 471–481. https://doi.org/10.5465/AMR.1984.4279680

Umpleby, S. A., & Dent, E. B. (1999). The origins and purposes of several traditions in systems theory and cybernetics. *Cybernetics & Systems, 30*(2), 79–103.

Von Bertalanffy, L. (1972). The history and status of general systems theory. *Academy of Management Journal, 15*(4), 407–426. https://doi.org/10.2307/255139

von Foerster, H. (1972). Perception of the future and the future of perception. *Instructional Science, 1*(1), 31–43. https://doi.org/10.1007/BF00053969

Von Foerster, H. (1979). Cybernetics of cybernetics. *Review: Literature and Arts of the Americas, 8*, 5–8. https://doi.org/10.1177/002194368402100104

Von Neumann, J., & Morgenstern, O. (1944). *Theory of games and economic behavior* (Vol. 625). Princeton University Press. https://doi.org/10.1177/1468795X06065810

Walker, B. M., & Winter, D. A. (2007). The elaboration of personal construct psychology. *Annual Review of Psychology, 58*, 453. https://doi.org/10.1146/annurev.psych.58.110405.085535
Weisbuch, G. (2006). Modeling complex systems: Do it! *Complexity, 11*(3), 25. https://doi.org/10.1002/cplx.20113
Wernerfeldt, B. (1984). A resource-based view of the firm. *Strategic Management Journal (Pre-1986), 5*(2), 171.
Winter, D. A. (2017). Personal construct psychology. In *Encyclopedia of personality and individual differences*. Springer. https://doi.org/10.1007/978-3-319-28099-8_1147-1
Wolstenholme, E. F. (1982). System dynamics in perspective. *Journal of the Operational Research Society, 33*(6), 547–556.
Wolstenholme, E. F. (1999). Qualitative vs quantitative modelling: The evolving balance. *Journal of the Operational Research Society, 50*, 422–428.
Wolstenholme, E. (2004). Using generic system archetypes to support thinking and modelling. *System Dynamics Review: The Journal of the System Dynamics Society, 20*(4), 341–356.

# Chapter 4
# Resource Agent Mapping of Healthcare and Pharmaceutical Systems

**Abstract** Healthcare and pharmaceutical markets are composed of multiple interdependent resources and agents who adapt their behaviours in response to one another and to changing external conditions. In this perspective, the resources of the healthcare and pharmaceutical markets include physical and human resources (such as medicines, medical equipment and personnel), financial resources (such as funding for research and development and healthcare services), and informational resources (such as medical research, drugs-related data, market data and patient data). The agents in these markets include healthcare providers, pharmaceutical companies, regulators, doctors and pharmacists, patients and other stakeholders.

A complex adaptive systems perspective highlights the interconnectedness of resources and agents in healthcare and pharmaceutical markets and emphasizes the importance of understanding how these interactions shape market outcomes and influence the delivery of healthcare services.

Chapter 4 presents a practical example of the design and application of the RAM methodology as a qualitative modelling approach, including steps for creating enhanced resource maps, agent interaction maps and agent behavioural maps.

## 4.1 Introduction

Roberts (2015) argued that 'accurate representations of complex realistic systems may require hybrid approaches that use components across multiple modelling types' and remarked that 'appropriate application of the dynamic methods … to the incredibly complex problems we face in healthcare today holds tremendous potential to improve the cost, quality, and efficiency of healthcare systems. Hopefully, dynamic simulation in healthcare may now come of age'.

According to the 'SIMULATE' checklist (Marshall et al., 2015), the healthcare and pharmaceutical systems are complex adaptive systems, having features like modelling multiple events, relationships, and stakeholders (System), including nonlinear or spatial relationships among stakeholders and their context that influence



R. Kazakov et al., *Understanding and Managing Socioeconomic Systems Behaviour*, Contributions to Management Science,
https://doi.org/10.1007/978-3-031-57057-5_4

behaviours and make outcomes in the system difficult to anticipate (Interactions). These systems have multilevel interactions that can be modelled from strategic, tactical, or operational perspectives (Multilevel). Therefore, to understand such systems decision makers need to use complex systems modelling methods (Understanding), capable of grasping feedback loops that change the behaviour of future interactions and the system outcomes (Loops), including multiple stakeholders with behavioural properties that interact and change the performance of the system (Agents). All these interactions are time dependent and exhibit dynamic transitions (Time), which lead to the emergence of macro level behaviour, following system interventions (Emergence).

There is abundance of modelling and simulation research studies in the healthcare field (Mustafee et al., 2015; Marshall et al., 2015; Mahsa Keshtkaran, 2015; Yan Li, 2014; Yu et al., 2010); however, there appeared to be a little number of published papers on a narrow topical variety when the focus is on pharmaceutical market and regulation. None of them presented a hybrid approach, that is, providing any form of combination (mixing, integration) among any of the above-mentioned modelling approaches in one enhanced multi-methodological framework.

The most explored topics are related to medicinal products prices, pharmaceutical planning, and pharmaceutical inventory, including availability and allocation. Price co-payment and pharmaceutical expenditure, drug reference prices and pharmaceutical products utilization have been also explored, with feu addressing pharmaceutical policy mix (product time-to-market, price co-payment, controlling doctors' prescribing behaviour), regulation impact, internal reference pricing, and generic drugs competition effect on prices.

Complex adaptive systems approaches like system dynamics and agent-based simulation modelling can provide a relevant option for tackling the challenges related to the pharmaceutical pricing regulation, like exploration of regulatory contextual effects on market competition and drug pricing.

For example, Kazakov and Petrova (2015) did a study related to policy evaluation and impact assessment of alternative/what-if policy decisions connected to reimbursement policy optimization. They employed mathematical modelling and simulation of the angiotensin converter enzyme (ACE) inhibitor antihypertension drugs market with the aid of computer modelling and simulation software. The focus of their study is designing and testing a reimbursement policy based on lower patient co-payment, while at the same time providing means for controlling pharmaceutical expenditure. The simulation experiments used prescription and market data by IMS Health. These data were analyzed and then used in a system dynamics model accounting for the doctor's prescribing behaviour, patient flows, and public expenditure, after which they explored alternative policy scenarios by interactive learning environment or the so-called management-flight simulator. Kazakov and Petrova (2015) have used management flight simulator system dynamic approach to the evaluation of alternative reimbursement policy scenarios; doctors, patients and public expenditure were conceptualized as key system stocks of resources flows subject to the variability in reimbursement level as one key influencing factor regarding prescribing and compliance behaviour. Main limitation of their study was the lack of account of doctor and patient decision/action routine. Taking account of agents' behaviours would bring further insights regarding managing the system, since these agents like drug suppliers, doctors and patients are key actors within the system.

Li et al. (2014) examined the social problem of unreasonably high pharmaceutical costs for patients in Chinese hospitals by system dynamics modelling. They have addressed two problems, that is, the unreasonably high prices of drugs and the high level of pharmaceutical fees relative to the medical costs of patients, aiming to suggest countermeasures and possible solutions. They found that if hospital and medical staff receive a higher kickback rate, they would be more likely to prescribe unnecessary expensive drugs to make greater profits, which results in unnecessary drug consumption and irrational drug use, and eventually leading to unreasonably high pharmaceutical fees. Further, they recommended that the benefit chain of the main drug suppliers needed to be cut off in order to break the link between the profits from pharmaceutical sales and the prescribing behaviour of physicians, and hospital incomes. They conclude that a reformed pharmaceutical distribution system would be needed to regulate physicians and hospital interaction. Li et al. (2014) applied system dynamic exploration of high drug prices in hospitals and drug expenditure and explored how the drug distribution system could be improved; doctors were conceptualized as stock of resource, influenced by financial incentivizing by drug companies; They identified a feedback loop reinforcing cycle between pharmaceutical sales and hospital income and accentuated on the ethical perspective and the need for better regulation over the interaction between drug suppliers and medical staff in hospitals. Main limitation was the lack of account of agent decision action procedure of doctors and drug suppliers.

Kunc and Kazakov (2013) developed a system dynamics simulation of the chronic cardiac disease in Bulgaria examining the dynamic behaviour of a cardiac drug molecule in the market. The objective of the study was to analyze the effect of different drug regulation policy options like providing timely access to market, influencing prescribing of generic medicines, implementing incentives for increasing the percentage of diagnosed patients. While the project developed my experience in system dynamics modelling, it revealed limitations like experimenting with only one drug molecule, and lack of capacity to model agent interaction with key market resources.

Kazakov and Kunc (2016) developed an interactive learning environment (ILE) by the application of system dynamics simulation model to aid the reformulation of a new generic drug launch plan. It also included account of pricing regulation changes in the future and rival pricing competition. That helped enhancing managerial cognition for exploring alternative product launch tactic and for finding optimal path of competitive action. The modelling experiment treated doctor behaviour, influenced by government and pharmaceutical company and patient flow, influenced by doctor allocation of drug therapy, by drug co-payment and by therapeutic compliance. The authors accentuated on the notion of managerial resource conceptualization through the resource-based theory (RBT) and anticipatory systems theory lenses. In addition, authors used the modelling and simulation interactive learning environment to support behavioural experimentation with the management team. Also, they applied combination of qualitative and quantitative simulation modelling. Main limitation of their study was the lack of account of agent behaviour dependent on different decision action routine.

Li et al. (2016) article introduced agent-based modelling by providing a narrative review of agent-based models of chronic disease and identifying the characteristics of various chronic health conditions that must be taken into account to build effective clinical- and policy-relevant models. Li et al. also identify barriers to adopting agent-based models to study chronic diseases and discuss future research directions of agent-based modelling applied to problems related to specific chronic health conditions. They have demonstrated that agent-based modelling is a promising systems science approach that can model complex interactions and processes related to chronic health conditions, such as adaptive behaviours, feedback loops, and contextual effects. However, they did not take into account in their work how agents interact and compete for limited resources.

Tang and Rosen (2014) also have applied AB modelling for an exploration of what incentives could overcome the widespread underuse of low cost, high benefit therapies (e.g. beta blockers and statins) and overuse of high cost, low benefit therapies (e.g. elective percutaneous coronary interventions). They use the agent-based modelling (ABM) to evaluate the health and economic impact of changing the financial incentives (out-of-pocket costs) faced by Medicare patients with CHD and to evaluate the incremental costs and quality-adjusted life expectancy of different policies. They argue that modelling behaviour change in both patients and physicians in response to targeted incentives to improve use of the most valuable therapies and reduce use of the least valuable therapies can be of great benefit both to the effort to improve efficiency and to understand the impact of these behaviours on the system. However, they took no account of drug companies' behaviour and doctors' prescribing behaviour regarding agent competition for limited resources like budget, prescribing doctors and buying patients.

A lack of broad hybrid system dynamics and agent-based modelling practice in pharmaceutical market systems, policy and regulation, and a growing need publicly announced Roberts (2015) have been pointing out the boundary of a widely underexplored healthcare policy and management territory. One of the few hybrid system dynamics and agent-based models recently provided in Djanatliev and German (2016). Kolominsky-Rabas et al. (2015) was focused on Prospective Health Technology Assessment (ProHTA) approach with the aim to explore the effects of new innovations early before the 'expensive and risky development phase begins'. The authors have considered two key questions related to 'economic prognoses and or impacts on patient's health' like 'How can a new technology be optimized prospectively after the observation of simulated effects?' and 'What innovation is required to reach desired output values?'

In their model they identified four modules as important ones which have conceptual relevance to my modelling project: population dynamics, disease dynamics, healthcare delivery, and healthcare financing. Djanatliev and German (2013) experimented with extending their proHTA model to combine system dynamics, discrete-event, and agent-based simulation by adding a middle layer due to the need to model the workflow of a mobile unit, providing an intermediate link from the micro agent level to the macro environment modelled by system dynamics.

In relation to the need of developing further a hybrid (multi-methodological paradigm) modelling framework, Lynch et al. (2015) proposed a multi-paradigm modelling framework (MPMF) for modelling and simulating problem situations. The benefit of the framework relates to identifying 'different levels of granularity (macro, meso, and micro)' which are linked to the relevant modelling paradigms in order to combine them for a more comprehensive modelling of the problem situation. Complex system behaviour can be reproduced better by holistic and comprehensive (Rosenhead, 2006; Ackermann et al., 2014) approach, rather than by requisite one, due to the purpose of the latter to approximate and simplify complex interactions (Phillips, 1984).

Further, Lynch et al. (2015) argued that multiparadigm modelling offers benefits over single modelling because it allows interactions representation of system elements at all levels of granularity, by the most appropriate paradigm. That approach provides means for reducing approximation of system elements and their interactions, thus increasing the level of correspondence between the model and the modelled environment.

Policy decision makers need to understand complexities of the healthcare system context emerging from the agent and resource interactions. Improving the efficiency of healthcare including pharmaceutical complex systems would require dynamic simulation modelling approach to the evaluation of healthcare policies and anticipation of interventions effect, because agents have adaptive non-linear decisions and actions changing over time, affecting resource levels and resource structures Marshall et al. (2015). Healthcare delivery systems including pharmaceutical subsystems and supply chain processes, have abundance of feedback, resource accumulations, resource flows, and time delays features in addition to autonomous and interacting agents. Hybrid modelling and simulation experimentation with different 'what-if' policies can provide an interactive learning apparatus for assumptions testing, and anticipation of the effects of different system scenarios. In that way policy decision makers are enabled 'to anticipate the consequences of unforeseen interactions in the system (emergence) and become prescriptive in nature, such that the models prescribe what actions/interventions to take, on the basis of scenarios tested through experiments' (Marshall et al. 2015).

## 4.2 Creating a Resource Agent Map

In general, the market resources (a medicine, public budget, etc.) provide the carrying capacity of a market system, which level can evolve through accumulation and depletion (by resources inflows and resources outflows), influenced by market agents interactive behaviour, other resources and endogenous systemic factors, including information feedback effects.

The mapping procedure included iterative steps involving analyzing system resources and agents, key influencing factors, the interrelations between all system components using arrows to denote the direction of influence or interdependence.

First, the enhanced resource map (RM) design encompasses several components aimed at exploring the effects of pharmaceutical pricing policies. This multifaceted approach involves the creation of a cognitive map (CoM) that outlines the main statements regarding these policies' impacts. At the macro level, a causal map (CaM) provides a global perspective on the causal relationships involved. Additionally, at the micro level, another CaM offers a more localized perspective on these dynamics.

An important aspect of this design is the mapping of the 'resources' concept within the micro CaM, allowing for a detailed analysis of how resources interplay in the local context. Furthermore, this enhanced RM design is implemented using software, enabling the visualization and analysis of complex relationships and feedback mechanisms.

Second, the AiM (agent interaction map) and AbM (agent behaviour map) designs focus on market actors' decisions and activities in response to pharmaceutical pricing policies. Initially, a cognitive map (CoM) captures the primary statements related to these policies, which are then refined and redesigned to accurately reflect the decisions and activities of market actors.

Subsequently, drafts of AiM and AbM are developed to model the interrelations and rules governing these market actors' behaviour. These drafts serve as crucial tools for analyzing the structural aspects and dynamics of agent interactions within the system.

Third, the resource agent map (RAM) design represents an integrated perspective, offering a holistic view of resources and agents within the context of pharmaceutical pricing policies. A new causal map (CaM) is drafted specifically for RAM, allowing for the positioning of resources and agents in a combined perspective.

This RAM design undergoes iterative development in software, incorporating insights and findings from a published journal paper authored by Kazakov et al. in 2021. This iterative process ensures that RAM accurately represents the dynamic interactions between resources and agents, providing valuable insights into the complex landscape of pharmaceutical pricing policies.

In summary, these designs—enhanced RM, AiM, AbM, and RAM—constitute comprehensive tools for researchers and decision makers to explore and analyze the intricate dynamics surrounding pharmaceutical pricing policies, from both global and local perspectives, and to facilitate iterative development and analysis through software implementation.

Figures 4.1, 4.2, and 4.3 provide an illustrative example. Initially a macro level causal map (CaM) of product pricing was constructed following main documented statements, regarding resource, agent and their interaction components of the pharmaceutical market. The goal of that map is to frame the system boundary and factors influencing drug pricing, like competition and information imperfection, and to support the design of the extended RM. A macro level like CaM related to the public drug price approval regulation has the goal of depicting also the contextual effect of

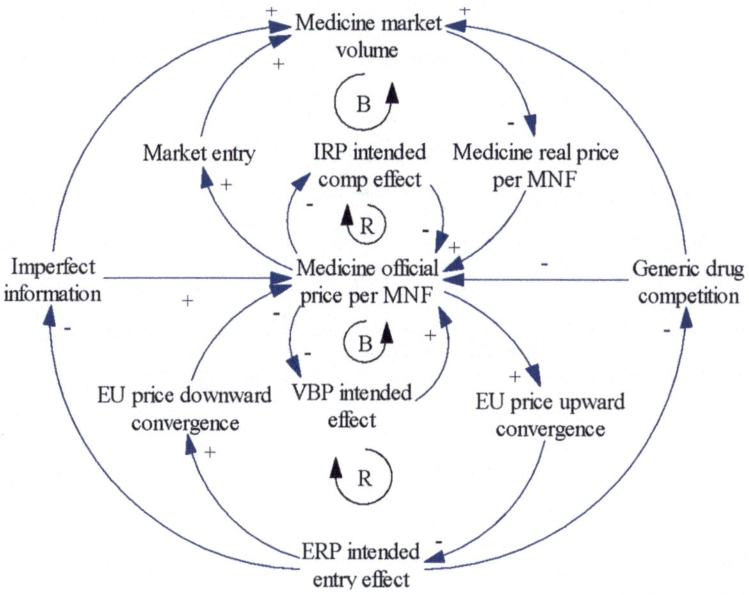


**Fig. 4.1** A macro level CaM related to the public drug price approval regulation and contextual effects

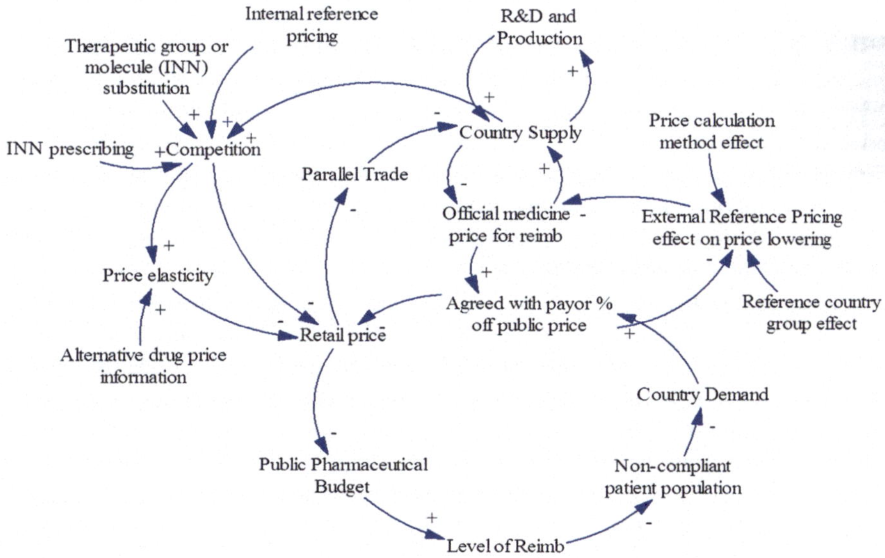


**Fig. 4.2** A micro level CaM of the regulation effect on the pharmaceutical market

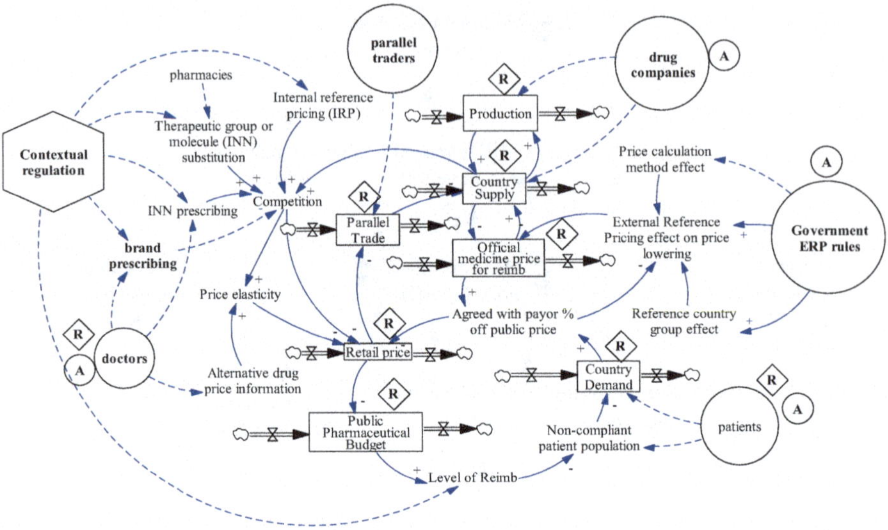


**Fig. 4.3** Reflecting on the micro level CaM of the pharmaceutical regulation effects on the market system, bringing resource and agent perspectives

pharmaceutical policy, internal reference pricing (competition based on molecule INN prices), and parallel trade (PT) on product market and product price developments (Fig. 4.1).

Key insights which we can get from Fig. 4.1 would be related to the effect of the external reference pricing, which could lead to the counterintuitive EU-wide upward price convergence or maintenance of a higher price for a longer period of time ('EU price upward convergence' on the CaM, which also inform 'market entry' and 'imperfect competition'). Another one could be that pharmaceutical pricing policies alone (without other regulation directed to product competition) would not produce the intended effect of lowering product price ('medicinal real price per MNF' and medicinal official price per MNF').

'EU price downward convergence' on the map was informed through the innovative and generic drug industries statements, which also inform 'medicine market volume' and 'generic drug competition'. In addition, a micro level CaM on Fig. 4.2 was made in a next iteration stage to transform the macro CaM components into a local market micro CaM, which to take account of and exhibits feedback relations among demand from patients and supply from drug manufacturers, constrained by budget resources, public and market retail price, contextual price regulation, and market competition. That micro level CaM followed the logic of interrelations within the macro CaM and had the goal to capture local market functional interrelations and effects.

'Medicine market volume' transformed into 'country supply' and 'country demand' linking them to 'official medicine price for reimb', 'agreed with payor % off public price', 'retail price', 'public pharmaceutical budget', and 'competition' including local contextual price regulation factors like 'INN prescribing' etc. and 'parallel trade'. Connections to the documented statements included in the CoM are evident and can be followed back to all of them, through the previous explanation of Fig. 4.2. A number of important interconnections and feedback loops have emerged on the micro CaM, like 'parallel trade' and 'country supply' and official public price, price discounting and retail price, competition and retail price and prices and 'country demand'. All these interrelations between factors, resources, and market actors' activities are affected through the regulation. Inadequate price regulation and inappropriate level of public funding would have negative effect on demand which in turn would keep the product price higher if not enough condition for market competition.

Reflecting on the micro level CaM of the regulation effects on the market system, further a next iteration of the map was created, containing drafted layer over the map from the perspective of main resources and actor's conceptualization within the market system (Fig. 4.3). For example, 'country supply' and 'country demand' factors were conceptualized as connected to drug stock resources and labelled with 'R' and a rectangular shape with incoming and outgoing flows notation. Other factors on the map which were conceptualized as resources were official drug price and retail price, parallel trade, and drug public budget. The main criterion for a resource was that resources or stocks of resources can increase, accumulate or decrease, following from main system dynamics concepts regarding stocks and flows and their graphical notation.

What was interesting, doctors and patients connected to the drug resources demand factor, were conceptualized both as resources 'R' and agents 'A'. On one side, they are strategic resources for the government and the drug companies, but on the other side they can take decisions and actions related to prescribing or buying a drug, this influencing on drug stock resources in a local market. Other important market agents are the government (pricing authorities) and drug companies (drug manufacturers and drug parallel traders), which have influence with their decisions on the policy rules and on drug resources supplied to a local market or traded among EU countries.

In that respect and line of working, a next version of the micro CaM emerged this time following the conceptualization of a resource map, reflecting on the market system resources from internal and external perspectives (explained in the theoretical framework), connected to the RBT and RDT.

A version of an enhanced RM is given on Fig. 4.4, which provides a qualitative model of the system conceptualized through SD perspectives and built from the collected information discussed in the previous section. Building the enhanced RM required elicitation of key feedback loops responsible for the endogenous dynamics in the system. This involved mapping the main resources and resource flows identified through the data analyzed.

Figure 4.4 provides this RM version on which 'drug supply' and 'country demand' factors from the second drafted version of the micro CaM were transferred into 'drugVolumeSupplied' and 'drugVolumeBought' on the enhanced RM. 'Parallel trade' was transformed into 'ParallelExport', 'public pharmaceutical budget' became 'DrugPublicExpenditure'. 'Official medicine price for reimb' was

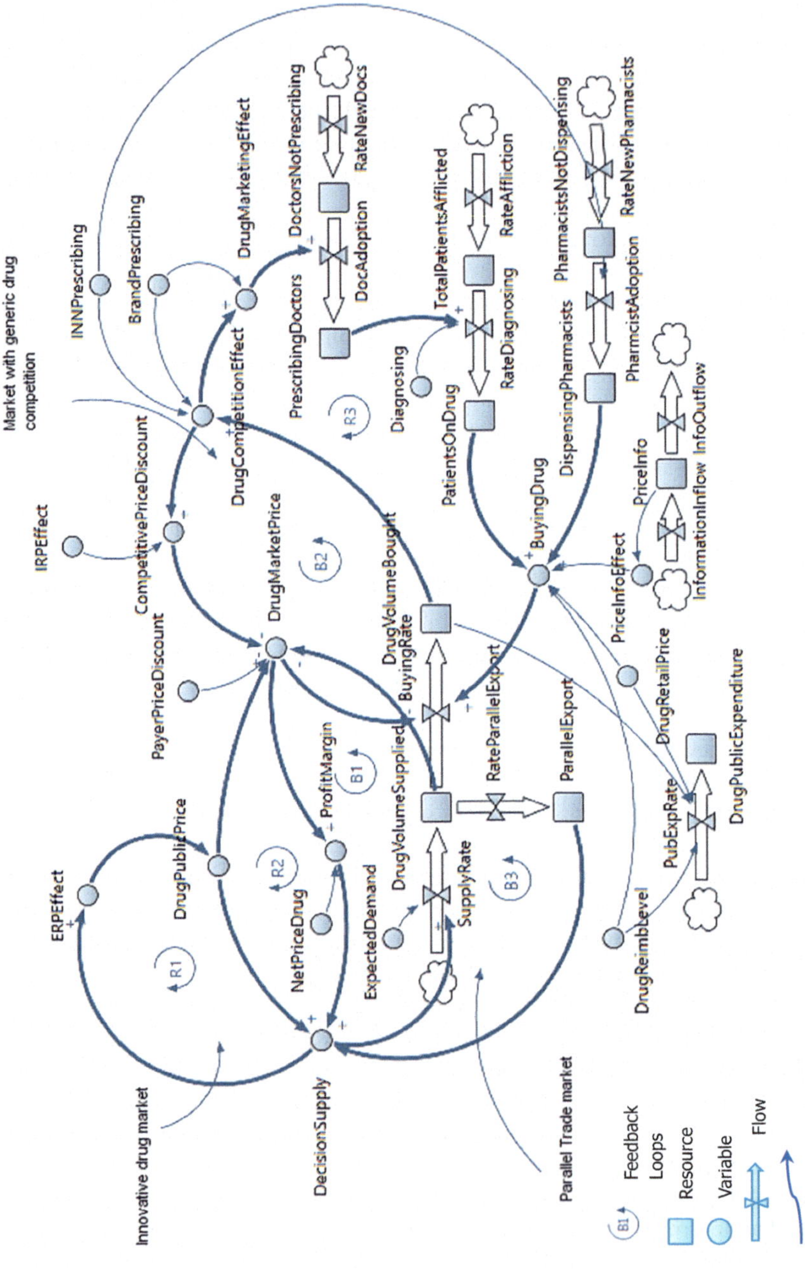


**Fig. 4.4** Enhanced resource map of the pharmaceutical market and regulation system (adapted from Kazakov et al., 2021)

transferred in 'DrugPublicPrice' and 'retail price' became 'DrugMarketPrice'. 'External reference pricing effect on price lowering' was relabeled to 'ExtRefprice' and 'pharmaceuticalPoliciesEffect'.

Boxes on the map represent stocks of resources, inflow and outflow arrows with converters denote rates of accumulation and depletion of resource levels. Circles are endogenous factors and variables influencing resource levels. All interrelations between resources and influencing factors are marked by connection arrows, denoting the direction of influence. All endogenous systemic factors included in the resource map can influence the level of market resources either positively or negatively, depending on their dynamic properties. The influencing factors include market agents' activity, market regulation, product price and information availability. The modelling graphical language is borrowed from the system dynamics practice and software.

Doctors and patients were included as resources on which competition ('DrugCompetitionEffect') has effect to prescribe or buy drugs. 'DecisionSupply' was included to denote important point of drugs entering into a local market, reflecting drug companies' decisions when to supply e drug to a chosen local country market. 'Agreed with payer % off public price' was included in the enhanced RM as 'PayerPriceDiscount'.

During the process of working and reflecting on the maps and their iterative versions and transferring them into an enhanced RM, thinking on the resource conceptualization of the pharmaceutical regulation effects on the drug market system, the notion of main market agents' decisions influencing on resource levels appeared to emerge. That was later developed in the process of drafting agent maps and when combining the enhanced RM with them into a hybrid RAM. Also, that notion was technically applied further in the software specification of the hybrid SD and AB simulation interactions between agent decisions and resource levels through making influence on stocks inflow and outflow rates. The pharmaceutical market and regulation system structure was differentiated by three different interconnected substructures: innovative drug market, market with generic drug competition, and parallel trade market. They emerged to have a separate and combined influence on the pharmaceutical market system in relation to resource levels and agents' behaviour.

The next phase of the mapping process included identification of important reinforcing (R) and balancing (B) feedback loops, which provided the non-linear dynamic state of the pharmaceutical market system. These loops were highlighted by examination of the interconnections between the system resources. A key variable in the market is product price (the officially approved price and the one used in the retail market). The higher the officially approved price of a medicine (drug molecule) in a price reference country, the higher the product public price in the referenced country (Loop R1), and the higher the capability for supply (volume) of that molecule (either under patent or off-patent), evident in Loop R2. However, this reinforcing feedback loop could produce the opposite cycle if the referenced and then the reference price start to decrease.

The higher the effect of the pharmaceutical regulation in one country on price lowering, the lower the level of the official drug price. In turn, there would be a lower willingness to supply the drug in certain countries for economic reasons and to evade circular country price benchmarking. Maintaining a higher market price per manufacturer would result in a higher profit margin, which would increase manufacturing and supply, which in turn would allow companies to relax the retail price in a monopolistic patent market, giving larger discount to the public payers (Loop B1); in addition a higher market price would decrease drug consumption in an off patent market which would produce competitive pressure on price discounting, leading to a decrease in market price (Loop B2). Another important factor on the market will be the level of the parallel trade (buying the imported medicine from a lower priced national market and re-exporting it to an EU country with a higher priced molecule), which would affect the local market drug volume negatively through reduced availability and a decision not to supply to that local market (Loop B3).

However, market competition (supply of the molecule by rival companies) could be able to offset the availability problem, either without or with a delay. The degree of market competition would be higher with the higher number of suppliers (generic medicine manufacturers) entering the off patent market, and would be generating higher demand through an increase in incentivizing activity and doctor prescriptions (Loop R3).

An agent interaction map of the pharmaceutical market is provided on Fig. 4.5. The key market agents influence each other's behaviour by interacting with each other within the constraints of the market environment and regulation. Manufacturers are influenced by pricing and reimbursement, and prescribing and dispensing regulation, including drug public price, controlled by the government's expenditure budget. Doctors and pharmacists are influenced by companies and government incentives. Patients are influenced by doctors and pharmacists and by the level of information they have regarding medicines price. The Agent interaction map on Fig. 4.5 describes the drug manufacturing (MNF) agent as following three main condition action rules: agent supply rule, market pricing rule, and doctor incentivizing rule, the first two of which are analyzed in more detail by the agent behaviour map in Fig. 4.6.

The agent supply rule, that is, manufacturing agent supply condition action routine is affected not only by the pharmaceutical regulation rule controlling the public price of the medicines, but also by a number of market factors such as the limited allocated public drug budget for which company agents compete, drug demand, market price competition, and drug actual price. Prescribing regulation influences doctors' prescribing patterns and doctor incentivizing rules, which in turn influence doctors' prescribing rule by brand incentivizing activity; dispensing regulation influences pharmacy dispensing rules and drug agent market pricing rules, which in turn influence further dispensing patterns by product price discounting; reimbursement regulation influences market pricing rules through drug market price competition and patient buying rules through the level of reimbursement and patient co-payment.

The agent interaction map reveals not only who influences who, but which agent behavioural rule influences other rules. The pharmaceutical regulation rule effect on drug manufacturing agent behaviour is imposed directly on agent decisions to

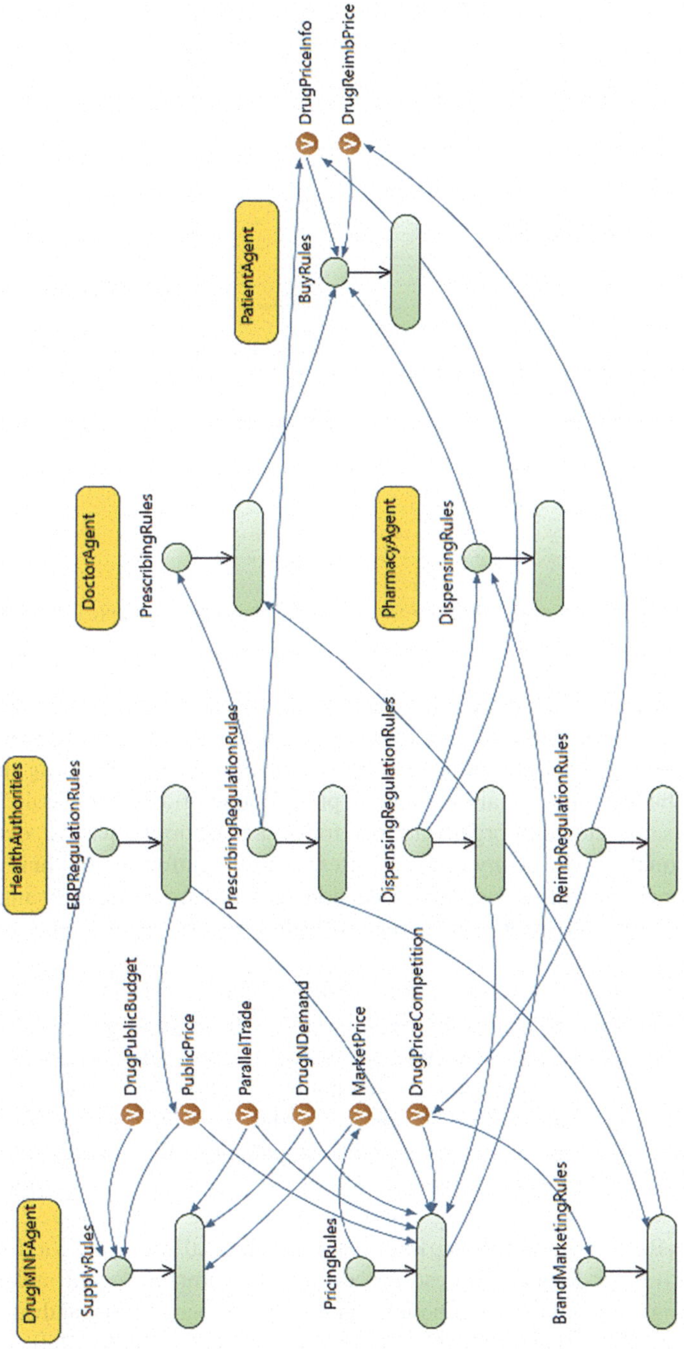


**Fig. 4.5** Agent interaction map (AiM) (adapted from Kazakov et al., 2021)

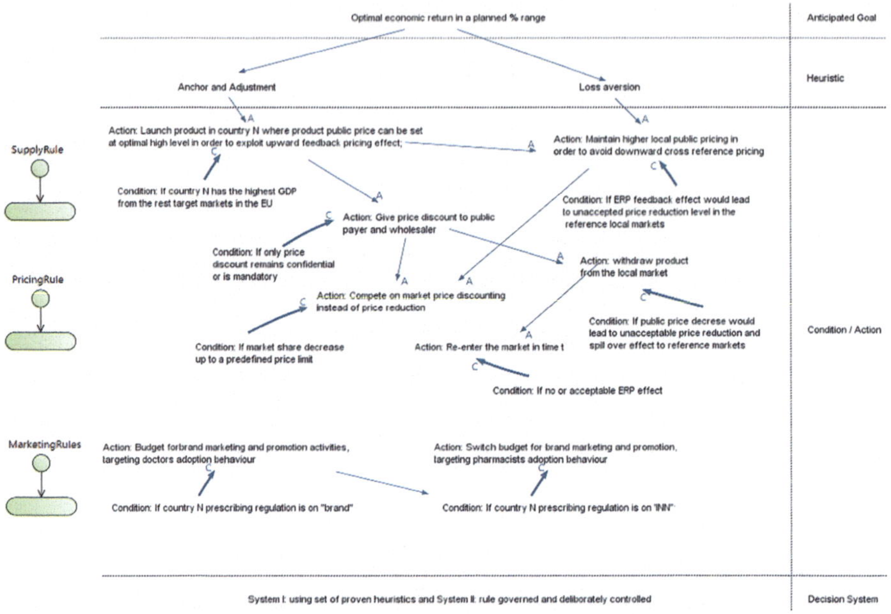


**Fig. 4.6** Agent behaviour map (AbM) for companies' behaviour (adapted from Kazakov et al., 2021)

supply through drug public price setting and indirectly on agent market pricing rules through the market price discount. Furthermore, a pharmaceutical firm agent supply and market pricing rules are influenced by key market factors like drug demand, drug public budget appropriation, market price competition, and parallel trade. Market agents, individual or organizational, follow a behavioural pattern, determining what action they take at any time and after what rule, informed by their perception of the environment and optimal decision making. Agents can change their behavioural pattern prospectively or reactively in order to adapt to the changing environment.

Main agents (market actors) on the regulation market system were identified from the documented assertions and working through the process of drafting and redrafting CoM, CaM, and enhanced RM, including conceptualization of agents' main behavioural rules in respect to the regulation effect on the market.

Each agent was positioned on the map in order from left to right, from drug manufacturer to government, doctor, pharmacist, patient, with corresponding labels for main behavioural rules of each actor. 'DrugMNFAgent' do mainly drug supply, drug price formation and drug marketing, so their rules were labelled: 'AgentSupplyRule', 'MarketPricingRule', and 'DocIncentRule' (rule for drug marketing incentivizing doctors to prescribe a drug). Government agent makes decisions regarding the regulation and policies tool set and other contextual drug pricing regulation, so 'GovernmentAgent' rules were labelled 'PharmaPoliciesRule', 'PrescribingRegulation', 'DispensingRegulation', and 'ReimbRegulation'. Doctors' prescribing decision rules are labelled 'PrescribingRule', pharmacists have 'DispensingRule' and patients buy medicines having 'BuyingRule', although there are other decisions and decision rules, the AiM includes main behaviours and associated rules which are relevant to the regulation effects on the system.

Also, important influencing factors (taken from the documented statements) were included among agents and their rules (drug budget, public price, parallel trade, drug market price and drug demand, price competition). Interconnections between each agent rules and important factors have been made in order to correspond to main documented statements and assertions. The agent behaviour routines emerged from the collected information and the agent interaction map analysis, and depicts the drug manufacturer forward looking behavioural model. This relates to the market agent's performance goals and to the agent's organization's future economic state. It is presented in Fig. 4.6 as a matrix of interlinked anticipated goals, heuristics, and conditions actions.

On the next drafting step, a next version of the agent behaviour pattern map was designed in software, reflecting further on connections between agents' sequence of activities and their relevant rules from the AiM, denoting arrows representing actions with label 'A' and arrows representing conditions with label 'C'. Also, an overarching goal (reflecting AST) and main guiding decision heuristics principles were included in order to denote agents' goal anticipated behaviour and behavioural decision making guiding scheme.

The agent behaviour map depicts each decision action routine for a chosen agent based on the agent interaction map. The depiction of agent behaviour, that is, decision action routine was informed by the collected data regarding stakeholder assertions on the regulations and policies effect and related drug companies response following a BDT and AST framework protocol. ABM represents a network matrix of agent condition/actions sequence based on agent-anticipated action-related goals, guided by the agent's main behavioural heuristic and decision system. The mapping starts from the top of the matrix using short phrases linked by unidirectional arrows that provide description of the agent's anticipated goal, the agent decision heuristic, the agent's actions and related conditions for each action, using arrows labelled 'A' for action and 'C' for condition. On the right side of the matrix the decision action routine is aligned to the goal, heuristic, condition action, and decision system protocol, while on the left side agent behaviour rules are mapped.

The drug manufacturing agent behaviour map in Fig. 4.6 provides insight about the behavioural routine of the pharmaceutical agents in response to the pharmaceutical regulation in EU. Drug manufacturing agents have an anticipated pay-off goal or an economic return on investment in R&D, attached to any product launch, in the form of a planned profit margin percentage ratio, with a minimum barrier which should not be overpassed. Their price decision making is driven by the dominant logic of the market (Bettis & Prahalad, 1995; Prahalad & Bettis, 1986; C. E. Helfat & Peteraf, 2015; C. Helfat & Peteraf, 2003), following anchor and adjustment and loss aversion behavioural heuristics in accord with the BDT principles.

The anchor and adjustment principle-related behaviour is translated into a sequential product launching activity in the EU country markets, 'anchoring' the local price in high GDP countries which can support higher price setting than other countries; and then 'adjusting' the public and market price through mandatory or nondisclosed price negotiation with local payers, and further through competitive discounting (Carone et al., 2012; Leopold et al., 2012; Vogler & Paterson, 2017; Vogler et al., 2014; Schneider, 2017). Further, the above price setting heuristic allows pricing the product at an optimal level and exploiting an upward feedback pricing effect through the external reference pricing regulation.

The loss aversion principle behaviour is translated into avoiding the external reference pricing feedback effect leading to price reduction in the referenced country, by maintaining higher local public pricing, competing on price discounting or even by product withdrawal on the condition that the pricing feedback effect could lead to unaccepted public price reduction in the referenced country and further to a spillover effect in other cross referenced country markets. Agents can re-enter the market if there is no pricing feedback effect or if there is an appropriate change in the pricing regulation.

The mapped agent activity pattern aims to unveil the pharmaceutical firm's pricing tactics related behaviour and their condition/action dependence. The map can also inform the modelling coding process through the links between agent behaviour and the rules and conditions it will be dependent on.

Figure 4.7 represents the decision-making pattern for prescribing doctors within a healthcare setting. It outlines IF THEN conditions and actions that guide a physician's choices in prescribing, anchored on the optimal medical benefit as the anticipated goal.

At the top level, we see the anticipated goal stated as the 'optimal medical benefit', which indicates that the primary objective of this system is to achieve the best possible health outcomes for patients. Two main decision paths are juxtaposed: one relies on the availability of drugs on the local market and the application of an 'anchor and adjustment' heuristic, which suggests a method of starting with an

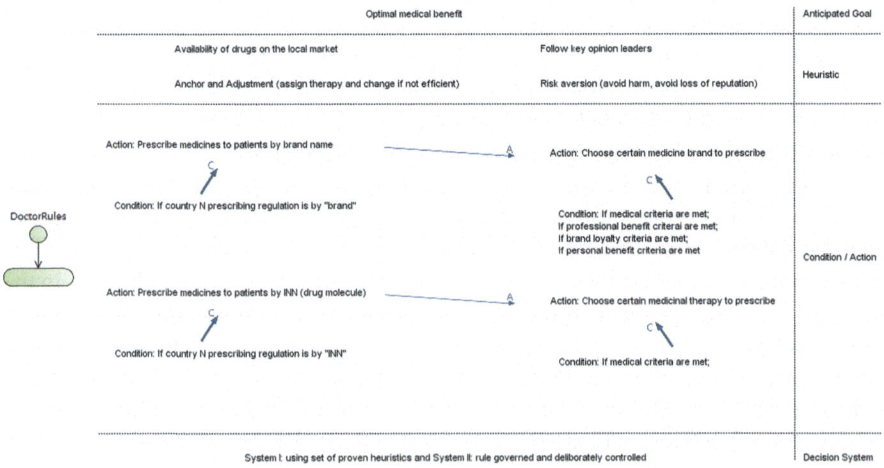


**Fig. 4.7** AbM for doctors behaviour

initial plan (anchor) and adjusting it as necessary based on efficacy; the other decision path involves following key opinion leaders, which could imply a reliance on expert consensus or recognized authority figures in the medical field.

One path of the ‘DoctorRules’ is contingent upon the country's prescribing regulations being brand-based; if so, the action is to prescribe medicines to patients by brand name. The alternative path is taken if the prescribing regulations are based on the international nonproprietary name (INN), which is the official generic name for pharmaceutical substances. In this case, the action is to prescribe medicines by their molecular name, implying a more generic, possibly cost-effective approach.

Both pathways follow a heuristic-based approach for final prescription choices, incorporating risk aversion strategies to avoid harm and protect the physician's reputation. Choosing a specific medicine brand or therapy to prescribe should comply with certain medical criteria, and potentially, professional or personal benefit criteria, indicating that there are multiple layers of considerations that could influence doctors’ prescribing decisions with the ultimate goal of maximizing medical benefits for patients.

Figure 4.8 represents the decision-making routine for the dispensation of medications within a pharmacy setting, delineating the pharmacists' actions based on regulatory conditions and predefined rules, and ultimately aimed at achieving optimal medical benefit and economic return.

The overarching goals guiding pharmacists’ decision process are achieving the ‘optimal medical benefit’ and ‘optimal economic return’. These goals suggest a dual focus on patient health outcomes and cost-effectiveness or profitability.

The two primary heuristics which are likely to influence pharmacists’ decision making are similar to the doctors’ decision protocol: ‘anchor and adjustment’ which involves initially using a standard approach (the anchor) and making subsequent adjustments based on the efficiency or effectiveness of the therapy, and ‘risk aversion’ which is geared towards minimizing potential harm and safeguarding the reputation of the pharmacist or the pharmacy.

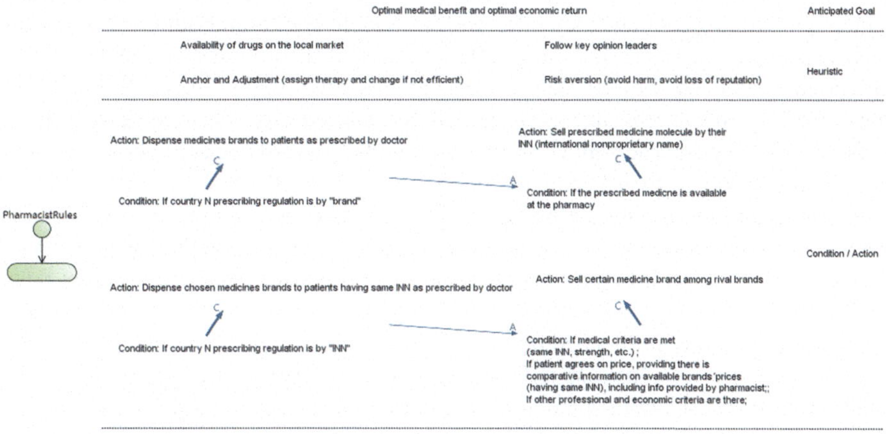


**Fig. 4.8** AbM for pharmacies´ behaviour

'PharmacistRules' are also guided through the drug dispensing regulation. If the country's regulation mandates dispensation by 'brand', then the pharmacist is to dispense the specific brands prescribed by the doctor. This path is based on the premise that certain regulations require or allow pharmacists to provide medications based on the brand names doctors prescribe. Alternatively, if the regulation is by 'INN' (international nonproprietary name), the pharmacist's action is to dispense the molecule as prescribed, without brand specification. This suggests a more generic approach to medication dispensation, which may focus on the active ingredient rather than the brand.

If the prescribed medicine is available at the pharmacy, the pharmacist will proceed to sell the prescribed medicine by its INN. In the case where multiple brands are available for a prescribed INN, the pharmacist will select a particular brand. This decision is based on several factors: medical criteria (such as the medicine's strength, dosage form, etc.), comparative information on available brands' prices, and additional information provided by the pharmacist. This implies a complex decision matrix where both professional judgement and economic considerations play a role.

The diagram's focus on conditions and actions suggests a logical flow where the pharmacist must balance regulatory compliance with professional discretion to make informed decisions about which medication to dispense. It incorporates a blend of rule-based and heuristic approaches, with the patient's health outcomes and the economic aspects of medication dispensation being the ultimate concerns.

Figure 4.9 illustrates a decision-making process from the perspective of patients within the healthcare system, specifically regarding the purchase of medications. The process is informed by 'PatientRules', referring to patient preferences, or other guidelines that influence their choices in relation to their main goal of 'optimal medical benefit', indicating that the primary concern for patients is to achieve the best possible health outcomes from the medications they purchase.

Patients may rely on simple, experience-based techniques for problem-solving and decision making, such as following key opinion leaders or using the anchor and adjustment strategy where they start with a default option and adjust it based on their experience or the medication's effectiveness. If the country's regulations dictate prescriptions by 'brand', then patients are expected to buy medicine brands as prescribed by the doctor and as dispensed by pharmacists. This suggests a more straightforward purchase behaviour where patients follow the specific brand recommendations made by their healthcare providers.

If prescriptions are regulated by 'INN' (international nonproprietary name), patients have the option to buy medicine brands having the same INN as prescribed by the doctor and as chosen by the pharmacist. This pathway indicates a more flexible approach, where patients may choose from different brands of the same generic medication, possibly influenced by the pharmacist's recommendations.

Patients might opt for a specific brand if it's prescribed after seeing a doctor, implying trust in the doctor's judgement. Alternatively, they may follow recommendations from the pharmacist, who ensures that medical criteria such as the INN, strength, etc. are met. This pathway also suggests that patients might consider

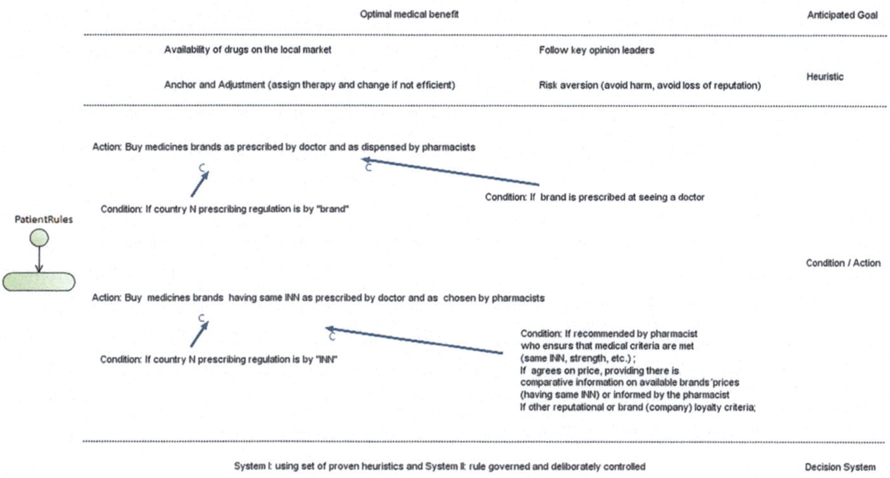


**Fig. 4.9** AbM for Patients' Behaviour Integrating Resource and Agent Maps to Create a Hybrid RAM

comparative price information on available brands provided by the pharmacist, as well as their own loyalty to certain brands or companies.

The resource and agent maps are then integrated (RAM), with the aim to highlight the main interdependencies among the key market agents and market resources in relation to the pharmaceutical regulation effects on the pharmaceutical market dynamics. The hybrid RAM analysis presents a rich cognitive model of the pharmaceutical market, driven by a number of important feedback loops and agents forward looking behavioural decision-making routines, exhibiting the supply and demand dynamics on a pharmaceutical country market without or with competition (on-patent or off-patent market). Integrating RM and AM supports a comprehensive hybrid exploration of the complex interrelations among market agents and market resources and can be used to become a blueprint for the integration of system dynamic and agent-based qualitative and quantitative modelling methodological frameworks, through the identification of the mediation effect of agent decision action routine on the resource system evolution.

The integration of the maps is usually done by simplifying the enhanced RM keeping key resources, inflows, outflows, and feedback loops in the modelled system with the influence arrows network realigned. And connecting the key agents rules included in the agent interaction map (AiM) and agent behaviour map (AbM) to their relevant decision points on the RM by using unidirectional arrows and denoting the decision points by the unified modelling language (UML) sign for a decision branch (a diamond shape).

The RAM key aim is to elicit the influence of the market agents upon the pharmaceutical system resource configuration through their decision action routine, and to find where the agent resource decision intersection points lie. These are denoted on the map by the use of an UML graphical symbol for decision branch for visual comprehension of the key turning points in the resource structure emerging out of agents' activity. The RAM is conceptualized not as a mechanical overlaying of the RM and AM, but as a higher-order integrated map which can help further understanding of the endogenous dynamic interdependence among agent decision action and resource accumulation and depletion, transforming the market system into a system of agent resource configuration sets. Using the hybrid RAM, turning points of the pharmaceutical market system were found where agents' decision action rules, that form their behavioural routine, can influence the system behaviour in counter-intuitive and nonobvious directions. For example, the drug manufacturer agent decision action rules related to drug supply, drug pricing, and doctor incentivizing could have a turning effect on the regulation purpose to reduce prices by turning the intended regulation induced price control feedback loop into a beneficial one through launch sequencing, maintaining higher price, and competing on nonpublic discounting and prescription incentivizing, evident in the RAM at Loop R1, Loop R2, and Loop B2.

In the drafting of the RAM, an initial resource agent map was produced attempting to conceptualize a comprehensive market and regulation system and interconnections among system components. Agents on the market are price authorities who control national regulation rules, innovative and generic drug manufacturers who make decision to enter or exit chosen local markets making decision on their drug local price influenced through local regulation and public price and through drug market price, doctors who decide what drug to prescribe influenced through drug market competition, pharmacists who have or do not have decision on drug dispensing, patients who decide to follow doctor's prescription etc., influenced through drug price and public funding. All actors influence the stock levels of the drug supplied on the local market, which influence the level of local market competition.

Figure 4.10 represents the initial RAM drafting and reflection on the resource and agents' interrelations in respect to the regulation effect and main criteria for regulation evaluation. That redrafting and notation over the initial draft supported the conceptualization of the positions of and connections among the components of the system, main important decision rules of main agents, main influencing factors and main statements from a combined resource agent perspective and from main criteria related to the evaluation of drug regulations and their effects.

Reflecting on all maps before and on the specific hybrid system, generated also considerations regarding ethical dimensions and regarding affordability vs. availability contradiction like a societal challenge and important public private policy question. Drug companies' decision to supply or withdraw a drug, including overpricing can produce 'moral hazard' and 'adverse selection' phenomena (Arrow, 2001; Stiglitz, 2000), all of which are connected to the regulation effects on market resources and agent decisions.

Key considerations elicited by the analysis of the RAM (Fig. 4.11), related to the pricing regulation effects on equitable drug access, availability and affordability on a national and EU-wide level, undermining patient medicinal treatment efficiency and health outcome are as follows:

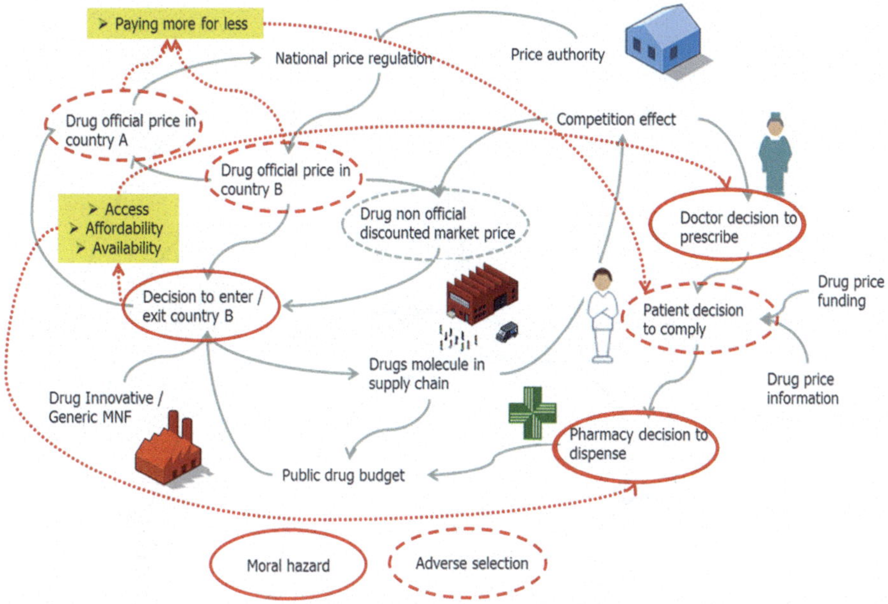


**Fig. 4.10** Initial resource agent conceptualization of a comprehensive market and regulation system and interconnections among system components

- A medicinal product could have a delayed entry in one EU country compared to another due to local drug regulation or other cross national pricing regulation (avoiding circular price referencing, sequential launching and other drug company activities) effect, manufacturing capacity or market competition avoidance effect.
- A medicinal product could become temporarily unavailable in one EU country due to a parallel trade effect or due to strategic withdrawal (a market tactic to exit and re-enter with higher price and not to interfere with another country's pricing and reimbursement regulation; or due to competition; or to be redirected to another country market due to a price/volume agreement with the government/payer).
- A product could have a low affordability level (having high reimbursement or high out-of-pocket value) by maintaining higher official and higher retail price for longer than it would have been capable of if there were no certain regulation or competition effects.

The above analysis was supported by the RAM through exploring the possible effect of the agents' condition action routines on the reinforcing or balancing loops identified in the enhanced RM, having influence on to the key turning points in the RAM. Being able to 'see the whole' complexity of the regulation effects through the application of hybrid RAM lead to the advantages pointed out by Ackermann (2012) such as '(a) ensuring the situation is explored from a range of perspectives,

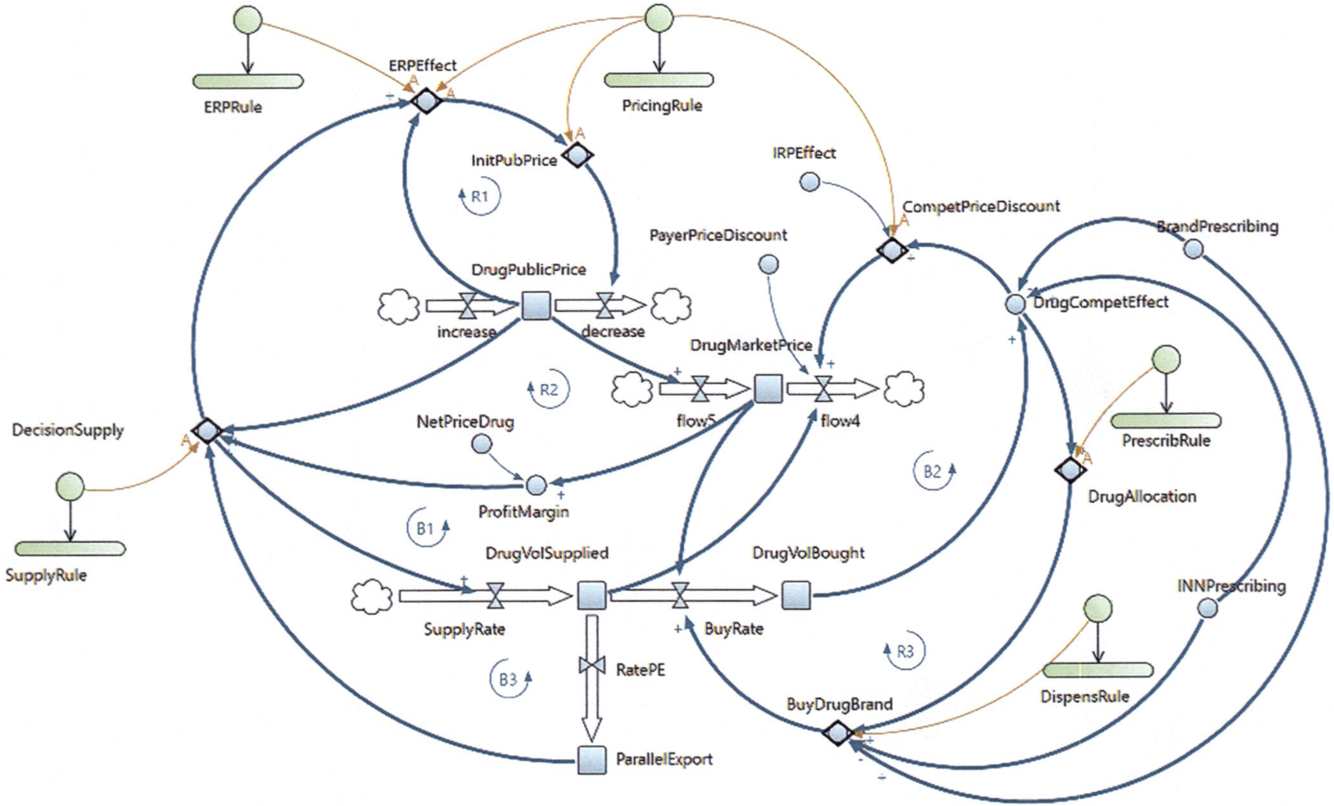


**Fig. 4.11** Hybrid RAM (adapted from Kazakov et al., 2021)

(b) widening the number of alternatives generated and (c) enabling new options to emerge'.

Figure 4.11 provides a hybrid RAM adapted from (Kazakov et al., 2021), exhibiting the map version, achieved after the journal editing procedure and communication with three anonymous journal reviewers.

The RAM depicts the complex interactions and feedback loops in a pharmaceutical market supply and regulation system and can be utilised also as a procedure for the design of a quantitative simulation of the behaviour of this complex systems over time.

The RAM includes the standard SD stocks and flows notation. Stocks are represented by rectangles, such as 'DrugVolSupplied' and 'DrugVolBought'. These are accumulations or quantities that can increase or decrease over time, depending on their flows. Flows are represented by thick arrows with valves, such as 'SupplyRate' and 'BuyRate'. These control the rate at which stocks change. Flows can be influenced by various factors, including decision rules and feedback from other parts of the system.

Agents decision rules are indicated by circles with 'Rule' in their label, such as 'SupplyRule', 'PricingRule', and 'PrescribRule'. These represent the policies or strategies that agents in the system use to make decisions. For example, the 'SupplyRule' defines how a supplier decides the rate at which to supply drugs to the market.

Feedback loops are indicated by circular paths that lead from a stock or decision rule back to itself or to another decision rule. These loops can be reinforcing (R) or balancing (B). Reinforcing loops (R1, R2, R3) tend to amplify changes, while balancing loops (B1, B2, B3) tend to resist changes and stabilize the system. 'ERP effect' and 'IRP effect' indicate the external reference pricing and internal reference pricing effects, respectively. These are mechanisms used by payers and regulators to control drug prices. 'CompEffect' and 'CompPriceDiscount' stand for competitive effects and competitive pricing discounts, which influence how drugs are prescribed and bought.

'NetPriceDrug' and 'ProfitMargin' indicate that the price of the drug affects the profit margin, which in turn influences the volume of drugs supplied and bought. 'DrugVolSupplied' and 'DrugVolBought' are central stocks that are affected by the supply and buying rates, which are influenced by various factors such as pricing rules, profit margins, and discounts. 'DrugMarketPrice' is influenced by multiple factors including public price, payer price discount, and competitive price discount, reflecting the complexity of pricing in the pharmaceutical market.

'INNPrescribing' and 'BuyDrugBrand' suggest a dynamic where generic (INN) prescribing might be balanced against branded drug purchases, reflecting real-world trade-offs between cost-saving measures and brand loyalty or preference. The 'ParallelExport' represents the practice of exporting drugs to other countries, which can affect supply and pricing dynamics within the market.

The RAM shows how various factors such as pricing, supply, demand, and regulation interact over time, and how decision rules by different agents in the market can influence these interactions.

## 4.3 Scenario Identification with RAM

Using the RAM, eight hypothetical scenario cases related to the pharmaceutical regulation effects on the pharmaceutical market were identified and commented further in the text. It is worth noting that these could also be used for simulation testing as working hypotheses. In general, researchers using a RAM constructed for a specific resource agent system can consider three aspects to generate and explore system scenarios:

- Variation in resource structure of the system (here, monopolistic or with competition or with or without parallel trade)
- Variation in the researched agent behaviour rules (here, regulation rules imposed by the government and behavioural rules of suppliers, intermediaries, and buyers)
- Contextually—related variations (here, local market differences in prescribing, dispensing, and reimbursement regulation), in order to analyze their mediating effect on the agent rule and resource system evolution

According to the different national market resource structure and government agent regulation rules influencing manufacturing agent condition action rule and the turning points feedback effect on resource evolution, the authors distinguished different effects on product delay, availability, and affordability level. Depending on the type of market system structure, that is, monopolistic (Loops R1 and R2 on Fig. 4.11) or with competition (Loops B1 and B2), without or with parallel export/import (Loop B3), the type of pharmaceutical policy methodological apparatus (government agent regulation rule), difference in the additional contextual factors linked to market competition such as local pricing regulation, prescribing, dispensing, and reimbursement regulation (Loop R3), the effect on market resource and market agent decision action routine dynamics might differ substantially.

Through hybrid qualitative analysis using the RAM, we can explore how different regulatory measures influence access, affordability, and availability in pharmaceutical markets. Various scenarios can be generated, encompassing system wide effects of monopolistic markets, competitive environments, parallel export, pricing methodologies, prescription types, and additional pricing regulations.

Scenario I: Pharmaceutical pricing regulation in monopolistic markets

In monopolistic markets, where only patented drugs exist, our analysis reveals that pricing regulation can have limited effects on delays of product entry. While it has no direct effect on affordability when reimbursement is full, it can strain public budget resources. Interestingly, it does not impact drug availability, indicating that exit rates remain unaffected.

Scenario II: Pharmaceutical pricing regulation in competitive markets

In markets with competition, encompassing both off-patent and generic drugs, pricing regulation can lead to delays in product entry. Affordability remains unchanged when reimbursement is full. However, as reimbursement decreases, affordability decreases due to higher copayments. Availability is contingent on price competition intensity and regulatory cross-references, which can lead to price convergence and drug exits.

Scenario III: Pharmaceutical pricing regulation with parallel export

The inclusion of parallel export in pricing regulation scenarios mirrors the findings from Scenario II. Parallel export does not interfere directly with pharmaceutical pricing regulation, but can have indirect price competition effects in exported markets.

Scenario IV: Pharmaceutical pricing regulation with variation in pricing methodology

This scenario highlights the intricacies of pricing methodology. Inappropriate country selection for price referencing can result in either overpricing or underpricing. The choice between minimum or average price calculation, without considering product volume and discounts, may lead to misleading price comparisons. Moreover, the timing of price revisions can significantly impact price variations.

Scenario V: Pharmaceutical pricing regulation and generic or branded drug prescription

Markets differences in prescription types yield varying effects on pricing. Countries with brand prescriptions tend to experience more inflated prices compared to those with INN prescriptions, indicating potential inefficiencies in the former.

Scenario VI: Pharmaceutical pricing regulation in branded markets with generic substitution

Comparing markets with branded drugs transitioning to INN replacements reveals that such markets achieve price convergence more rapidly. This highlights the efficiency gains associated with regulatory changes.

Scenario VII: Pharmaceutical pricing regulation in markets with variation in reimbursement level

Reimbursement levels play a pivotal role in determining access, availability, and affordability. Higher reimbursement levels improve access, availability, and affordability, while lower reimbursement levels increase copayments and reduce these factors. The higher is the reimbursement, the higher is local market attractiveness and lower the market price competition.

Scenario VIII: Pharmaceutical pricing regulation in markets with additional pricing regulation.

The introduction of additional pricing regulations, such as internal reference pricing (IRP), price linkage, and mandatory discounts, can create barriers to competitive actions by pharmaceutical companies. This can limit market competition and reduce the potential for price reductions.

The hybrid RAM analysis highlights the complex effects of various regulations and market factors on drug access, affordability, and availability. A full evaluation of the pharmaceutical pricing regulation effects should take account of local market structure and drug regulatory specifics, and that a hybrid SD/AB simulation interactive learning environment could further enhance researchers and policy-makers capacity for the analysis and evaluation of these effects on drug equitable access, affordability, and availability. The use of such a hybrid simulation modelling technique would provide means for rich scenario testing with the capacity to inform further a more efficient and sustainable drug pricing regulatory environment.

## 4.4 Discussion and Future Potential for RAM Applications

Combinations of agent-based and resource-feedback approaches have traditionally been carried out from the individual perspectives of resource structure or agent behaviour, or opposing macro to micro, quantity of stock levels to quality of agent behaviour patterns, and resources to agents, and without the application of a joint conceptual qualitative hybrid model building procedure, leaving calls for hybridization of both SD and AB unattended from conceptual and theoretical perspectives (Guerrero et al. 2016; Hans Jochen Scholl 2001; Schieritz 2002).

In addition to the application of the RAM as a novel problem structuring tool, the enhanced RM and the novel AiM and AbM tools can be applied either individually or in an integrated RAM method as a hybrid qualitative conceptual modelling procedure for resource and agent interactive systems such as pharmaceuticals and healthcare. A hybrid RAM can have the capability to strengthen the integration process between the two modelling approaches and the confidence building among modellers and users.

In addition, the AiM and AbM could be applied to enhance the agent-based conceptual model building process in relation to more accurately collecting and interpreting data and analyzing agent behaviour and their decision-making pattern, taking into account the behavioural decision and anticipatory systems theoretical perspective proposed here. Integrated with RM to form RAM has the potential to enhance hybrid SD/AB conceptual model building and validation. Applying RAM as a novel hybrid tool for conceptual qualitative modelling and as a blue print for quantitative hybridization of SD/AB modelling approaches can further reveal new theoretical, methodological, and practical avenues for research focusing on more comprehensive integration of the two methods, and on the behavioural exploration of complex adaptive systems.

Integrating system dynamics with agent-based modelling and simulation provides extended benefits to understanding complex systemic behaviour due to the combination of two modelling approaches which address both dynamics on a whole system-macro and individual micro agent-behaviour perspective. Testing what if policy changes in a constraint environment can reveal hidden gaps, information asymmetries and key leverage factors for optimal policy decision making. RAM method provides novel and powerful means for a comprehensive exploration of agent resource systems and their complex adaptive dynamics.

## References

Ackermann, F. (2012). Problem structuring methods 'in the Dock': Arguing the case for Soft OR. *European Journal of Operational Research, 219*(3), 652–658.

Ackermann, F., Franco, L. A., Rouwette, E., & White, L. (2014). Special issue on problem structuring research and practice. *EURO Journal on Decision Processes, 2*(3–4), 165–172. https://doi.org/10.1007/s40070-014-0037-6

Arrow, K. J. (2001). Uncertainty and the welfare economics of medical care. *Journal of Health Politics, Policy and Law, 26*(5), 851–883. https://doi.org/10.1215/03616878-26-5-851

Bettis, R. A., & Prahalad, C. K. (1995). The dominant logic: Retrospective and extension. *Strategic Management Journal, 16*(1), 5–14. https://doi.org/10.1002/smj.4250160104

Carone, G., Schwierz, C., & Xavier, A. (2012). Cost-containment policies in public pharmaceutical spending in the EU. In *Economic and financial affairs*. https://doi.org/10.2765/27111.

Djanatliev, A., & German, R. (2013). Prospective healthcare decisions-making by combined system dynamics, Disrete-event and agent-based simulation. *Winter Simulation Conference, 2013*, 270–281. https://doi.org/10.1109/WSC.2013.6721426

Djanatliev, A., & German, R. (2016). Towards a guide to domain-specific hybrid simulation. *Proceedings Winter Simulation Conference, 2016*, 1609–1620. https://doi.org/10.1109/WSC.2015.7408281

Guerrero, C. N., Schwarz, P., & Slinger, J. H. (2016, March). A recent overview of the integration of system dynamics and agent-based modelling and simulation. In *System dynamics conference* (pp. 1–13).

Helfat, C. E., & Peteraf, M. A. (2015). Managerial cognitive capabilities and the microfoundations of dynamic capabilities. *Strategic Management Journal, 36*, 831–850. https://doi.org/10.1002/smj

Helfat, C., & Peteraf, M. (2003). The dynamic resource based view: Capability lifecycles. *Strategic Management Journal, 24*(10), 997–1010.

Kazakov, R., Howick, S., & Morton, A. (2021). Managing complex adaptive systems: A resource/agent qualitative modelling perspective. *European Journal of Operational Research, 290*(1). https://doi.org/10.1016/j.ejor.2020.08.007

Kazakov, R., & Kunc, M. (2016). Foreseeing the dynamics of strategy: An anticipatory systems perspective. *Systemic Practice and Action Research, 29*(1), 1–25. https://doi.org/10.1007/s11213-015-9349-0

Kazakov, R., & Petrova, P. I. (2015). The market for statins in Bulgaria: System dynamics perspective for efficient resource optimization. Conference: 27th EURO 2015 conference, Glasgow.

Kolominsky-Rabas, P. L., Djanatliev, A., Wahlster, P., Gantner-Bär, M., Hofmann, B., German, R., Sedlmayr, M., Reinhardt, E., Schüttler, J., Kriza, C., … Miethe, M. (2015). Technology foresight for medical device development through hybrid simulation: The ProHTA project. Technological Forecasting and Social Change, 97, 105–114. https://doi.org/10.1016/j.techfore.2013.12.005.

Kunc, M., & Kazakov, R. (2013). Competitive dynamics in pharmaceutical markets: A case study in the chronic cardiac disease market. *Journal of the Operational Research Society, 64*, 1790–1799.

Leopold, C., Vogler, S., Mantel-Teeuwisse, A. K., de Joncheere, K., Leufkens, H. G. M., & Laing, R. (2012). Differences in external price referencing in Europe-A descriptive overview. *Health Policy, 104*(1), 50–60. https://doi.org/10.1016/j.healthpol.2011.09.008

Li, M., Zhu, Y., Xue, C., Liu, Y., & Zhang, L. (2014). The problem of unreasonably high pharmaceutical fees for patients in Chinese hospitals: A system dynamics simulation model. *Computers in Biology and Medicine, 47*(1), 58–65. https://doi.org/10.1016/j.compbiomed.2013.09.024

Li, Y., Lawley, M. A., Siscovick, D. S., Zhang, D., & Pagán, J. A. (2016). Agent-based modeling of chronic diseases: A narrative review and future research directions. *Preventing Chronic Disease, 13*, E69. https://doi.org/10.5888/pcd13.150561

Lynch, C., Padilla, J., Diallo, S., Sokolowski, J., & Banks, C. (2015). A multi-paradigm modeling framework for modeling and simulating problem situations. *Proceedings Winter Simulation Conference*, 1688–1699. https://doi.org/10.1109/WSC.2014.7020019

Mahsa Keshtkaran, L. C. (2015). Stroke care systems: Can simulation modeling catch up with the recent advances in stroke treatment? *Proceedings of the 2015 Winter Simulation Conference, 53*(9), 1689–1699. https://doi.org/10.1017/CBO9781107415324.004

Marshall, D. A., Burgos-Liz, L., IJzerman, M. J., Osgood, N. D., Padula, W. V., Higashi, M. K., Wong, P. K., Pasupathy, K. S., & Crown, W. (2015). Applying dynamic simulation modeling methods in health care delivery research—the SIMULATE checklist: Report of the ISPOR simulation modeling emerging good practices task force. *Value in Health*. https://doi.org/10.1016/j.jval.2014.12.001

Mustafee, N., Powell, J., Brailsford, S., Diallo, S., Padilla, J., & Tolk, A. (2015). Hybrid simulation studies and hybrid simulation systems: Definitions, challenges, and benefits. *Proceedings of the 2015 Winter Simulation Conference*, 1678–1692. https://doi.org/10.1007/s13398-014-0173-7.2

Phillips, L. D. (1984). A theory of requisite decision models. *Acta Psychologica, 56*(1–3), 29–48. https://doi.org/10.1016/0001-6918(84)90005-2

Prahalad, C. K., & Bettis, R. A. (1986). The dominant logic: A new linkage between diversity and performance. *Strategic Management Journal, 7*(6), 485–501. https://doi.org/10.1002/smj.4250070602

Roberts, M. S. (2015). Dynamic simulation in health care comes of age. *Value in Health, 18*(2), 143–144. https://doi.org/10.1016/j.jval.2015.02.006

Rosenhead, J. (2006). Past, present and future of problem structuring methods. *Journal of the Operational Research Society, 57*(7), 759–765. https://doi.org/10.1057/palgrave.jors.2602206

Schieritz, N. (2002b, July). Integrating system dynamics and agent-based modeling. In *Proceedings of the XX international conference of the system dynamics society*.

Schneider, P. (2017). *Euripid best practice report on external reference pricing (ERP)* (Vol. 2014, Issue European Commission Grant 'Statistical data for medicinal product pricing' under the call HP-PJ-2014 (No.664317)).

Scholl, H. J. (2001, January). Agent-based and system dynamics modeling: A call for cross study and joint research. In *Proceedings of the 34th annual Hawaii international conference on system sciences* (pp. 8–pp). IEEE.

Stiglitz, J. (2000). The contributions of the economics of information to twentieth century economics. *The Quarterly Journal of Economics, 115*(4), 1441–1478. https://doi.org/10.1162/003355300555015

Tang, C., & Rosen, A. B. (2014). *In search for the MOST COST-effective strategy: A coronary heart disease policy analysis* (pp. 4049–4050).

Vogler, S., & Paterson, K. R. (2017). Can Price transparency contribute to more affordable patient access to medicines? *PharmacoEconomics Open*. https://doi.org/10.1007/s41669-017-0028-1

Vogler, S., Zimmermann, N., & Habimana, K. (2014). *Study of the policy mix for the reimbursement of medicinal products: Proposal for a best practice-based approach based on stakeholder assessment*. (pp. 1–92).

Yan Li, N. K. (2014). *Assessing lifestyle interventions to improve cardiovascular health using an agent-based model* (pp. 1221–1232). WSC.

Yu, X., Li, C., Shi, Y., & Yu, M. (2010). Pharmaceutical supply chain in China: Current issues and implications for health system reform. *Health Policy (Amsterdam, Netherlands), 97*(1), 8–15. https://doi.org/10.1016/j.healthpol.2010.02.010

# Chapter 5
# Hybrid SD and AB Simulation Experimentation for Policy Decision Making

**Abstract** The novel RAM presented in the previous chapter is applied as a procedure for hybrid quantitative simulation. This chapter provides a practical example of this hybridization procedure for the exploration and evaluation of various pharmaceutical policies, related to medicines prescribing and pricing regulations.

The procedure includes the transfer of the qualitative RAM to main SD and ABM components' functions, that is, stocks and flows of resources and agents, their attributes and their behaviour, including main parameters and behavioural assumptions.

The analysis of the pharmaceutical regulation in this chapter presents a number of what if scenarios conceptualized through the RAM approach and performed through the use of a public policy scenario simulator. They have the task to elicit the effects of the regulation tool box and its elements in combination with important contextual regulatory and market competition factors. It extends further the practice of public policy evaluation through simulation, bringing a comprehensive approach and providing interactive learning environments, where decision makers can design and test policies through experimentation. Using simulation helps to illustrate why intendedly rational policies can lead to policy resistance and can support the design and testing of robust interventions, accounting for the counterintuitive nature of policy problems.

## 5.1 Introduction

The purpose of the hybrid SD and AB quantitative simulation modelling is to demonstrate the use of the qualitative RAM for further design of a numerically and operationally sound representation of a researched system. In this respect, the hybrid simulation must be built with the capability for scenario experimentation and simulation testing of the qualitative scenarios generated by the RAM, analysis of the simulation results, and for sustaining policy recommendations.



R. Kazakov et al., *Understanding and Managing Socioeconomic Systems Behaviour*, Contributions to Management Science,
https://doi.org/10.1007/978-3-031-57057-5_5

The novel RAM developed in previous chapters is applied as a conceptual procedure for hybrid quantitative model building and as a functional specification for the coding of the simulation model resource structure and agents' behavioural routine.

Anylogic software has been used for quantitative hybrid simulation due to its capability to handle multimethod modelling and simulation, namely combination of an SD macro with an AB micro perspective. In the above respect, anylogic software is capable of integrating mathematical (continuous) with java programming (discrete) simulation integration, providing flexibility in respect to any type of SD and AB combinations (Borshchev & Filippov, 2004).

Anylogic technical functionality allows application of agent classes, and multiple types of agents and structures. Agent behaviour modelling is supported by visual tools like state charts and action charts. The software also has full feature for SD stock and flow diagrams, and supports SD simulation. It allows control over continuous and or discrete time, continuous and or discrete space, agents' mobility, and communication between agents (e.g. message passing).

## 5.2 Hybrid SD and AB Simulation Modelling Procedure

The simulation design procedure main stages include conceptual specification, then functional specification, and then technical specification. Following these stages, a full documentation on the simulation design can be provided, from its initial conceptualization to the implementation phase, capturing all the components of the hybrid system dynamics and agent-based simulation designs and can support simulation modelling validation and reproducibility requirements.

The functional specification of the hybrid simulation model is tightly linked to the hybrid RAM. The RAM now is used as a hybrid quantitative simulation building procedure (Ackermann et al., 2014), apart from its qualitative analytical merit, bringing a comprehensive perspective to the management of CAS.

The procedure of building a hybrid SD and AB simulation model followed a number of steps aiming at translating the RAM into a formal functional and technical specification of the quantitative model. The functional specification included the transfer of the qualitative RAM to a description of the main SD and ABM components' functions, that is, stocks and flows of resources for the first and agents, their attributes and their behaviour for the second, including main connected parameters and behavioural assumptions characterized in tables.

Initially, main resources and resource flows were taken from the RAM and, together with main agents and related parameters (and attributes), have been initialized in graphical, mathematical, and program code, following the principle 'from simple to complex' components and interconnections (Ghaffarzadegan et al., 2011; Gilbert et al., 2018). Then, next step included testing, reflection, and editing resource and agent simulation model structure, allowing for conceptual and technical corrections, in order to reach to a maximally close technical representation of the RAM.

The drug supply chain (SD component) was technically reconceptualized to provide separate (individual drug firm agent) supply chain for each drug (drugA, drugB, drugC, etc.), similar to the SD notion for using 'subscripts'. This followed to further accounting for market price competition, produced between all drugs. This led to variables addition for 'drug market value' (linked to specific drug firms pricing strategies, connected to changes in their market share). Drug price entry strategy was conceptualized in pseudocode. Another reflection was made, related to 'PublicPriceRuleA' rule of the pricing authorities, who need to set up pricing and prescribing rules and calculate drug public prices.

Other considerations included agents' behaviours. Drug manufacturers agents ('drugMNF') were initially conceptualized to have one innovative and two generic drug suppliers and to variate in number. Also, market drug price discounts are unknown and to vary between a minimum to maximum interval within the simulation runs. Patients are conceptualized as agents which buy medicines following specific rules, related to brand or generic prescribing by doctor agents, and dispensed by pharmacists agents.

Next, the technical specification included the building of stock and flow diagrams and coding of mathematical equations, representing the relations between the SD elements (resource levels and resource flows, parameters, variables, and feedbacks); and the coding of agents' state charts and or actions' charts related to their 'IF THEN' behavioural algorithm and parameters (attributes) in the programming language of the software used.

## 5.3 Hybrid Simulation Modelling and Experimentation for Pharmaceutical Policy and Regulation

The first group of agents described here are drug firms that manufacture both innovative and generic medicines. The main parameters associated with drug firms include their name, number, maximum and minimum price, entry year, market share, marketing allocation, and conditions for price decrease depending on market share. The main functions of drug firms include supplying (launching) their products in EU countries, starting from the most attractive one (with the highest GDP), calculating market share, allocating marketing budgets, and changing product prices due to competition.

The second group of agents listed are parallel traders. They are characterized by their name and number, the country they buy drugs from, entry year, time to investigate drug market prices, and market share. The main functions of parallel traders include investigating drug markets and price differences, buying from the country they are located in, and selling to the country with the highest price difference.

The third group of agents listed are countries, which are characterized by their name and ID number, GDP index, public price policy (minimum or average calculation), time period to review and change public price, and countries used in the reference price basket. The main function of countries is to calculate public price according to a price formula, time period, and country basket selection.

The fourth group of agents listed are doctors, characterized by their population (number) and allocation of drugs by brand or by molecule (e.g. for hyperlipidaemia). The main function of doctors is to prescribe (allocate) drugs to hyperlipidaemia (hl) patients according to the type of prescribing regulation (by brand or by molecule) and the marketing budget influence of drug firms.

The fifth and final group of agents are patients, characterized by their hyperlipidaemia (hl) population, consumption of drugs per month, and buying drugs allocated by doctors (if prescribed by brand) or buying available drugs according to price (if prescribed by molecule).

Main resources (stocks) and resource flows in the hybrid simulation and the variables that influence their levels include drugs supplied and drugs bought on the country market. The inflow and outflow of drugs are determined by the rate of supply and demand, respectively. The variables that influence the level of this resource include the planned demand per year, the decision to supply (launch) a particular drug, and the public price of the drug.

The inflow of drugs is determined by the rate of demand or consumption, while the outflow is determined by the number of patients buying drugs. The variables that influence the level of this resource include the competition among drug suppliers, the consumption per year, the demand for relevant drugs, the marketing budget, the market share, and the prescribing regulation (by brand or by molecule).

Another resource is drugs bought and drugs sold by parallel traders. The inflow of this resource is determined by the rate of parallel trader buying, which is influenced by the public price difference among EU countries. The outflow of this resource is determined by the rate of parallel trader selling, which is influenced by the demand for relevant drugs, the prescribing regulation, and the public price.

Main parameters and the scenarios in which they can be used are as following. The first parameter is the number of drug manufacturing agents, which can be varied to examine the level of competition in the market, ranging from one on patent drug (a monopolistic market) to two, three, or more rival drugs in the off-patent market. The second parameter is the minimum and maximum drug price, which can be varied to examine the level of target profit margin. For example, the maximum price can be set at 10 monetary units, and the minimum price can be set at 5 monetary units.

The third parameter is the time of entry of innovative drugs, which can be varied to examine the period of patent protection. For example, the patent protection period can be set at 15, 10, or 5 years. The fourth parameter is the marketing strategy or marketing allocation condition, which can be varied by changing the percentage allocation from sales for the marketing budget. For example, the percentage allocation can be set at 15%, 10%, or 5% or other.

Another parameter is the pricing strategy or price decrease condition, which can be varied by changing the percentage of price decrease related to the variation in product market share. For example, the price can be decreased by 15%, 10%, or 5% or other if the market share decreases by 10% or other. The sixth parameter is the drug price regulation-related variables that are the external reference pricing country basket, which can be varied in terms of the number and combination of price reference countries in the reference price countries basket. For example, the basket can contain 15, 10, or 5 different countries for each experiment; and the drug public price formula, which can be varied by referring to the minimum or average price of the same drugs among a reference countries basket.

Prescribing regulation parameter used is the variable representing if drugs are prescribed by brand or by molecule. In addition, parallel traders parameter is also included, which can be varied to examine the intensity level of parallel trade (i.e., the number of parallel traders).

Initially, this can be assumed that there are three multinational drug manufacturing agents which decide where to launch their drug, based on each local country's GDP index. They launch first in the country with the highest GDP index, setting their maximum desired price if they are the first supplier. Public price regulation reflects the actual situation in Europe. The three drug agents compete on drug market value (market share), and if it decreases by predefined percentage for each agent, that company decreases its drug price by a chosen percentage.

Patients buy the cheapest drug available in a country, or they can buy a certain drug brand if the prescribing regulation is by molecule or by brand. If the manufacturing agent drug's public price becomes equal to or below a predefined minimum threshold, then that agent would stop supplying. If a country's price is equal to or below the predefined minimum MNF drug price, then the MNF agent will not start supplying to that local market.

External reference pricing-related parameters per country are set to reflect the actual situation in EU countries and are referenced to official surveys. Drug firms' supplying, pricing, and marketing strategies (market behaviour) reflect published research and theoretical framework. Drug firms have a predefined goal of a certain profit margin, according to which they set their maximum desired drug price. The first drug firm registers its maximum (desired) price in the most attractive country market, after which it adjusts its price in other countries according to the local public price and competition, reflecting the behavioural decision principle of price 'anchoring and adjustment'. A drug firm exits a country market if the local public price decreases to its minimum price threshold, reflecting the principle of profit margin 'risk aversion'.

Doctors allocate (prescribe) a branded drug of a certain company, influenced by each drug firm's marketing budget or randomly. Or a doctor agent can allocate (prescribe) a non-branded drug (drug molecule INN), which means that the patient can choose which drug to buy in the pharmacies chain. If a drug firm's marketing budget is higher than the other drug firms' marketing budgets, then doctor agents will prescribe that drug with a higher probability. Drug firms can have two general market strategies: they can try to win doctor agents by increasing their marketing budget or try to win patient agents by decreasing the drug price or combining both.

Patient agents buy the drug that the doctor agent allocated (if by brand) or choose to buy a cheaper drug with a predefined probability (if prescribing is by drug molecule INN). Doctors and patients' behaviour reflect two main general situations related to the state of prescribing regulation (by brand or by molecule). Drug firms compete either through marketing budgets targeting doctors and patients (if prescribing by brand) or through price decrease (if prescribing by molecule).

Parallel traders buy cheaper drugs from one local market and export them to another local market with the highest difference in drug price. They have their own 'parallel' supply chain, affecting the relevant drug volume supplied by drug manufacturers and drug volume bought by patients, which, in turn, affects drug firms' pricing, marketing, and supplying strategies related to each local market. Parallel traders' behaviour reflects published research.

Using the qualitative RAM as a tight procedure for the specification and building of a hybrid simulation model ensures that the right model is being build and a conceptual validation is achieved (transferred from qualitative to quantitative model). This can be proved by comparing the RAM with the hybrid simulation model representation in software, showing a sufficient structural and logical similarity between both.

## 5.4 Simulation Analysis

The simulation analysis of the pharmaceutical regulation presented here comes as a second step of the hybrid resource agent qualitative and quantitative modelling framework. The simulation design and analysis follows the RAM qualitative model and applies it as a hybrid quantitative simulation building procedure, described in Kazakov et al. (2021).

The analysis of the pharmaceutical regulation presents a number of what if scenarios, conceptualized through the RAM approach and performed through the use of a public policy scenario simulator. They have the task to elicit the effects of the regulation tool box and its elements in combination with important contextual regulatory and market competition factors. It extends further the practice of public policy evaluation through simulation, bringing a comprehensive approach (Rosenhead, 2006), building upon and combining the following two principle perspectives related to system dynamics and agent-based modelling and simulation applications to the topic:

- How small system dynamics models can help the public policy decision making and evaluation process (Ghaffarzadegan et al., 2011)
- Computational modelling for evaluation of public policy: Reflections on practice (Gilbert et al., 2018)

The principles of the above two perspectives applied here are related to the practice of simulation models to provide interactive learning environments, where modellers and policy-makers can design and test policies through experimentation and gaming (Ghaffarzadegan et al., 2011). Using simulation helps to illustrate why intendedly rational policies can lead to policy resistance and can support the design and testing of robust policies, accounting for the counterintuitive nature of policy problems. Also, simulations can help to build consensus and can allow policy-makers to explore how behaviours are created endogenously, through a broad model boundary.

In relation to policy evaluation, simulations can provide means for comparing behaviour 'patterns' between simulated and real data and an apparatus for 'accurate' representation of the simulated real systems (Ghaffarzadegan et al., 2011, pp. 29 and 30).

Policy evaluation can be performed through developing a computational model and running simulations with and without implementation of a policy, and then compare formally the two model outcomes with each other and with reality (with the policy implemented), using quantitative analysis through multiple simulations, sensitivity analysis, and 'what if' tests (Gilbert et al., 2018).

This allows for the exploration of alternative interventions and policy options, simply by trying out numerous parameter variations, and experimenting with context-specific scenarios along different horizons. Such simulation modelling experiments enable recursive learning by stakeholders, who can achieve system competence and practical skills through testing different scenarios and learn 'by doing' how to manage complex situations.

## 5.5 Scenario Setting Experimentation

The hybrid simulation experimentation is set with connection to the scenarios generated using the qualitative RAM analysis.

The purpose of the scenario setting and experimentation is to examine the effects of what if changes in the regulation and market system components, together with contextual changes related to local drug prescribing regulation (having effect on local market price competition) and parallel trade activity (having effect on supply and price competition across country markets). This ensures that the regulation effects will be analyzed not as an isolated mechanism but interfering with important contextual price regulatory and market competition factors locally and across connected EU markets.

Main input parameters used in the scenario experiments are as follows:

- Changes in the external reference pricing tool box (reference countries basket variation, time period for price revisions and recalculation)
- Local prescribing regulation variation (brand or generic prescribing)
- Parallel trade competition
- Competition strategies related to drug price setting, marketing budget and allocation, and other

In all presented scenarios, parallel traders and local prescribing regulation are taken as a controlling factor for comparing output indicators. Here in this example of a user dashboard, such output observable variables are product launch time, price evolution over a simulated time horizon, product market exit time, public budget spending, and prices of parallel traded drugs connected to drug access, affordability, and availability criteria.

The input and output variables above have been selected according to the following criteria:

- Input variables need to present options for varying the regulation tool set, connected to price calculation formula (calculating min or avg. value of a drugs price in reference countries basket), reference countries basket (changing selected countries for price benchmarking and their number), time period for price revision (how often a drugs price is benchmarked and recalculated), contextual factors of importance like parallel trade competition and prescribing regulation
- Output variables need to provide options to observe regulation and competition effects related to the research question criteria of equitable access, affordability, and availability of medicinal products (launch time, price evolution, market exit, and public budget expenditure)

The purpose of this scenario setting is to provide what if scenario situations for experimentation with changing important regulation related input parameters and contextual factors, like the ones described above. This will provide an interactive simulation environment where regulation and competition effects can be observed and evaluated against the main criteria of drugs access, availability, and affordability. Some of the what if scenarios are connected to global (EU wide) regulation tool box and contextual factors variation, while other what if scenarios can be experiments with regulation and contextual factors variation on a local market scale.

The simulation model has been tested with real public price data for all EU countries and compared to public price evolution for strengthening the user confidence in its capabilities to provide a trustful representation of the pharmaceutical market public price behaviour.

## 5.6 Analysis of 'Price Convergence' Concept Due to External Reference Pricing Regulation

Another counterintuitive outcome is related to the concept that the external reference pricing regulation must have convergence effect on drug prices around the countries applying this regulation (Vogler & Habimana, 2014), while the simulation shows no evidence for converging drug prices, but just on the opposite.

Price evolutions of drugs A, B, and C, exhibited on Figs. 5.1 and 5.2 each show that even each drug is set to enter all markets at one and the same price value, during the whole simulated time period, difference appear with lowest drug prices for Bulgaria and Slovakia, middle-level prices for Poland and Latvia and highest level prices for Austrian and Hungarian markets. This should come out due to the fact that external reference price regulation rules do not 'act' in isolation. Instead, there are contextual effects (market and drug price competition, prescribing regulation, and

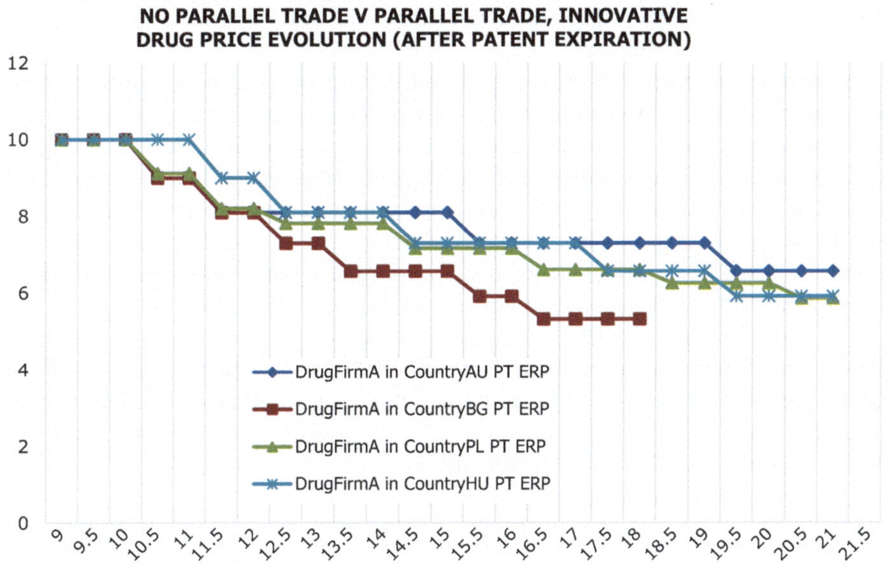


**Fig. 5.1** Innovative drug A price evolution (after patent expiration) across four EU markets selected for comparative reasons (Austria, Bulgaria, Poland, Hungary)

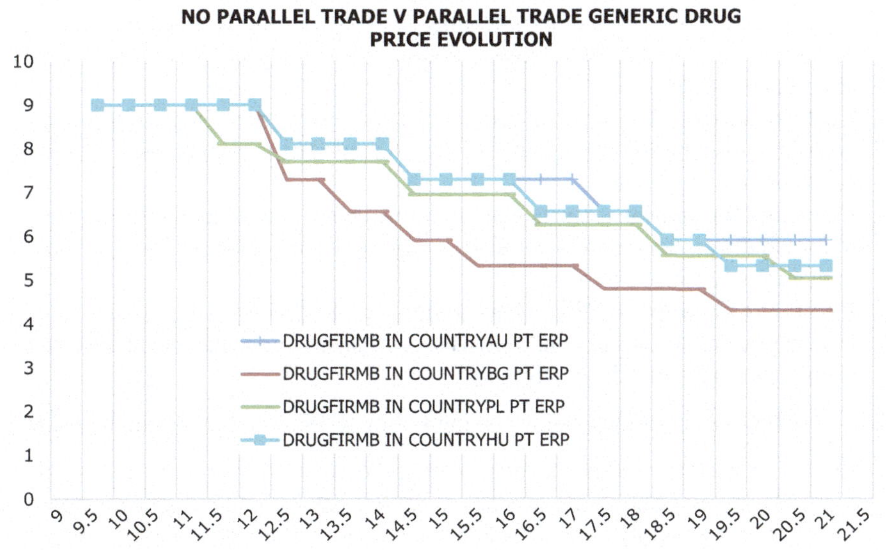


**Fig. 5.2** Generic Drug B price evolution in the same four EU countries

other), that interfere with that regulation rules, and could hinder, amplify, or produce counterintuitive outcomes, like described above.

However, it could be acknowledged that certain convergence of prices could occur among price referencing countries which refer to each other. This raises further questions about the reference price baskets composition and suitability in regard to achieving more equitable and at the same time affordable price levels. An important remark should be made here, regarding the price benchmarking method and if it should be adjusted to local price purchasing parity (PPP) levels, since one drug price could be regarded affordable in one country but in another it could be at a higher or at a lower level when adjusting for the local PPP criterion.

The provided graph indeed suggests a divergence in the price of DrugFirmB across four different countries (AU, BG, PL, HU) when parallel trade (PT) and external reference pricing (ERP) are applied. While one might expect prices to converge due to the harmonizing intentions of PT and ERP, the graph shows that prices start at a similar level but evolve differently over time.

This divergence can be attributed to several factors:

1. **Market conditions**: Different local market conditions, such as supply and demand dynamics, can lead to divergent prices. For instance, if demand in CountryAU is higher than in CountryBG, prices in CountryAU may remain higher due to market pressures.
2. **Regulatory differences**: Even with ERP, the implementation and regulatory framework can vary by country, leading to price variations. Each country may use a different basket of reference countries or apply ERP rules differently, affecting the final price.
3. **Cost structures**: The cost of bringing a drug to market, including logistics, taxes, and distribution costs, can vary significantly between countries, contributing to price divergence.
4. **Currency fluctuations**: Exchange rate movements can affect the local price of imported drugs, leading to divergence when prices are converted back to a common currency for comparison.
5. **Parallel trade impact**: PT can have unpredictable effects on drug prices. It may lead to price decreases in countries where drugs are imported but can also cause supply shortages that drive prices up.

Given these observations, the following policy recommendations can be made:

- **Review of ERP formulas**: Regulators should review ERP formulas and consider a more harmonized approach to reference pricing that could mitigate divergence.
- **Strengthening supply chains**: Policies to strengthen supply chains and mitigate shortages can help stabilize prices and reduce the impact of PT.
- **Market surveillance**: Continuous surveillance of drug markets can help identify and respond to factors contributing to price divergence.
- **Collaborative policy development**: Countries could benefit from collaborative policy development, sharing best practices, and harmonizing regulatory approaches where possible.

- **Cushioning currency impacts**: Hedging strategies or currency adjustment factors could be introduced in ERP calculations to minimize the impact of currency fluctuations on drug prices.

The graph serves as an important reminder that while PT and ERP aim to harmonize and reduce drug prices, the actual outcome can be influenced by a myriad of factors leading to price divergence. Therefore, policies should be dynamic and responsive to the complex realities of pharmaceutical pricing in a global context.

## 5.7 Analysis of the Effects If External Reference Pricing Is Not Applied in all EU Countries

Figure 5.3 presents the price evolution for a 'no external reference pricing, without parallel traders' vs. 'no external reference pricing with parallel traders' scenario for drug A in Austria and Hungary

This scenario is testing the effects of a 'no external price referencing' on the market if there were or there were not any parallel traders. In this scenario, price evolution is left to be depending on price competition effect among all market agents supplying a given drug (drug manufacturers and parallel traders) on a local market.

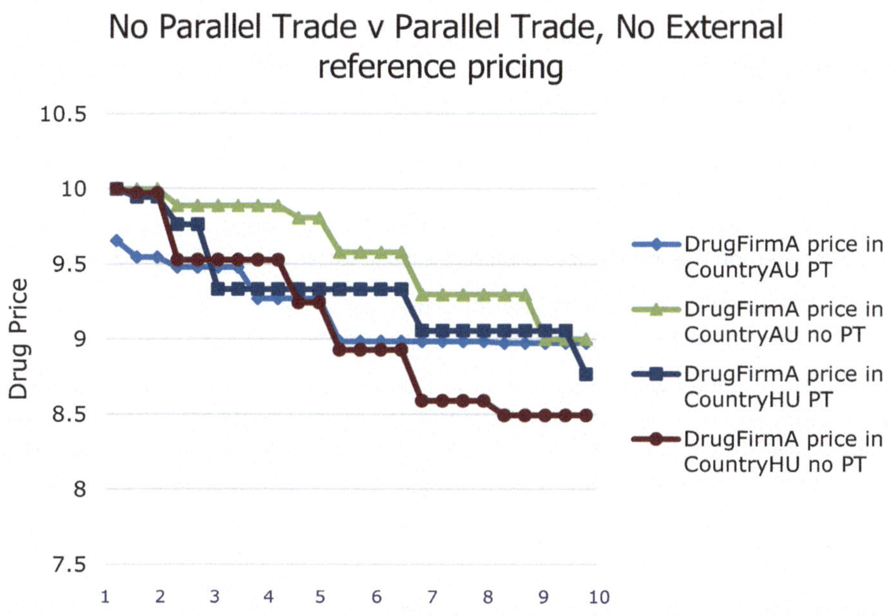


**Fig. 5.3** Price evolution for a 'no external reference pricing, without parallel traders' vs. 'no external reference pricing with parallel traders' scenario for drug A in Austria and Hungary

Price evolution will also be dependent on contextual local prescribing regulation, which could be either by brand or by molecule and which is influencing the buying behaviour of consumers. Prescribing by brand usually means that patients buy drugs by their brand, and that drug manufacturers compete on marketing budgets allocated for doctor adoption, without having incentive to decrease their drug price. If prescribing is by molecule, patients usually buy more affordable (cheaper) drugs and drug firms compete on mostly on price, which increase further price competition intensity and can lead to faster price decrease.

If there are no parallel traders in this scenario, originator drug prices remain higher for longer period of time in countries like Austria and Hungary, but if included then prices decrease faster due to the competition effect of parallel traders' activity on drug prices and on drug market share of each drug company agent.

## 5.8 Scenario Experimentation for One Local EU Market

The hybrid simulation model presented here is capable also to provide opportunity for scenario experimentation related to a chosen country and for exploration of the pharmaceutical pricing regulation market effects in a parallel trade and prescribing regulation context and what if interventions for policy optimization. Here an example is provided for one country, Bulgaria. Pricing regulation in this country is applied at the minimum price referencing level, price revisions are made every year and the price reference country basket contains the following countries: Denmark, Estonia, Finland, France, Germany, Latvia, Lithuania, Slovakia, Slovenia, Sweden, and Switzerland. Local prescribing is mainly made by brand and parallel traders exist. An initial reference mode, tailored to the real price and contextual regulation parameters for all included countries is exhibited on Fig. 5.4 (with parallel trade).

Figure 5.4 exhibits price evolution of drugs A (innovative), B (generic), and C (generic) explored in two different market scenarios:

- 'ERP, parallel trade' (brand prescribing market)
- 'No ERP, parallel trade' (brand prescribing market)

Clearly, a market with ERP regulation could provide means for more favourable price affordability levels on one side, but on the other it could have effect on drug market exits (drug A exits at year eight after its patent expiration and its monopolistic position on the market, after which it experienced market and price competition from generic drug rivals coming to the market).

Also considering prescribing by molecule would ensure higher price competition local effect. In countries with limited market and price competition (with fewer rival drugs and or local prescribing is done on brand), ERP configured to regular benchmarking with drug prices from local markets with higher competition level could be a good tool to offset oligopolistic pricing behaviour on that local market.

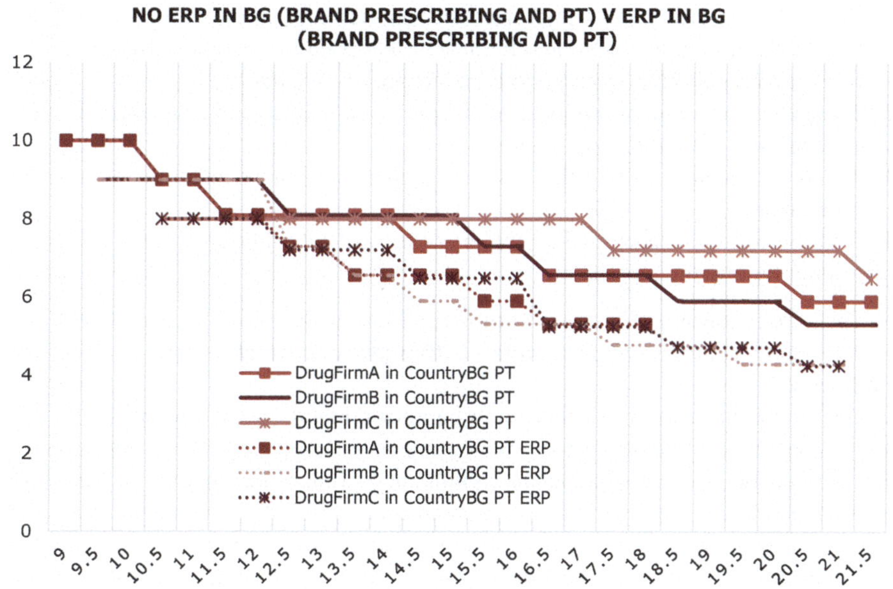


**Fig. 5.4** Comparing 'ERP, parallel trade' reference mode scenario and 'no ERP, parallel trade' scenario, brand prescribing market

## 5.9 Generic Drugs Competition After Patent Expiration of the Innovative Drug

Exploring further the evolution of drug prices after drug A patent expiration and the entering of two generic drug rivals in year 9 and year 10 (Fig. 5.4) shows that prices start to decrease for all available drugs, due to market share competition. In regard to the affordability criterion, public drug budget spending becomes lower. In this, like in the previous scenario, the pricing regulation is set to capture competitive price discounts in full and to use them to change public prices due to which it can further transfer changed public prices among reference basket countries with different price competition level.

## 5.10 Uncertainty Analysis Related to Market Competition Price Discounts

Here four scenarios will be further explored, consisting simulating uncertainty experiments related to the market competition drug price discounts. They are combined with parameter variation, including price calculation formula (min or avg), local prescribing regulation (brand or generic), parallel trade, and state price discounting.

1. The first scenario is about pharmaceutical policy regulation with price calculation on minimum price among reference basket countries and prescribing regulation on molecule INN (international nonproprietary name).
2. The second scenario is the same as the previous one but without external reference pricing regulation application.
3. The third scenario is like the first one, but prescribing regulation is on drugs brand name.
4. And the fourth scenario is like the previous one but without external reference pricing regulation application.

The simulation was done in 100 runs for each of the above scenarios with the goal to capture enough wide sample of drag price distribution within a 95% of confidence.

Due to the uncertainty of the level of capturing market price discounts, 100 different drug price distributions have been grouped and analyzed. The results showed that all distributions are statistically significant and mark the interval in which all possible average price distributions can be placed with 95% of certainty. Also, the analysis proves that the market price discount has an influence and plays significant role in all four scenarios and that the results of the scenarios (each run) are not due to random factors.

All this means that public price levels depend on the degree of capturing market price discounts through the external reference pricing regulation, but also this can produce effects of market withdrawals of drugs and drugs unavailability on a local market (only on one or more markets which are referencing public prices among each other).

This produces an important question about the contradiction and trade-off between drug price affordability and drug price availability and how public price authorities should find a way to cope with this issue. Drug price statistical means of all scenarios have been compared for all simulated drug prices (drug A, drug B, and drug C).

Statistical means of drug price values can also capture and exhibit for observation the behavioural 'pattern' of all drug price distributions. This ensures that statistical means of drug prices can be used for representative comparison purposes among all scenarios, taking account for the uncertainty related to the level of market price discounts captured within the drug pricing regulation.

Figures 5.5, 5.6, 5.7, 5.8, 5.9, and 5.10 provides comparative results of the drug price distribution statistical means.

Here, counterintuitive results can be observed: price affordability level in scenario when there is no external reference price regulation with prescribing on molecule almost coincides with the scenario when there is external reference price regulation, but prescribing regulation is on 'brand' for drugs A, drugs B, and is even better for drug C.

This observation questions the usefulness of external reference price regulation in connection to the contradiction between drug price affordability and drug availability. This proves the hypothesis that drug price competition plays the main role in

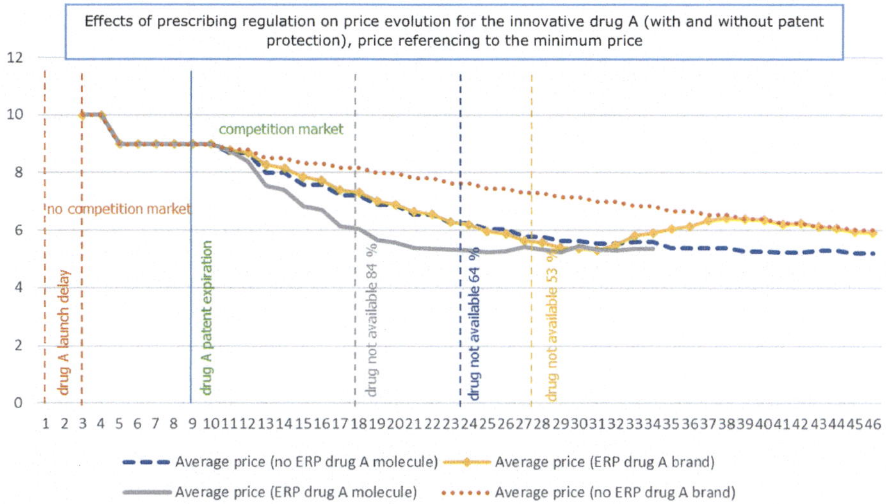


**Fig. 5.5** Comparing the effects of prescribing regulation on drug price competition and price evolution for the innovative drug A (with and without patent protection)

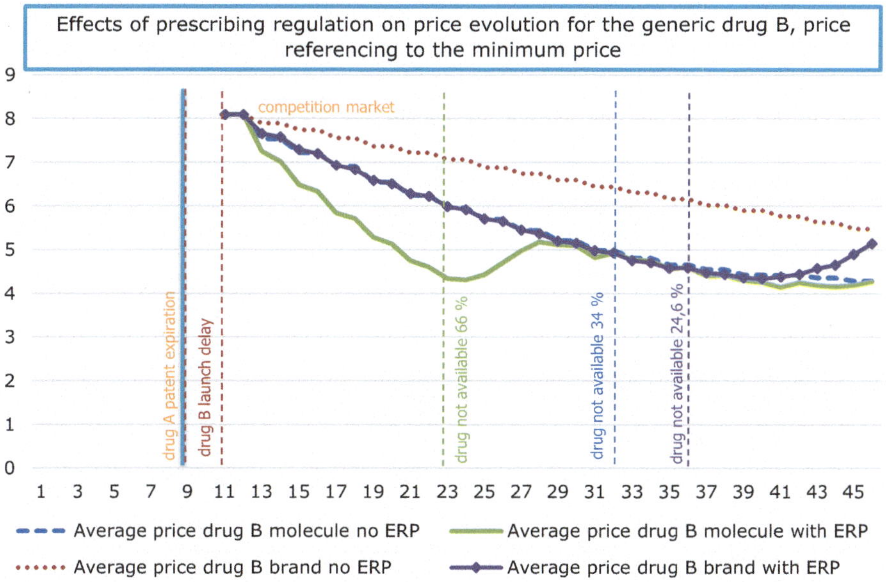


**Fig. 5.6** Comparing the effects of prescribing regulation on drug price competition and price evolution for the generic drug B

rising drug price affordability levels, while external reference pricing regulation can just transfer direct or indirect price levels from one competitive market to other less competitive markets and or vice versa.

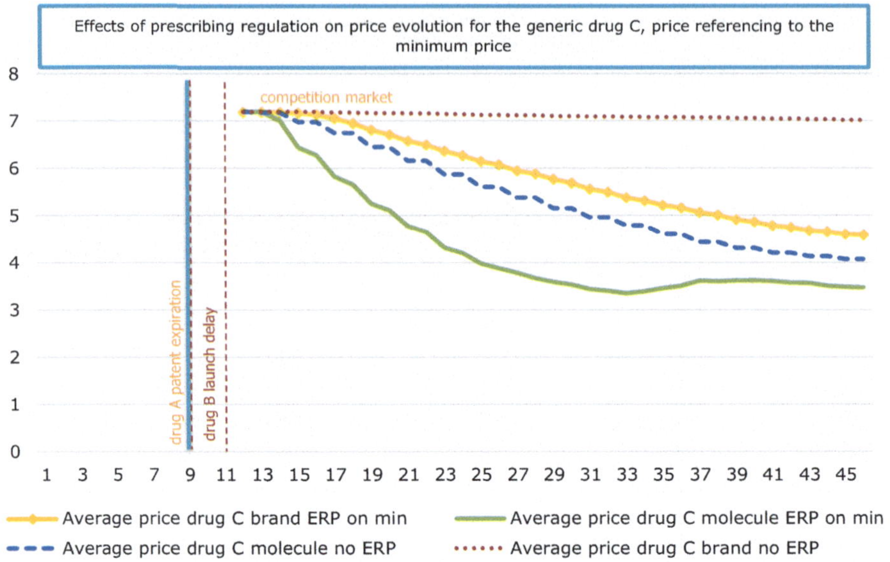


**Fig. 5.7** Comparing the effects of prescribing regulation on drug price competition and price evolution for the generic drug C

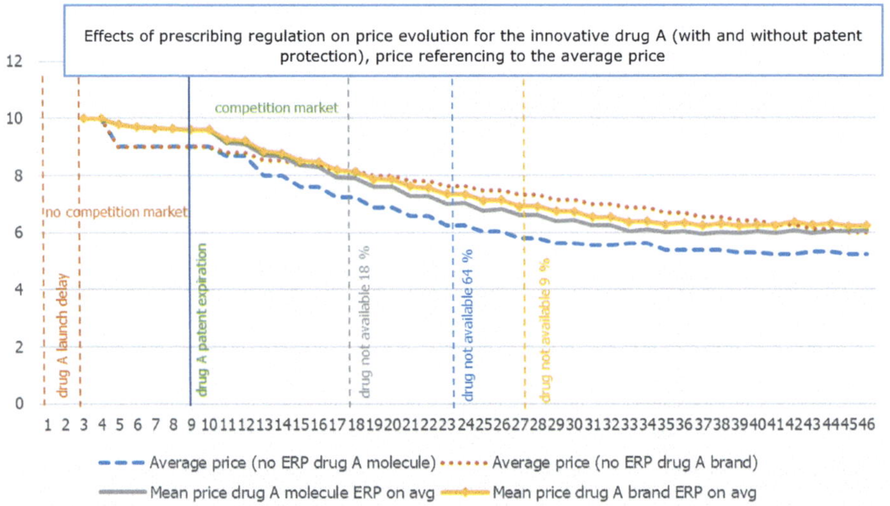


**Fig. 5.8** Comparing the effects of prescribing regulation on price evolution for the innovative drug A (with and without patent protection), price referencing to the average price among the reference basket countries

The price inflation hypothesis is also proved in the patent-protected markets and in markets where external reference price regulation coexists and interferes with brand prescribing regulation, this way transferring higher level prices compared to the scenario with 'molecule' prescribing regulation which fosters higher market price competition.

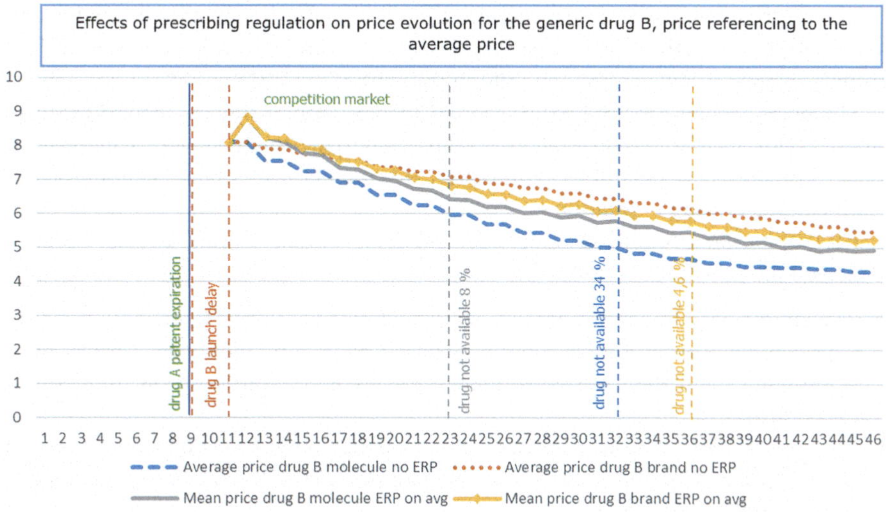


**Fig. 5.9** Comparing the effects of prescribing regulation on price evolution for the generic drug B, price referencing to the average price

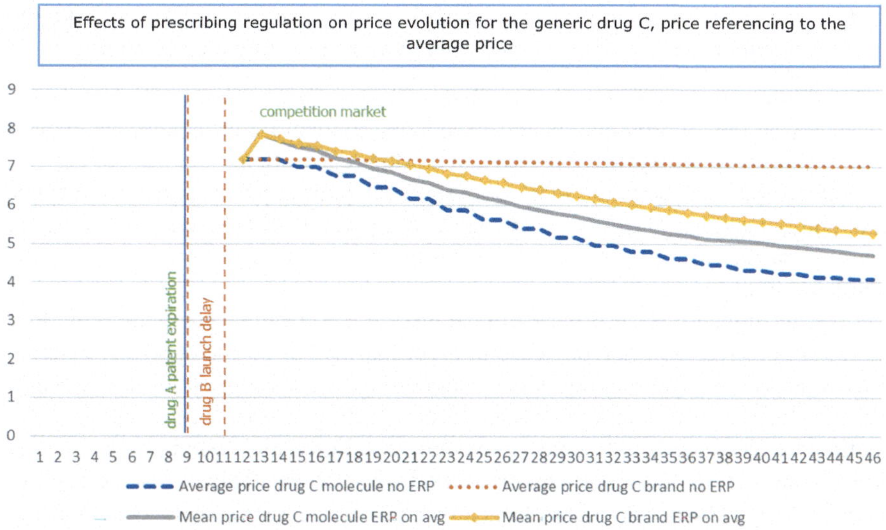


**Fig. 5.10** Comparing the effects of prescribing regulation on price evolution for the generic drug C, price referencing to the average price

The purpose of this comparative scenario analysis is to assess the effects of brand vs. generic prescribing regulation in regard to price competition, in both situations when there is external reference price regulation applied and if there is no external price regulation on the market.

This approach follows main principles for public policy evaluation through using computation simulation for comparing different 'policy' scenarios and their effectiveness against selected outcome criteria (Gilbert et al., 2018).

The above scenarios are taking account of the parallel traders' activities, drug suppliers pricing and market strategies, connected to their market sales volumes and share, drug budget expenditure, public price discounts for reimbursement purposes, and local prescribing regulation.

All graphs show four drug A, drug B, and drug C price scenario evolutions for a simulated 45-year time period, where

1. The simple grey line represents the statistical means of drug A, drug B, and drug C price when prescribing regulation is based on generic medicines (drug's molecule name) and the external reference price calculation is set on 'min' referenced drug
2. The yellow diamond line represents the statistical means of drug A, drug B, and drug C price when the local prescribing regulation is based on the medicine's brand, ERP calculation is on 'min'
3. The blue dashed line represents the statistical means of drug A, drug B, and drug C price when prescribing is on 'molecule' name and there is no external reference pricing regulation
4. The dotted line represents the statistical means of drug A, drug B, and drug C price when prescribing is on 'brand' and there is no external price referencing

In addition, the graph shows the effect of a state price discount of 10% introduced at year two of drug market entry and a requirement for drug presence in three countries prior to drug price approval and market registration.

Vertical lines on the graph mark drug time delay, drug patent protection expiration, and percentage of drug A unavailable on the market like averaged number of years when the drug is not present on the market for all 100 runs divided to the simulated time period.

Looking at the graph, first period of patent protection and no competition of drug A shows no effect on price decrease in all scenarios but on the opposite, external price referencing supports drug prices maintaining on their highest level. Even after the introduction of a public price state discount, drug A price decreases once and continues to stay stable until patent protection expiration and coming of the generic drugs' competition. Drug A enters the market with 2 years delay due to the requirement for drug presence in at least three other EU markets prior to its local launch.

The effect on price affordability is highest after the patent protection period, decreasing drug A price do the lowest level compared to the other scenarios. On other side, the effect on maintaining drugs' availability is lowest compared to the other scenarios (84% not available on the local market). The public price is higher when prescribing is on brand, but it almost coincides with drug A price when there is no external reference pricing and prescribing is on molecule. In both scenarios, drug A could be unavailable in 53% and 64% of the simulated time period. If there were no external reference pricing and the prescribing were on brand, then drug A would have achieved the highest price; hence, the lowest level of affordability for public budget and out-of-pocket expenditure.

The above results present a contradiction leading to an important trade-off conflict within the external reference pricing regulation and to a need to find how to strike a balance between this trade off tension between the affordability and the availability criteria. These results also confirm that the external reference pricing regulation just 'controls' prices, which are officially registered on the public price lists and thus can transfer their evolution between reference basket countries.

Further, these results, as also evident on the Fig. 5.5 (presenting statistical mean drug prices for the four scenarios explained above), provide the insight that the local prescribing regulation, can have interfering effect with the external reference pricing regulation and on drug price evolution, due to affecting price competition tactics of drug companies: 'brand' prescribing sustain higher drug prices and lower rate of price decrease in time, in comparison to 'generic' prescribing regulation, which fosters price competition and quicker price decrease. Also, prescribing and pricing regulations have interfering effects with the effects of parallel trading and state drug price discounts.

All the above insights are evident on the other drug price evolution graphs, which present parameter variation uncertainty results for generic drugs B and C.

Figure 5.6 exhibits the mean price evolution of drug B under the same environmental and agent-specific conditions described in relation to drug A. Here, drug B price follows similar behaviour and shows that when prescribing is on brand (scenario 2 and scenario 3) and there is external price referencing, the outcome effect is very much similar with the scenario when there was no external price referencing, but prescribing is on 'molecule' (yellow diamond line and blue dashed line). Using external price referencing with calculation on 'min' when local market prescribing is on 'molecule' can undermine drug availability level (up to 66% possible market exits of all simulated runs). Like in drug A scenario options, here a branded prescription market without external price referencing would not be recommendable, because it favours the highest drug price levels throughout the whole simulated time period. In markets with prescribing on 'molecule', and with no external price referencing regulation, ensuring market competition on price through providing quicker market access to innovative and generic drug rivals, can avoid spillover effects and induced drug market exists. On the opposite, in local markets with prescribing on 'brand', external price referencing regulation with price calculation on 'min' can increase drug price level of affordability for the public budget and out-of-pocket spending.

This situation with drug B first entering the generic market is repeated with its second generic rival drug C (Fig. 5.7) even on a higher extent showing that drug C price affordability level is and stays even higher in a generic prescribing competition market without ERP (scenario 3), compared to market with prescribing on 'brand' and ERP (scenario 2).

The three graphs on the price evolution of drug A, B, and C are showing that pricing regulation is not an isolated tool and it interferes with local competition, price tactics of drug companies, and prescribing regulation. It is important to take into account local prescribing regulation and number of drug rivals on the market in designing and adjusting a proper and adequate pricing regulation tailored not only to each local market but also to innovative and generic drugs.

The next three graphs on Figs. 5.8–5.10 exhibit drugs A, B, and C price evolution in an external reference pricing market with price calculation on 'avg', compared to a no external reference pricing market and local prescribing on 'brand' or 'molecule' variation. Here, the 'no ERP' market with prescribing on 'molecule' outperforms all other policy options, although it could lead to a 64% and 34% drug A and drug B withdrawals, but due to price competition and not to ERP regulation induced price spillover effects.

In this scenario, price calculation formula is changed from minimum ('min') price taken out of the reference country basket price of the same drug, to taking the average ('avg') of all prices. Price averaging seems to have a moderate (smoothing) price decrease effect with no abrupt changes in price and no drug exits for the simulated 10 year period, compared to the scenario with minimum price calculation.

In this scenario, changing the local prescribing regulation from 'brand' to 'molecule', while the price calculation is done on the average and not on the minimum of the reference drug prices, brings a little to the affordability effect. It provides an insight about the capability of the external price referencing to compensate for the differences in the local prescribing regulation in different countries (if by 'brand' or by 'molecule'), due to the averaging effect of the reference drug prices.

Another favourable effect of this policy scenario is related to the drug availability criterion, since no drug exits occur in the explored local market. However, this does not prevent drug exits indirect effects in any of the rest of the price referencing markets.

External reference pricing regulation using 'avg' price calculation policy favours higher drug prices compared to price calculation based on the 'min' price, but on the other side, it keeps unavailability level lower. However, public price state discounts could be not utilized in full or even are neutralized due to the price averaging effects. In general, following the observations of the simulated scenarios and policy options, it could be stated with confidence that off patent markets with generic competition and local prescribing regulation on 'molecule' provide more sustainable conditions for achieving higher levels of drug access, availability, and affordability without external price referencing in comparison with other options. However, if prescribing regulation is on 'brand', then external price referencing regulation can bring value in relation to all three criteria, especially on affordability of drugs on an 'off-patent' market. External price referencing brings no or limited effect on increasing access, affordability, and availability of on-patent drugs but on the opposite, it could hinder or delay drugs market access and provoke drug market exists, due to reference basket countries price benchmarking avoidance tactic, on one side, but on the other it could support higher drug price transfer among local markets in EU.

## 5.11 Discussion and Policy Recommendations

Initially, during the patent protection period, the pricing of the innovative drug is not affected through the ERP. The introduction of ERP correlates with a noticeable drop in the average price of drug A. This suggests that ERP is effective in reducing drug prices in the absence of market competition. The introduction of competition after the patent protection period in the market is indicated by a further drop in drug prices.

Drug B price shows a similar drug A evolution. However, the price of the generic version with ERP appears to decline more sharply than the branded version, suggesting that generics are more sensitive to the effects of the ERP regulation.

The introduction of generic drugs has a significant impact on reducing innovative drug prices, which is amplified when ERP is further applied. This underscores the importance of generics in the pharmaceutical market as a tool for cost containment. Policies encouraging the early entry and uptake of generic drugs could be more effective at reducing drug prices than ERP alone. Additionally, ensuring a stable supply of generics is important to prevent price spikes due to temporary non-availability.

In markets without competition, ERP can be a limited tool to control drug prices and should be considered by policy-makers as part of a broader drug pricing regulation strategy. The introduction of competition is associated with a reduction in drug prices, highlighting the importance of prescribing regulation to stimulate price competition when prescribing is on drug molecule name. Policies that promote the entry of generic drugs and biosimilars, including molecule prescribing, can enhance competition and lead to lower prices.

Both ERP and competition reduce prices, but the long-term effects should be monitored. Policies should be adaptable to changing market conditions, in order to prevent negative effects on drug availability.

Finally, a comprehensive approach to drug price regulation should be adopted, combining ERP, prescribing and competition policies, and consideration of innovation incentives to ensure both the affordability and the continued development of pharmaceuticals.

When ERP is based on average prices rather than minimum prices, this may result in higher reference prices since outliers on the lower end would have less impact on the calculation, potentially leading to less aggressive price reductions (Figs. 5.8–5.10).

If the goal is to achieve lower drug prices, policy-makers may consider using the minimum reference price for ERP calculations instead of the average, as it can lead to more competitive pricing. The data reaffirms that competition is effective in reducing drug prices. Policies that facilitate the entry of generic drugs, biosimilars, and new market entrants can be beneficial in driving down prices.

Implementing a tiered approach to ERP where both average and minimum prices are used in different scenarios or for different classes of drugs might balance the need for lower drug prices with the sustainability concerns of pharmaceutical companies.

The observed result that the price of drug B becomes lower in the absence of ERP compared to a scenario with ERP, where prices are calculated on averages, is an interesting outcome that may be counterintuitive to the original intent of ERP systems.

ERP is designed to regulate drug prices by referencing the costs in other countries, with the objective of preventing excessive pricing. However, when ERP calculations are based on average prices, this can result in less aggressive price reductions. This is because the averaging method dilutes the impact of the lower prices that would be more influential in a minimum price reference system. Therefore, if the reference basket includes countries with high drug prices, the average price will be higher than the minimum price, potentially leading to higher reference prices under ERP.

In a no ERP scenario market forces, particularly competition, are the primary drivers of drug pricing. Each of these graphs suggests that these market forces have led to a situation where the price of drug B falls below the price it would have had in an ERP system that uses average pricing. This indicates that the competitive dynamics in the market are more effective in reducing prices than the regulatory impact of ERP in this particular case.

All the simulation experiments show the complexity of drug markets and drug pricing and the need for careful design and monitoring of pricing regulations to ensure they meet their intended goals.

## References

Ackermann, F., Howick, S., Quigley, J., Walls, L., & Houghton, T. (2014). Systemic risk elicitation: Using causal maps to engage stakeholders and build a comprehensive view of risks. *European Journal of Operational Research, 238*(1), 290–299.

Borshchev, A., & Filippov, A. (2004). From system dynamics and discrete event to practical agent based modeling: Reasons, techniques, tools. In *22nd international conference of the system dynamics society, 25–29 July 2004*, p. 45.

Ghaffarzadegan, N., Lyneis, J., & Richardson, G. P. (2011). How small system dynamics models can help the public policy process. *System Dynamics Review, 27*(1), 22–44. https://doi.org/10.1002/sdr.442

Gilbert, N., Ahrweiler, P., Barbrook-Johnson, P., Narasimhan, K. P., & Wilkinson, H. (2018). Computational modelling of public policy: Reflections on practice. *JASSS, 21*(1). https://doi.org/10.18564/jasss.3669

Kazakov, R., Howick, S., & Morton, A. (2021). Managing complex adaptive systems: A resource/agent qualitative modelling perspective. *European Journal of Operational Research, 290*(1), 386. https://doi.org/10.1016/j.ejor.2020.08.007

Rosenhead, J. (2006). Past, present and future of problem structuring methods. *Journal of the Operational Research Society, 57*(7), 759–765.

Vogler, S., & Habimana, K. (2014). Pharmaceutical pricing policies in European countries.

# Chapter 6
# Managerial Dynamic Cognitive Capabilities in a Complex Market Environment

**Abstract** This chapter demonstrates how simulation modelling of complex adaptive systems can enhance managerial dynamic cognitive capabilities. SAFE ARCS framework is introduced, which offers a comprehensive analysis for strategic decision-making and related dynamic cognitive capabilities, consisting of four key stages: Search, Articulate, Find, and Evaluate Agent Resource Configurations. The SAFE ARCS correlates with essential cognitive capabilities like strategic imagination, strategic conversation, strategic innovation, and strategic surprise. Strategic imagination involves the capability to envision plausible future scenarios and identify avenues for strategic change. This aligns with the 'search' cognitive phase, which is supported by the RAM framework. Strategic conversation is the capability of engaging with stakeholders within and outside the organization. It revolves around fostering dialogues and diverse perspectives, creating an environment for strategic idea generation and alignment. This relates to the 'articulate' aspect and is again supported by the RAM methodology. Strategic innovation encompasses the capability to communicate alternative options for competitive advantage. The 'find' phase aligns with this capability, guiding managers in identifying game-changing strategies, supported by scenario simulation experimentation. Strategic surprise emphasizes the capability for proactively responding to future changes. In this context, the 'evaluate' cognitive phase relates to the process of comparing and selecting optimal strategic paths.

## 6.1 Introduction

Managerial dynamic cognitive capabilities (MDCCs) refer to a manager's ability to adapt to changing and complex business environments through cognitive processes related to managerial learning, reasoning, and decision making.

MDCCs represent a manager's skill in processing information and adjusting their behaviour in the ever-evolving business landscape. These capabilities include perceiving, analyzing, and applying information, which leads to decisive actions.



R. Kazakov et al., *Understanding and Managing Socioeconomic Systems Behaviour*, Contributions to Management Science,
https://doi.org/10.1007/978-3-031-57057-5_6

These cognitive processes include attention, memory, perception, problem-solving, creativity, and decision-making, all of which are essential for effective leadership in complex environments (Helfat et al., 2007; Helfat & Peteraf, 2015).

There are various methods for assessing MDCCs. Surveys and questionnaires are commonly used, focusing on aspects such as problem-solving, creativity, and judgement skills. Cognitive tests are also employed to measure similar abilities. In some research areas, MDCCs are evaluated through decision-making simulations and other behavioural tasks (Cepeda & Vera, 2007).

Research indicates that MDCCs contribute to organizational success. Managers with strong MDCCs demonstrate greater adaptability, decision-making skills, and the ability to foster innovation among their teams. They are also skilled at navigating the complex and uncertain terrain of modern business. The importance of MDCCs underscores the need for organizations to invest in enhancing these competencies among their managerial staff (Lin & Wu, 2014).

Helfat and Peteraf (2015) explored the role of managerial cognitive capabilities in the development of dynamic capabilities. The authors argue that managerial cognition plays a key role in shaping the firm's ability to identify and respond to changes in the market environment. They propose a model of the micro foundations of dynamic capabilities that emphasizes the role of managerial cognitive capabilities in facilitating the acquisition, integration, and reconfiguration of resources.

Cepeda and Vera (2007) examined the relationship between dynamic capabilities and operational capabilities from a knowledge management perspective. The authors argue that dynamic capabilities are necessary for firms to adapt and respond to changes in the market environment, while operational capabilities are necessary for firms to efficiently and effectively implement their strategies. They propose a framework that integrates these two types of capabilities and emphasizes the importance of knowledge management in supporting both.

Sher and Lee (2004) explored further the role of information technology in facilitating the development of dynamic capabilities through knowledge management. The authors argue that information technology can enable firms to more effectively manage their knowledge assets and respond to changes in the market environment. They propose a model that emphasizes the importance of knowledge management processes and the use of information technology tools in supporting dynamic capabilities.

Lin and Wu (2014) examined the relationship between dynamic capabilities and firm performance from a resource-based view framework (Barney et al., 2001). The authors argue that dynamic capabilities are a key source of competitive advantage for firms, enabling them to adapt and respond to changes in the market environment. They propose a conceptual framework that emphasizes the role of dynamic capabilities in creating and leveraging valuable, rare, inimitable, and non-substitutable (VRIN) resources (Barney, 1986, 1991; Ulrich & Barney, 1984).

Ambrosini (n.d.) expounded on dynamic managerial capabilities, accentuating a manager's ability to adapt and maintain an adequate response to evolving market situations. The pivotal role of these capabilities in fostering and upholding a firm's competitive advantage is accentuated. Their framework notably underscores strategic agility, foresight, and improvisation-related cognitive capabilities as pillars for nurturing managerial dynamic capabilities.

In a collaborative perspective, de Souza and Forte (2021) explored the interaction between managerial cognitive abilities and dynamic managerial capabilities. Their consensus centres on the main role of managerial thinking in enhancing a firm's ability to utilize dynamic capabilities. They have proposed a conceptual framework that emphasizes managerial cognitive abilities as enablers for acquiring, integrating, and transforming resources. Their insights offer practical strategies for firms to improve and shape dynamic managerial capabilities.

The connection between MDCCs and gaining a competitive edge through VRIN resources is evident. VRIN resources, which represent assets that are challenging for competitors to replicate or replace, serve as a cornerstone for maintaining competitive superiority (Lin & Wu, 2014). In this context, MDCCs play a vital role in identifying and accumulating VRIN resources. Proficient managers can recognize emerging opportunities, survey the environment for critical information, and introduce innovative ideas. This dynamism leads to the acquisition of VRIN resources.

A manager enriched with MDCCs demonstrates skill in moulding and utilizing organizational resources, transforming them into VRIN resources. Their cognitive abilities enable them to create resources that are unique and formidable, resistant to imitation, resulting in the development of rare resources. Additionally, their ability to combine these resources produces assets that are irreplaceable.

Furthermore, such managers employ their cognitive tools to continuously refine these VRIN assets, resulting in unparalleled resources. Through constant adaptation and rejuvenation, these resources can be maintained as competitive assets in the long run. In essence, the synergy between MDCCs and the attainment of VRIN resources highlights the importance of honing MDCCs in managerial roles. By enhancing these cognitive faculties, managers can effectively identify, accumulate, nurture, and leverage VRIN resources, setting a path toward sustained competitive advantage and business success.

In the realm of business analytics, managerial skills are crucial for conducting insightful analyses, for example, using Porter's Five Forces and PESTLE frameworks, which are key tools for understanding competitive landscapes and external factors that impact a firm's trajectory (Ambrosini & Altintas, 2019).

Porter's Five Forces framework focuses on the competitive landscape of an industry, identifying threats posed by new entrants, the bargaining power of suppliers and buyers, the risk of substitute products or services, and the intensity of competition. This framework helps businesses understand industry dynamics and formulate their strategic position against competitors. On the other hand, PESTLE analysis focuses on external factors that influence a company's performance, encompassing political, economic, socio-cultural, technological, legal, and environmental aspects. This comprehensive perspective enables firms to assess their external environment and identify potential opportunities and threats.

To effectively conduct a meaningful analysis using Porter's Five Forces and PESTLE frameworks, managers require a set of essential skills. Firstly, analytical and critical thinking abilities are crucial for unravelling and evaluating the numerous factors shaping the industry and the company's vitality. This involves tasks such as data collection, interpretation, trend analysis, and pattern recognition. Additionally, a thorough understanding of the industry and a comprehensive grasp of the broader business environment are essential. Familiarity with market dynamics, competitive landscapes, and a wide range of external influences, spanning from political, societal, ethical to environmental aspects, becomes indispensable for managers.

Effective communication is a fundamental managerial skill, essential for conveying the outcomes of comprehensive analyses conducted using Porter's Five Forces and PESTLE frameworks to an organization's stakeholders (Ambrosini & Altintas, 2019). This entails not only presenting complex information clearly but also skilfully encapsulating findings in persuasive presentations that inspire informed actions.

Well-developed managerial cognitive abilities support insightful strategic industry analyses and provide means for identifying hidden threats and opportunities, charting the way for strategic initiatives and, consequently, optimizing organizational performance. In relation to the above, the incorporation of simulation modelling in managerial routines enhances managerial cognitive capabilities, creating a space to prototype various market and regulatory scenarios. Scenario simulations enable managers to explore diverse scenarios pathways, challenge dominant assumptions, and evaluate potential optimal decision paths. The resulting comprehensive insights into market behaviour and regulatory dynamics sharpen their decision-making skills, allowing them to navigate complex information landscapes, anticipate challenges, and make informed decisions in uncertain situations.

Additionally, scenario simulations enhance the cognitive flexibility in managers, showcasing their ability to switch between different perspectives and problem-solving approaches. By engaging with a variety of scenarios, a repertoire of strategies can be explored and assessed, preparing companies for the complex adaptive systems nature of the market and regulatory environments.

Furthermore, simulations contribute to strategic awareness and planning navigation expertise. By exploring diverse scenarios, strategic opportunities become clear, facilitating the creation of effective action plans aligned with the organization's values and objectives. Therefore, in the context of enhancing managerial cognition, simulation modelling is a powerful and efficient tool.

## 6.2 SAFE ARCS Framework

The SAFE ARCS framework offers a comprehensive analysis for managers strategic decision-making and related dynamic cognitive capabilities, consisting of four key phases: Search, Articulate, Find, and Evaluate Agent Resource Configurations (Table 6.1), all with the aim of identifying optimal agent-resource configurations that can enable transitioning the company's performance to an improved future state (Kazakov & Kunc, 2016).

**Table 6.1** SAFE ARCS Framework

| Phase | Description |
|---|---|
| Search | Gathering information from both internal and external sources, related to the market system behaviour. Critical elements under scrutiny include competitive dynamics, market trends, regulatory environment, and other aspects related to the 'five forces' and PESTLE analysis.<br>This stage includes also qualitative modelling of optional scenarios to address future challenges. |
| Articulate | Conversation and co-understanding of the strategic challenges, desired outcomes and alternative strategic options relating to optimal acquisition, configuration or reconfiguration of internal and external system agents and resources.<br>This involves defining the problem, mapping out the desired goals, and comparing strategic decision options. |
| Find | Selecting a set of optimal competing agent-resource configurations for utilizing best future alternatives. The ability to choose best options to align with the organization's mission. |
| Evaluate | Most promising strategies are selected and assessed against the organization's values and objectives. This phase also entails risk assessment and the development of contingency plans. |

Table 6.1 presents a structured breakdown of the managerial strategic decision-making process. Decision-making plays a pivotal role in shaping the course of an organization's actions and future outcomes. The four phases outlined in the table, namely Search, Articulate, Find, and Evaluate, provide a comprehensive framework for guiding decision-makers through complex scenarios. Integrating simulation techniques can enhance the effectiveness of these phases by providing a dynamic and data-driven perspective to decision-making.

The 'Search' phase involves gathering information from various sources, both internal and external, to understand the dynamics of the market system. This phase emphasizes on data collection and analysis. Scenario simulation can be integrated into this phase to model various scenarios and assess their impact on decision outcomes, supported through problem structuring methods.

The 'Articulate' phase focuses on effective conversation and the mutual understanding of an agreement on strategic challenges and options. This phase emphasizes the importance of clear articulation and alignment of strategic options to the firm's goals, which are critical in decision-making.

The 'Find' phase involves the selection of a set of optimal configurations of agents and resources that align with the organization's mission. Decision-makers often seek the best possible options to achieve their objectives, and this phase can involve scenario simulation comparative experiments.

The 'Evaluate' phase focuses on assessing selected strategies (optional best scenarios) against organizational values and objectives and compared to each other, including risk assessment and contingency planning. This phase is crucial for decision-makers to ensure that chosen strategies align with the organization's goals and values.

When designing strategies and plans, several cognitive challenges come to the fore, which have the potential to hinder effective strategic planning:

Linear vs. non-linear thinking: Linear thinking follows a structured, sequential problem-solving approach, which can sometimes lead leaders to overlook market ambiguities. On the other hand, non-linear thinking promotes adaptive strategies (Henderson & Clark, 1990).

Behavioural coupling: Another challenge is the phenomenon of behavioural coupling, where managers tend to mimic competitors rather than charting distinctive strategic paths. Such imitation stifles originality and erodes competitive advantage (Delgado et al., 2014; Porter, 1998).

Complexity downsizing: The peril of oversimplification is a significant challenge. Leaders may attempt to simplify intricate market dynamics for easier understanding, but this can potentially lead to skewed predictions and hinder proactive market adaptations.

Cognitive opposition: Lastly, cognitive opposition reflects divergent cognitive perspectives within strategic teams, which can result in disputes and hinder consensus in decision-making. Such opposition dilutes strategic cohesion, prolongs decision-making processes, and may even derail strategic trajectories (Nelson & Winter, 1982).

The above cognitive phenomena can limit the managerial ability to build a better cognitive model of market dynamics and take effective strategic decisions. It is important for managers to be aware of these phenomena and develop strategies to mitigate their impact on the strategic planning process. This may involve adopting a more flexible and creative approach to problem-solving, pursuing unique and differentiated strategies, engaging in scenario planning and simulation, and risk analysis, and fostering open communication and collaboration within the team.

These cognitive phenomena are related to the heuristics described in behavioural decision theory (Kahneman & Tversky, 1979). Behavioural decision theory examines how people make decisions under conditions of uncertainty and complexity, and it identifies a number of heuristics or mental shortcuts that people use to simplify the decision-making process. These heuristics can lead to cognitive biases that can affect the accuracy of decision-making.

For example, the complexity downsizing phenomenon can be related to the availability heuristic, which refers to the tendency to rely on easily available or accessible information when making judgements or decisions, rather than considering the full range of available information. This can result in oversimplification and inaccurate predictions, as managers may not fully consider the complexity of the market dynamics.

The cognitive opposition phenomenon can be related to the confirmation bias, which refers to the tendency to seek out information that confirms one's pre-existing beliefs or hypotheses, while disregarding information that contradicts them. This can lead to a lack of consensus and delays in decision-making, as team members may hold different cognitive models and perspectives on the market dynamics.

The behavioural coupling phenomenon can be related to the imitation heuristic, which refers to the tendency to imitate the behaviours and strategies of others, rather than pursuing unique and differentiated strategies. This can limit the ability to gain a competitive advantage and construct an innovative competitive strategy.

The cognitive phenomenon of linear-type thinking can be related to several heuristics identified in behavioural decision theory. One is the representativeness heuristic. This heuristic refers to the tendency to judge the likelihood of an event based on how closely it resembles a typical example or prototype. This can lead to oversimplification and inaccurate predictions, as managers may rely too heavily on typical or prototypical examples when making judgements or decisions, rather than considering the full range of available information.

Another heuristic that can be related to linear thinking is the anchoring and adjustment heuristic. This heuristic refers to the tendency to rely on an initial piece of information (the "anchor"), and then adjust subsequent judgements or decisions based on that anchor. This can lead to biased and inaccurate predictions, as managers may be too influenced by the initial anchor and not adjust their thinking sufficiently based on new information or changing circumstances.

That is why it is important to understand these decision heuristics and their potential impact on decision-making. By being aware of these heuristics, managers can take steps to mitigate their impact on the strategic planning process and make more accurate and effective decisions. Such managerial cognitive phenomenon can frequently impede board and organizational effectiveness in relation to strategic decision-making in a complex market and regulatory environment.

Kazakov and Kunc (2016) conducted a participatory action research behavioural experiment with a management team of directors responsible for the finance, business development, R&D, marketing and legal functions, at a manufacturing firm, related to the task of strategic market environment analysis, including political, socio-economic, technological, ecological, and legal perspectives. The experiment was conducted with the help of a scenario simulator, with the intention for analyzing managerial cognitive capabilities and phenomena related to them. Their research found evidence of the above managerial cognitive processes, capabilities, and cognitive phenomena: **linear and non-linear-type thinking phenomenon** limiting managerial ability to build a better cognitive model of the market dynamics in the future; **behavioural coupling phenomenon**, limiting the managerial ability to construct an accurate cognitive model of the market dynamics in a way different to firm's competitors; **complexity downsizing phenomenon**, limiting ability to anticipate larger sets of market dynamics scenarios and agents' interactions; and **cognitive opposition phenomenon**, limiting the team ability to form strategic consensus.

Kazakov and Kunc (2016) also discovered that a manager's capacity to pinpoint "cognitive distant opportunities" (Gavetti, 2011, 2012) correlates with four dynamic cognitive capabilities: strategic imagination, strategic conversation, strategic innovation, and strategic surprise. Notably, managerial strategic imagination inversely correlates with complexity downsizing; strategic conversation inversely correlates with cognitive opposition; strategic innovation directly correlates with linear or non-linear managerial thinking; and strategic surprise inversely correlates with behavioural coupling (Table 6.2).

The SAFE ARCS paradigm correlates with essential dynamic cognitive abilities crucial for making astute strategic decisions. These encompass strategic imagination, strategic conversation, strategic innovation, and strategic surprise.

**Table 6.2** Overview of dynamic cognitive capabilities and their descriptions

| Dynamic cognitive capability (DCC) | Cognitive capabilities explanation |
|---|---|
| Strategic imagination | Perceived key market environment resources and agents, and potential alternate resource agent configurations |
| Strategic conversation | Ability to concur on a pivotal resource agents configuration |
| Strategic innovation | Discovering a resource agent configuration not identified by another team |
| Strategic surprise | Identifying unanticipated resource agent configurations |

Strategic imagination involves the dynamic cognitive capability to envision plausible future scenarios and identify avenues for achieving strategic dominance. It requires creativity and vision to explore uncharted territory in agent-resource configurations, transcending existing market paradigms. This aligns with the 'search' cognitive phase, which encourages managers to embark on innovative explorations to clarify strategic challenges and objectives.

Strategic conversation is the cognitive art of engaging with stakeholders both within and outside the organization. It revolves around fostering transparent dialogues and incorporating diverse perspectives, creating a rich environment for strategic idea generation and alignment. This closely relates to the 'articulate' facet, where managers skilfully communicate strategic imperatives and welcome collaborative insights (Agbejule et al., 2021; Kristensen et al., 2022; Sterman, 2001, 2006).

Strategic innovation encompasses the dynamic cognitive ability to conceive and implement innovative solutions, establishing enduring competitive advantage. The 'find' phase aligns with this capability, guiding managers in identifying game-changing strategies.

Strategic surprise emphasizes adaptability, which is a cognitive capability in effectively responding to unforeseen environmental disruptions. In this context, the 'evaluate' cognitive phase resonates by guiding strategic discussions and promoting the use of simulations to anticipate risks and develop innovative strategic approaches, challenging prevailing market norms.

These dynamic cognitive proficiencies play a vital role in the SAFE ARCS paradigm, enabling managers to navigate the complexities of strategic decision-making and contribute to the organization's quest for sustained success and competitive dominance.

Kazakov and Kunc (2016) emphasized on anticipatory systems thinking as an advancement in strategic planning and decision-making over traditional methods. Traditional strategic planning, often anchored in linear thinking, tends to overlook market complexities. In contrast, anticipatory systems thinking adopts a dynamic, holistic stance, considering organizations as adaptive complex systems.

Central to this perspective is the managerial cognitive process of search-articulate-find-evolve with respect to anticipating alternative resource configurations. Active pursuit of novel opportunities, grasping market dynamics, assessment of potential options, and evaluation of optimal adaptations are main issues of analysis.

Teece et al. (1997) argue that a firm's competitive advantage emerges from timely discernment and reaction to internal and external cues, allowing for primacy in accessing resources and opportunities. This precognition in understanding market dynamics and swift resource realignment is vital for a sustainable competitive performance.

Various scholars underline the importance of grasping the co-evolutionary dynamics of organizational capabilities to orchestrate valuable resources vis-a-vis changing environments (Cockburn et al., 2000; McKelvey, 1999; Olsen & Haslett, 2002). Extending this paradigm, Leydesdorff and Franse (2009) advocate for organizations to craft predictive models encapsulating their interplay with the competitive environment. Organizations, viewed as anticipatory complex systems, can devise dynamic strategic pathways stemming from envisioned future market states. Recognizing this "anticipatory process" is of main importance, underpinning a firm's dynamic managerial capabilities (Helfat et al., 2007) in fostering performance heterogeneity.

Kazakov and Kunc (2016) exemplified their proposition by studying a pharmaceutical firm's senior management team. In this behavioural study, they employed a simulation-based learning environment during the product market strategy development for a new drug launch. Their objective was to explore how managers conceptualize, structure, and synchronize the resources and capabilities that are foundational for competitive advantage. This innovative theoretical perspective integrates anticipatory systems theory (Rosen, 1985), Resource-based view theory (Barney et al., 2001; Peteraf, 1993), and dynamic capabilities literature (Teece et al., 1997), and is further enriched by insights from complexity and configuration standpoints.

Anticipatory systems theory posits that entities utilize internal predictive models of their future states and environments to influence their behaviour, rather than merely reacting to past behaviour and environmental signals, a perspective that departs from traditional cybernetic or feedback control (Rosen, 1985). Consequently, resource and capability conceptualization, organization, and synchronization proceed through an anticipatory process, encapsulated in the SAFE ARCS stages.

Managerial cognition aligns also with cognitive science proposition, which identifies anticipation as a cornerstone cognitive process, facilitating the mental projection of potential outcomes of interactions with external environments in the future (Butz et al., 2007; Pezzulo, 2008). If we recognize organizations as complex socioeconomic entities (Leydesdorff & Franse, 2009), anticipation emerges as a main cognitive process in both individual and collective decision-making linked to strategic behaviour. Through anticipation, entities envisage potential decision scenarios, design adaptation paths, and steer actions based on optimizing future resource agent configurations.

## 6.3 Anticipating Agent-Resource Configurations

The essence of strategic management is devising and orchestrating distinct agent-resource configurations to cultivate competitive leverage over rivals (Peteraf, 1993; Sirmon et al., 2007). Strategic mastery also necessitates sensing and seizing emergent patterns (Teece et al., 1997) in line with the SAFE ARCS process of managerial cognition, described above.

Recognizing organizations as complex compositions of interconnected structures of resources and agents, and interactions, there is a challenge in understanding their intricate cause-and-effect relationships and non-linear connections when relying solely on linear causation (Gary et al., 2007; Kunc & Morecroft, 2010; Fiss, 2007). The ability to anticipate potential but latent agent-resource configurations empowers firms to create adaptable structures, thereby strengthening their resilience in the face of environmental changes (Meyer & Szirbik, 2007; Miller, 1986).

The process of agent-resource configuration dynamics is connected with actual performance and the anticipation of possible performance outcomes, in connection with the process of agent-resource configuration conceptualization and agent-resource configuration management, as shown in Fig. 6.1.

Figure 6.1 exhibits the agent resource configuration conceptualisation process and the managerial strategic foresight in terms of anticipating possible future performances. The scope of search horizons, as elaborated by Teece (2007) and Kauffman (1995), spans a continuum from narrow boundaries (focused on local opportunities) to expansive landscapes marked by long-reaching leaps. Shifting from limited to broader search horizons often requires significant investments due to their dependence on prior paths. In the face of an uncertain future, managers develop informed predictions about the journey ahead. These predictions remain open to adjustments as new data emerges. Such anticipatory processes involve constructing models that encompass a range of potential trajectories. Organizations, utilizing these models, can simulate numerous paths, each leading to diverse outcomes. This simulation capability empowers managers to transcend organizational limitations, thereby envisioning novel configurations of value that have the potential

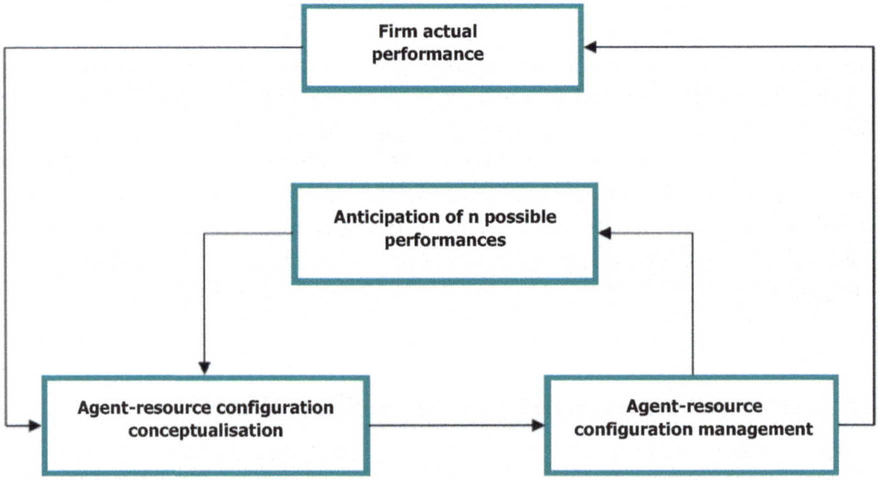


**Fig. 6.1** Agent-resource configurations (ARCS) conceptualization in relation to managerial strategic anticipation

to benefit stakeholders, including customers and shareholders, often in ways previously unimagined. This enables organizations to break free from existing market constraints.

Kazakov and Kunc's behavioral investigation unveiled that prior to the implementation of scenario simulation learning environments, the strategy search and selection process for product market was considerably constrained, focusing on a handful of pivotal resources and presenting a rather simplistic view of resource configuration possibilities. However, post the integration of this learning environment, the process underwent a metamorphosis. As posited by Kunc and Morecroft (2010), the scope of search expanded significantly, encompassing a more extensive configuration setting of agents and resources.

Such research underscores the proposition that the ability to conceptualize and configure diverse resources is intrinsically linked with anticipatory capabilities—a faculty to create state and pay off predictive models of market system dynamics (Pezzulo, 2008). Tools such as simulation models can further augment these anticipatory capabilities, thereby amplifying the boundaries of the search and selection process, enabling exploration of configurations that previously seemed out of reach (Leydesdorff & Franse, 2009).

Managerial cognition is instrumental in guiding their strategies and is contingent upon how they foresee the multifaceted cascading effects of their decisions. These effects can pertain to resource allocation, capability enhancement, or reconfiguration (Teece, 2007). When organizations harness predictive models to refine their anticipation, they position themselves favourably in the competitive landscape. These predictive models enable them to navigate and adapt their performance to anticipated system changes and objectives.

The path of strategic decision-making is not a straightforward one; it weaves together various anticipatory processes, each with its distinct implications. For example, predicting future sales performance, forecasting the strategic moves of competitors, or assessing how an organization will respond to upcoming strategic changes are all aspects of this complex process. As a result, the SAFE ARCS framework becomes essential in the domain of strategic decision-making. The effectiveness of this framework relies on the dynamic cognitive capabilities of the managers leading the strategic change. Equipping these managers with tools such as system dynamics or agent-based simulations can expand their cognitive horizons and enhance their strategic capabilities.

A synthesis of anticipatory systems perspectives with Gavetti's (2012) behavioural strategy theory can produce further insights on how firms can manage strategic challenges arising from the principles of bounded rationality (Simon, 1984, 1991) and from cognitive restrictions related to the boundaries of firms′ strategic explorations (Baumol et al., 1964).

Illustration of the use of qualitative and quantitative RAM method for supporting managerial cognitive capabilities.

The RAM on Fig. 6.2 represents the relationships between various resources and agents on a pharmaceutical market in connection to a product market strategy.

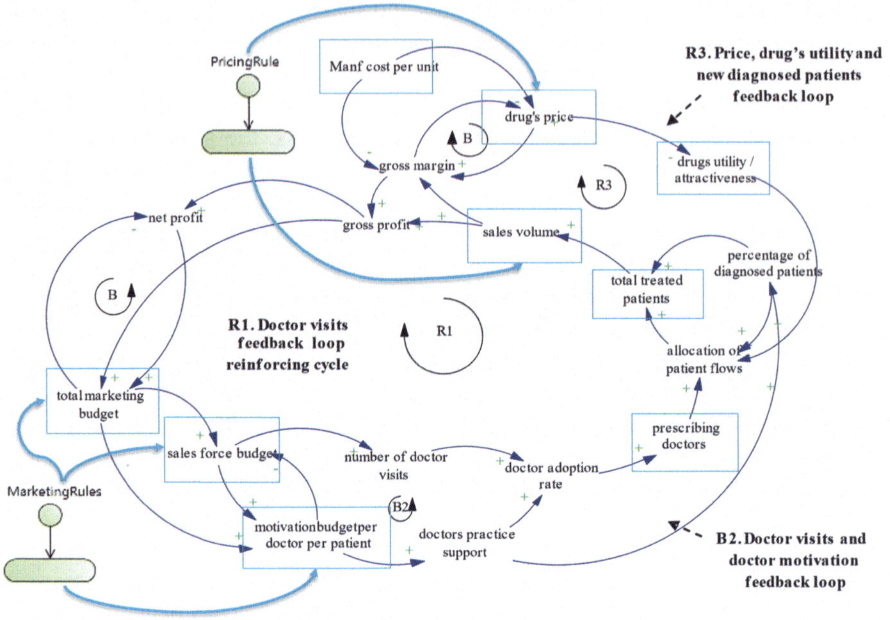


**Fig. 6.2** RAM on main resources and agent rules on a pharmaceutical market

Pharmaceutical companies have marketing rules which affect the budget allocation for sales force (medical representatives) and budget per doctor for support of their medical practice and continuous education. This means that the rules that govern the company's marketing activities impact the amount of money that is allocated to the sales team and the budget for supporting doctors' practices. The sales force (medical representatives) budget and budget per doctor then impact the doctors' adoption rate and prescription rate. The more money that is available for sales force and for supporting doctors and their practices, the higher the adoption rate and prescription rate.

The doctors' adoption rate and prescription rate then influence the number of patients diagnosed and drugs allocation. When the number of patients who are diagnosed with that condition increases, doctors prescribe more of a particular drug. The medicinal product utility and product price impact the drug sales volume and value on the local market. If a product is perceived as useful and valuable by doctors and patients, sales volumes and values are likely to be higher.

The prices of the drugs are set based on the drug company pricing rules, which are linked to product manufacturing variable costs and profit goal. The cost of manufacturing a drug is a significant factor in determining its price. Finally, all of these activities impact the product market performance regarding sales and gross and net profit. The success of a drug in the market depends on its sales volume and value, as well as the costs of manufacturing and marketing it. If the sales volume and value are high, and the costs are low, then the gross and net profit will also be high.

This resource agent map represents a complex system with multiple feedback loops and agent rules affecting stock levels and their incoming and outgoing flows. For example, if the sales volume and value of a drug are high, this can lead to more money being available for supporting doctors, which can then lead to higher adoption rates and prescription rates, and ultimately more patients being treated. This, in turn, can lead to even higher sales volumes and values.

On the other hand, if the medicinal product utility and price are not perceived as favourable by doctors and patients, this can lead to lower sales volumes and values, which can reduce the amount of money available for supporting doctors and their practices. This can lead to lower adoption and prescription rates, and ultimately lower sales volumes and values. This RAM highlights the interdependent relationships between various resources, agents, and factors that contribute to the success of a pharmaceutical product in the market.

The managerial dynamic cognitive capabilities play an essential role in foreseeing and navigating product market performance in the pharmaceutical industry. The pharmaceutical market is highly complex, and there are many variables that can impact the success of a product, such as changing market dynamics, shifting regulatory requirements, and emerging competitive threats. To navigate this complex landscape, managers need to have strong cognitive capabilities, such as the ability to analyse data, interpret and anticipate market trends, and make strategic decisions. They also need to be able to adapt quickly to changing circumstances and make decisions based on incomplete or uncertain information.

An efficient, risk free, and insightful way that managers can use their cognitive capabilities to navigate product market performance is by using simulation and scenario analysis tools. These tools can help managers to test different scenarios and evaluate the potential outcomes of different decisions. By running simulations and scenarios, managers can gain insights into the potential risks and rewards of different strategies, which can help them to make better-informed decisions.

Using scenario simulation can foster also a culture of learning and improvement within their organization. This involves involving managers and employees in serios simulation-based gaming, as well as providing them with the training and resources they need to enhance their cognitive capabilities.

Ultimately, the ability of managers to foresee and navigate product market performance in the pharmaceutical industry will depend on their ability to leverage their cognitive capabilities to make strategic decisions and adapt to changing circumstances. By doing so, they can position their organizations for success in a highly competitive and rapidly evolving marketplace. Scenario simulation plays an essential role in supporting managerial cognitive capabilities by providing a powerful tool for analysing complex systems and evaluating the potential outcomes of different decisions. Scenario simulation involves creating models of complex systems and testing different scenarios to evaluate the potential impact of different decisions. In the pharmaceutical industry, scenario simulation can be used to evaluate the potential impact of different marketing and pricing strategies, as well as the potential impact of changes in regulatory requirements or competitive dynamics. By running simulations, managers can gain insights about alternative strategies, which can help them to make more informed decisions.

One of the key benefits of scenario simulation is that it allows managers to test different scenarios and evaluate the potential outcomes without having to take on the risks associated with real-world experimentation. This can be particularly important in the pharmaceutical industry, where the costs of bringing a new product to market can be very high. Another benefit of scenario simulation is that it can help managers to identify potential uncertainties that may not be immediately apparent. By running simulations, managers can gain insights into how different variables may interact with each other, which can help them to identify potential constraints or areas of vulnerability.

Scenario simulation is a powerful tool for supporting managerial cognitive capabilities in the pharmaceutical industry. By using this tool, managers can gain insights into the potential impact of different decisions and evaluate the potential outcome of different strategies. The SAFE ARCS process of searching, articulating, finding, and evaluating agent resource configurations can be greatly enhanced by the use of scenario modelling and simulation tools. Using the RAM presented on Fig. 6.2, managers can conceptualize their search for agent resource configurations that can help the organization achieve its goals. Agents can include employees, suppliers, distributors, partners, and other stakeholders who can contribute to the success of the product in the market. Once potential agent resource configurations are identified, managers need to articulate their comparative characteristics, in relation to their goals and objectives, and then create a clear understanding of how they can fit into the overall strategy.

The next step in this process involves finding and selecting a set of optimal agent-resource configuration to be compared and evaluated for a best fit. The next step in this process involves evaluating the future performance of each agent-resource configuration conceptualized as optimal strategic scenarios. This involves measuring and comparing key output performance indicators related to the selected options and identifying ones meeting objectives and contributing best to the success of the product in the market.

The SAFE ARCS process requires understanding of the market, the competition, and the overall business environment. Managers must be able to identify the key factors and agent-resource configurations that will drive success in the market and design a strategy that leverages their strengths to achieve these goals.

This process also requires effective communication and collaboration between all stakeholders involved in the strategy. Managers must be able to clearly articulate the strategy and shape consensus, delegate responsibilities, and provide feedback and guidance to ensure the effective implementation of the selected strategy and course of action.

Effective cognitive capabilities can provide several advantages:

1. Faster decision-making: With better cognitive capabilities, managers can process information more quickly and make better-informed decisions in a timely manner. This can help companies stay ahead of their competitors and respond more effectively to changes in the market.

2. Better market insights: A better cognitive process can help managers gain a better understanding of market trends and consumer behaviour. This can help companies develop more effective strategies and products that are better aligned with the needs and preferences of their target audience.
3. Improved innovation: Companies with better cognitive capabilities are more likely to be able to develop innovative products and services that meet the changing needs of the market. This can give them a significant competitive advantage over their rivals.
4. Enhanced problem-solving: A more productive cognitive process can help managers to identify problems and challenges more quickly and effectively. This can help companies to respond more rapidly to challenges and make changes to their strategies as needed.

Companies that invest in developing and leveraging their dynamic cognitive capabilities can gain a significant competitive advantage over their rivals. By making faster and better-informed decisions, gaining superior market insights, driving innovation, and enhancing problem-solving, these companies are more likely to succeed in today's highly competitive business environment.

Companies in the pharmaceutical industry often use various strategies to increase the adoption of their products among doctors. One common approach is to allocate marketing budgets and sales force resources strategically to maximize their impact and effectiveness, as shown on Fig. 6.2 exhibiting the resource agent map of the pharmaceutical market.

The marketing budget is typically used to fund promotional activities such as direct-to-physician advertising, medical conferences, and other marketing materials aimed at increasing the visibility and desirability of a particular drug among physicians. Companies with larger marketing budgets may be able to reach more doctors and influence their prescribing behaviours more effectively than companies with smaller budgets.

Sales force effectiveness, on the other hand, refers to the ability of a company's sales representatives to build relationships with physicians and educate them about the benefits of their products. Companies with more effective sales forces may be able to achieve higher rates of adoption among doctors, even with smaller marketing budgets. In general, companies use a combination of both marketing and sales force strategies to increase doctor adoption of their products. The exact mix of strategies may vary depending on the characteristics of the product, the competitive landscape, and the target market.

For example, a company with a new drug that targets a niche market may rely more heavily on sales force effectiveness to educate physicians and build relationships. In contrast, a company with a more established drug in a competitive market may need to allocate more resources to marketing to differentiate their product and maintain market share. The doctor adoption strategy and of pharmaceutical companies depend on their ability to effectively allocate their marketing budget and sales force resources to reach and influence physicians, while also considering the competitive landscape and market conditions.

A scenario simulator can exhibit the dynamics over time of the medical doctors adopting and prescribing new medicines on a given local market. On selected output plots, managers can observe the effects of their alternative marketing strategies to inform about the characteristics of their new medicinal products and motivate doctors prescribing behaviour. Using a scenario simulator like that, managers can enhance their cognitive capabilities in designing optimal market strategies and anticipate their effects on the agents behaviour on a given market of interest, whether local, regional or global.

Such simulation tools are especially valuable for providing insights into complex market dynamics, which often involve numerous interconnected factors such as competitive pricing, regulatory conditions, and customer (in this case, physician) preferences.

## 6.4 Scenario Simulation Experiments in Relation to Changes in Pricing Regulation

As an illustration of the role simulation modelling can have to support managerial cognitive capabilities and strategy practice, a number of scenario simulation experiments have been done, using a simulation model of the pharmaceutical market. These experiments involved changes in the main pricing regulation tool set and local prescribing parameters in a local EU market (price calculation on 'min' or 'avg', time period for revision of prices on 1 or 2 years, and local prescribing on 'brand' or 'molecule').

Comparing scenario experiments on variations in main price regulation tool set and local prescribing parameters can support companies market strategies and preparedness to changes in the regulation environment, consistent with market agents behaviour and market logic.

Figures 6.3, 6.4, and 6.5 for drugs A, B and C exhibit each eight simulation scenarios. It can be clearly observed on all of the graphs, that highest prices occurred when the pricing regulation uses drug price calculation on 'avg' and price revision period on 2 years, combined with local drug prescribing regulation on 'brand name'. On the contrary, the lowest drug prices can appear if the regulation uses drug price calculation on 'min' and price revision period on 1 year, combined with local drug prescribing regulation on 'molecule'.

Main insight from the above is that contextual prescribing regulation on 'molecule INN' (generic prescribing) plays an important role in fostering local market price competition, which can be transferred to other price referencing countries, but when local prescribing is on 'brand name' then prices are kept higher, which again are transferred through the external reference pricing rules to other local markets. Also, it is clear that neither of the variations in the selected parameters influence prices of innovative drugs, when they are having a patent protection.

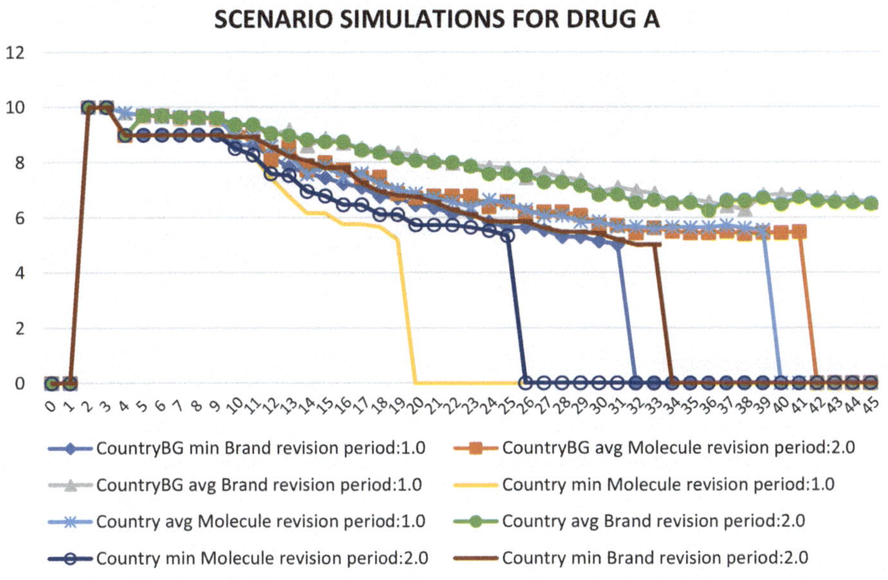


**Fig. 6.3** Scenario simulation for innovative drug A: External price referencing on 'min' and on 'avg', revision period of one or two years and prescribing on 'brand name' or 'molecule INN'

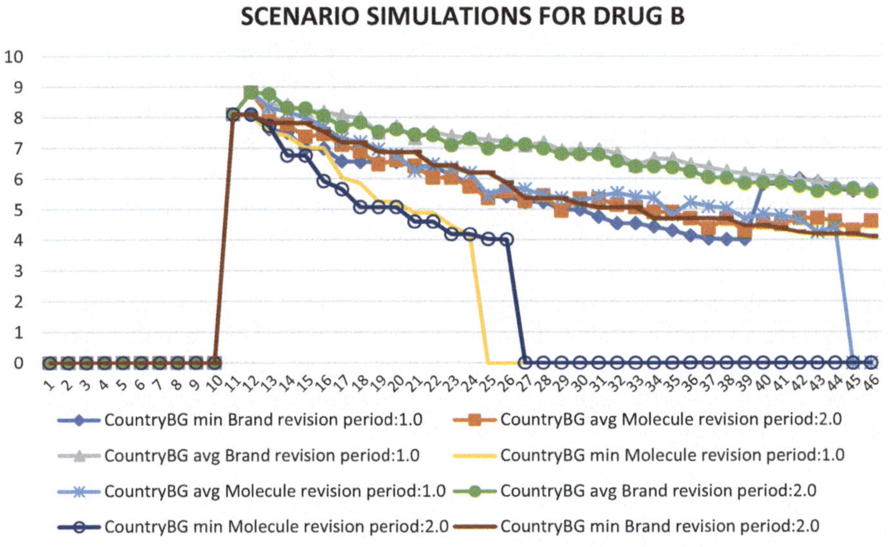


**Fig. 6.4** Scenario simulation for generic drug B: External price referencing on 'min' and on 'avg', revision period of one or two years and prescribing on 'brand' or 'molecule'

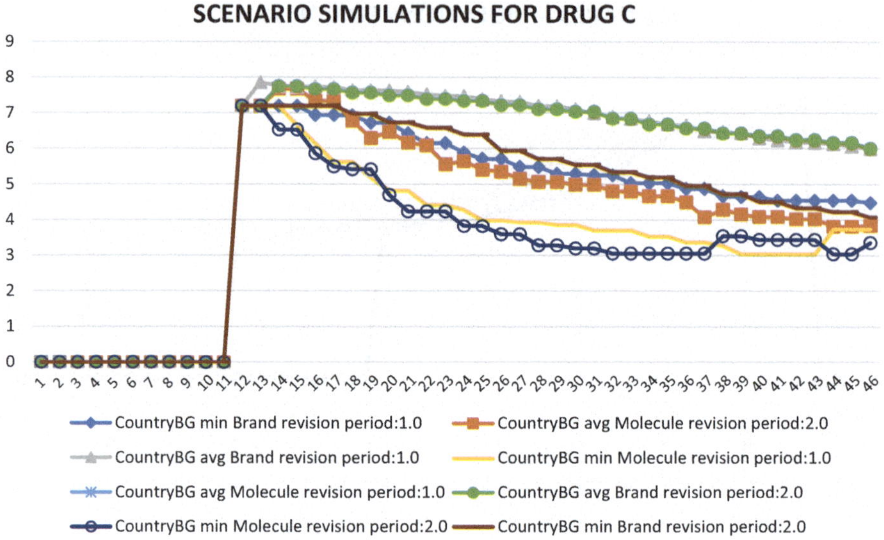


**Fig. 6.5** Scenario simulation for generic drug C: External price referencing on 'min' and on 'avg', revision period of one or two years and prescribing on 'brand' or 'molecule'

When pricing regulation cannot capture competitive market price discounts (where drug companies compete on hidden price discounts along the value chain), then public prices are higher and are transferred throughout the reference basket local markets using the external reference pricing regulation, while the market prices can change more often due to hidden competitive discounts which remain uncaptured. However, if the pricing regulation could take account of market price competition and price discounts in full, then drug price affordability level would be much higher but can lead to drug market exists, except in most favourable combination of the reference price regulation components (price calculation on avg. and not on min, longer price revision time period) and local prescribing regulation on 'brand name' v 'molecule INN'. Because of the above described effects, a trade-off occurs between the aim of the pricing regulation to provide higher affordability and at the same time keep drug availability levels. In this respect, external price referencing can be more suitable for application in countries with local prescribing regulation on 'brand', providing market competition is high.

## 6.5 Policy and Managerial Implications

Based on these observations, the following policy recommendations can be suggested (Table 6.3):

Public authorities can consider a shorter price revision period, such as annually, to help ensure drug prices reflect current market conditions more accurately, which could lead to faster price reductions. Policies that reference to the minimum price within the basket of comparison countries can lead to more significant cost savings

**Table 6.3** Public policy considerations

| Public policy | Description |
|---|---|
| Shorter revision periods | A shorter revision period, such as annually, could help ensure drug prices reflect current market conditions more accurately and lead to faster price reductions. |
| Minimum price referencing | Policies that reference the minimum price within the basket of comparison countries can lead to more significant cost savings for healthcare systems. |
| Encouraging molecule-based prescribing | Encouraging or mandating the prescribing of drugs based on the molecule rather than the brand name could foster a more competitive market and lead to lower prices. |
| Tailored country policies | The impact of EPR varies by country, suggesting that policies should be tailored to the specific healthcare and market environments of each country. |
| Monitoring and adjustment | Continuous monitoring of drug prices under different EPR methods is crucial. Policies should be adjustable in response to market dynamics and outcomes. |
| Balancing affordability with innovation | While aggressive price reduction strategies can lead to cost savings, they should be balanced with considerations for pharmaceutical innovation and a stable supply of medicines. |

for healthcare systems. Encouraging or mandating the prescribing of drugs based on the molecule INN rather than the brand name could foster a more competitive market, especially with the entry of generics, leading to lower prices.

Policies also should be tailored to the specific healthcare and market environments of each country and should include continuous monitoring of drug prices in order to be adjusted in response to observed market dynamics and outcomes to ensure they meet healthcare affordability and access goals.

While aggressive price reduction strategies can lead to cost savings, they should be balanced with considerations for pharmaceutical innovation and competition, ensuring a stable supply of essential medications.

The above scenario experiments and policy implications can inform the design of strategies aligned to the following managerial recommendations (Table 6.4).

Effective management requires regular strategic pricing reviews, which can be done annually, to stay competitive and adjust to market changes. These reviews make sure that the company's pricing strategy stays in line with industry trends and regulatory requirements. When negotiating prices with healthcare providers and payers, it is important to consider how drug regulation can affect prices.

Managing costs becomes especially important when drug policies and regulation aims to control prices and affordable access. This might involve improving the supply chain, reducing production costs, and efficiently managing operational expenses to keep making money even when prices are lower.

Segmenting markets based on drug regulation can further inform tailored strategies for each segment. For example, in markets where the lowest price is used as a reference, managers may need to focus on increasing sales volume or offering extra services to make up for lower prices. Different price trends for branded and generic drugs mean that separate strategies are needed in regard to future policy changes, especially related to

**Table 6.4** Insights for managerial decision making

| Strategy | Description |
|---|---|
| Strategic pricing reviews | Management should schedule regular strategic reviews of pricing, potentially on an annual basis, to remain competitive and responsive to market changes, aligning with industry trends and regulatory environments. |
| Negotiation tactics | Consider the impact of reference pricing variations when negotiating with healthcare providers and payers, developing tactics that protect the bottom line while complying with external referencing rules. |
| Cost management | Focus on cost management, especially if reference pricing policies drive prices down. This could involve optimizing the supply chain, reducing production costs, and managing operational expenses to maintain profitability. |
| Market segmentation | Segment markets based on the drug regulation, tailoring strategies to each segment's dynamics. Adjust strategies according to the drug regulation future changes in different markets. |
| Brand and generic strategies | Develop distinct strategies for branded and generic drugs, considering the different price trajectories in respect to different regulation effects. |
| Adaptation to policy changes | Anticipate and prepare for policy changes in drug pricing and reimbursement regulation. Use simulation scenario planning to predict future changes and develop adaptable strategies. |
| Value communication | Strengthen communication of the drug's value proposition, especially where brand prescribing is prevalent. Focus on demonstrating clinical benefits, cost-effectiveness, and patient outcomes. |
| Innovation investment | Balance innovation investment with potential reduced revenues due to drug price regulation. Evaluate the portfolio and pipeline focusing on areas with unmet needs and higher willingness-to-pay. |
| Global pricing strategy | Develop a global pricing strategy that considers various regulation effects across different markets to optimize global revenue. |
| Stakeholder engagement | Engage with stakeholders, including payers, healthcare providers, and patient advocacy groups, to understand perspectives on drug pricing and access, informing more nuanced and responsive pricing strategies. |

drug pricing and reimbursement. Scenario simulation planning can help anticipate future changes and develop flexible strategies that can quickly adapt to new policies.

Creating a comprehensive global pricing strategy that considers various drug regulations and how often prices change in different markets is also needed for optimizing global revenue. Engaging with stakeholders, including payers, healthcare providers, and patient advocacy groups, to understand their perspectives on drug pricing and access can further support more nuanced and adaptive pricing strategies, aligning them with the evolving healthcare landscape.

## 6.6 Simulation Experiments Informing Companies Marketing and Competitive Pricing Strategies

Another simulation experiments that can be made are related to the companies' marketing and competitive pricing strategies, in relation to perceived changes in the prescribing regulation and or pricing regulation.

Figures 6.6, 6.7, 6.8, 6.9, 6.10, and 6.11 exhibit possible price evolution for one innovative and two generic drugs, in different regulatory conditions like prescribing on 'brand name' or generic prescribing based on 'molecule INN'.

The price evolution of a medicinal product in a country with local prescribing regulation on 'brand' and with different marketing strategies and pricing tactics can be influenced by several factors.

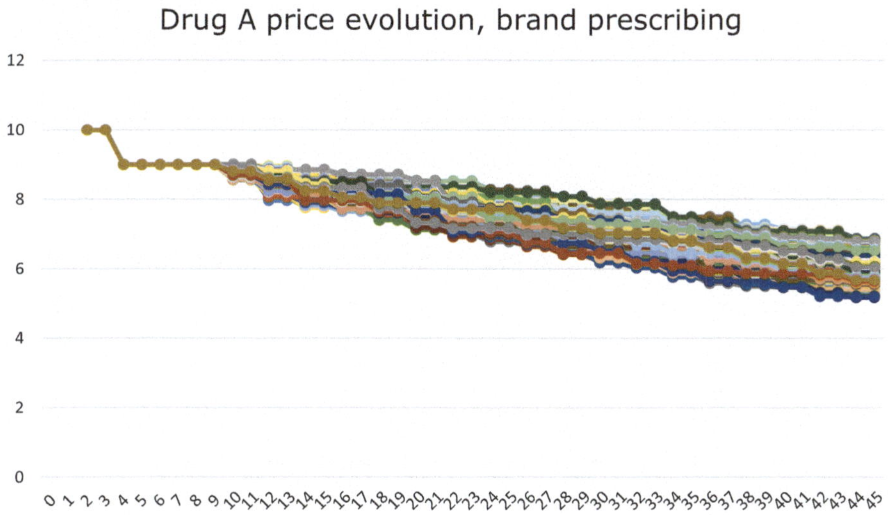


**Fig. 6.6** On innovative drug A price evolution if prescribing regulation is on brand, with variation in marketing strategy and pricing tactics

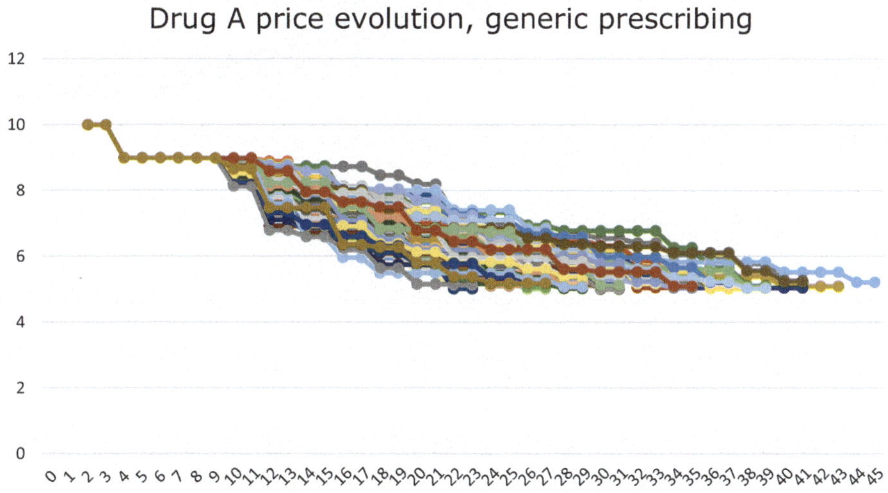


**Fig. 6.7** On drug A price evolution if prescribing regulation is on molecule, with variation in marketing strategy and pricing tactics

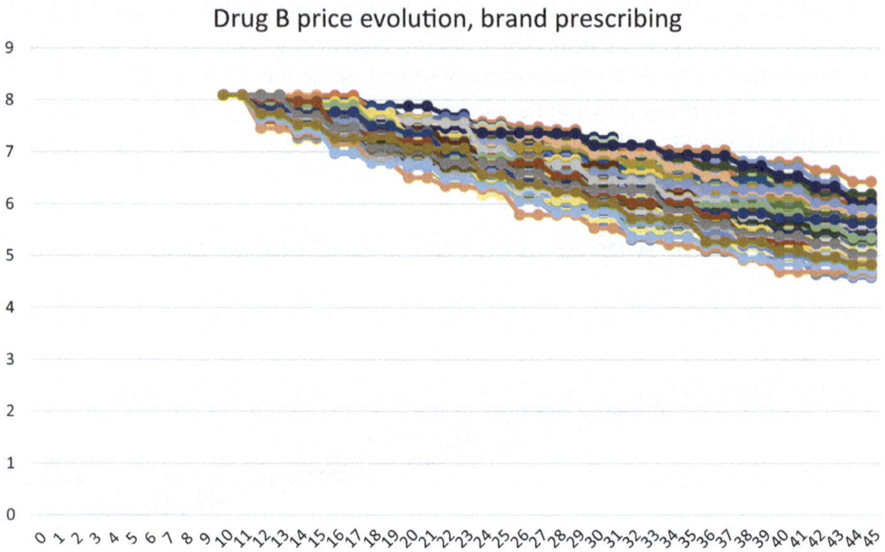


**Fig. 6.8** On the first generic on the market drug B price evolution, if prescribing regulation is on 'brand', with variation in marketing strategy and pricing tactics

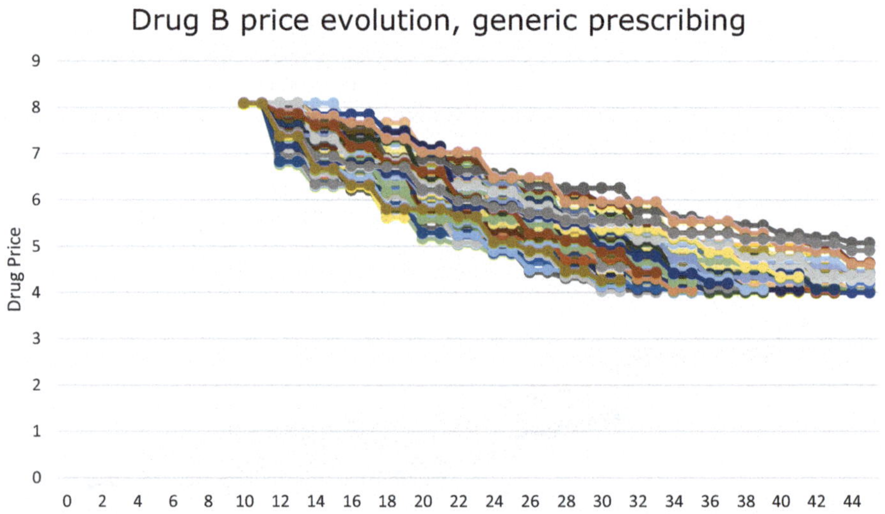


**Fig. 6.9** On the first generic drug B price evolution if prescribing regulation is on 'molecule', with variation in marketing strategy and pricing tactics

1. Competition: If there are several pharmaceutical companies marketing similar products in the same therapeutic area, pricing tactics will likely be more aggressive, and prices may be lower than if there were only a few companies. This is because competition tends to drive prices down as companies try to gain market share.

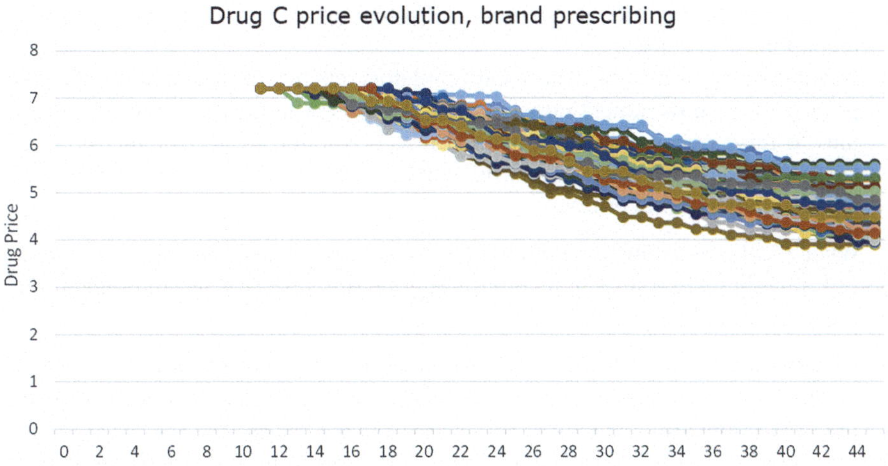


**Fig. 6.10** On the second generic on the market, drug C, price evolution if prescribing regulation is on brand, with variation in marketing strategy and pricing tactics

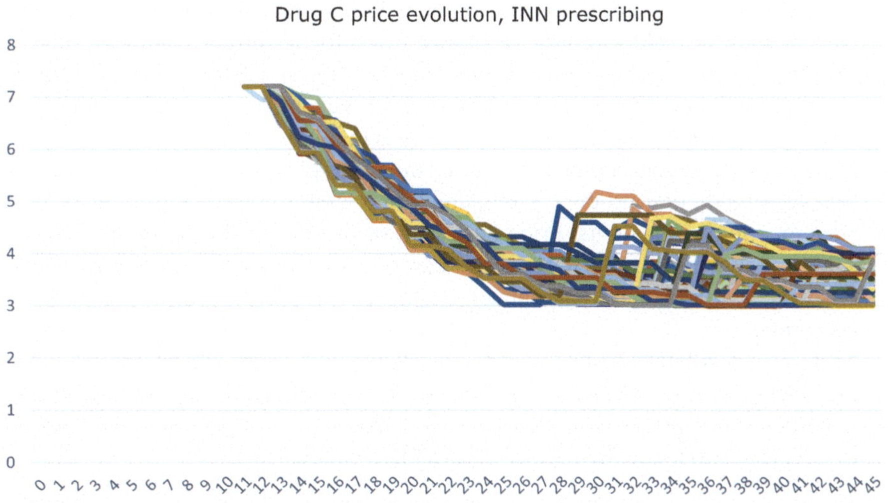


**Fig. 6.11** On the second generic product coming to the market, drug C, price evolution if prescribing regulation is on molecule, with variation in marketing strategy and pricing tactics

2. Product differentiation: If a company has a product that is perceived as superior to its competitors in terms of efficacy, safety, or convenience, it may be able to charge a higher price for that product (if the local prescribing regulation is on 'brand'). This is because customers are willing to pay more for products that they perceive as better.
3. Marketing expenses: Companies often spend a significant amount of money on marketing their products to doctors and patients. These expenses are typically passed on to consumers in the form of higher prices. If a company is spending

more on marketing than its competitors, it may need to charge higher prices to recoup those expenses.

4. Regulatory environment: The local regulatory environment can also influence pricing. If the government imposes price controls or limits the ability of companies to raise prices, this can limit the price evolution of a medicinal product. Conversely, if the regulatory environment is more permissive, companies may be able to charge higher prices.

When local prescribing regulation is based on a drug's molecule, the price evolution of a medicinal product in a country may be different than when regulation is based on the brand name.

1. Generic competition: If the drug's molecule is off-patent and there are several generic manufacturers producing the same molecule, this may lead to lower prices as competition among generics drives down prices.
2. Price controls: Governments may impose price controls on drugs based on their molecule. This can limit the price evolution of a medicinal product, as manufacturers are not able to charge more than the regulated price.
3. In a market with more generic drug options available, which can lead to increased competition and lower prices. If a company holds a patent on a particular molecule, it may be able to charge a higher price for its product until the patent expires, and generic versions of the drug become available. Once the patent expires, other companies can produce and sell generic versions of the drug at a lower price, which can lead to further price reductions.
4. Marketing strategies and pricing tactics may also play a role in the price evolution of a medicinal product. Companies may employ various pricing tactics, such as volume discounts, price bundling, or promotional pricing, to increase sales and market share. These tactics can result in lower prices for customers, but they can also have an impact on the profitability of the drug and the company.
5. Moreover, regulatory bodies such as the pricing authorities and health insurance providers can also influence the price evolution of a medicinal product. They can negotiate lower prices with pharmaceutical companies or impose price caps on certain drugs to make them more affordable for patients.

The above Fig. 6.6 exhibits the possible price dynamics for an innovative medicinal product (on-patent and becoming off-patent), if the prescribing regulation is on 'brand', subject to variations in companies' price tactics and marketing strategies. The observation of the price evolution provides means for search and selection of the most suitable pricing tactics and marketing strategies in certain regulatory conditions, which include the presence of state price discounts for product entry and reimbursement, prescribing regulation on 'brand name' or on 'molecule INN', and external reference pricing policies.

The above Fig. 6.7 exhibits the possible price dynamics for the same innovative medicinal product exhibited on Fig. 6.6, but if the prescribing regulation is on 'molecule', subject to variations in companies' price tactics and marketing strategies.

The above Fig. 6.8 exhibits the possible price dynamics for the first generic medicinal product on the market, coming after the patent expiration of the innovative reference product, if the prescribing regulation is on ‘brand’, subject to variations in companies’ price tactics and marketing strategies.

The above Fig. 6.9 exhibits the possible price dynamics for the first generic medicinal product on the market, coming after the patent expiration of the innovative reference product, if the prescribing regulation is on ‘molecule’, subject to variations in companies’ price tactics and marketing strategies.

The above Fig. 6.10 exhibits the possible price dynamics for the second generic medicinal product on the market drug C, coming after the first generic drug B, if the prescribing regulation is on ‘brand’, subject to variations in companies’ price tactics and marketing strategies.

The above Fig. 6.11 exhibits the possible price dynamics for the second generic medicinal product on the market drug C, coming after the first generic drug B, if the prescribing regulation is on ‘molecule’, subject to variations in companies’ price tactics and marketing strategies.

Again, all the above observations of the innovative and generic medicines price evolution provide means for search and selection of the most suitable pricing tactics and marketing strategies in a regulatory context including variations in drug public policies.

Observing the results, a clear pattern emerges, distinguishing pricing dynamics in scenarios where generic drugs are prescribed from those involving brand-name drugs. Notably, the data highlights a pronounced trend of accelerated price reduction in the generic drug market. This swifter decline can be attributed to the presence of generic competition, a well-known driver of price reduction due to the increased number of players and the standardization of drug molecules.

The faster decline in drug prices occurs also when doctors prescribe medications by their molecule name, rather than specifying a particular brand or trade name. When doctors prescribe medications by their molecule name, it allows pharmacies to dispense generic versions of these drugs. Generic drugs are essentially identical to their brand-name counterparts in terms of active ingredients and therapeutic effects, but they tend to be more affordable. This creates immediate price competition as multiple generic manufacturers can produce and sell the same drug, often at significantly lower prices.

Another critical aspect is the promotion of price transparency. Prescriptions by molecule name enable patients and healthcare providers to easily compare prices among different generic versions of the same medication. This transparency incentivizes pharmacies to offer competitive pricing to attract customers, as patients and their healthcare providers can readily identify the most cost-effective option. Furthermore, the competitive landscape is shaped by pharmacy rivalry. With multiple generic versions of a prescribed medication available, pharmacies engage in higher competition to provide the lowest price. This competitive environment often leads to price reductions as pharmacies strive to capture a larger share of the market.

The freedom of choice afforded to patients when they are prescribed medications by their molecule name plays also an important role. Patients can select where to purchase their drugs based on price and convenience, exerting additional pressure on pharmacies to maintain competitive prices. Insurance companies and government healthcare programs also influence the preference for generic drugs. They often incentivize the use of generics by offering lower co-payments or higher reimbursement rates for these medications, further increasing the demand for generic versions of prescribed drugs. Additionally, the proliferation of generic drugs in the market, facilitated by prescriptions using molecule names, contributes to a more competitive landscape. As generic manufacturers compete for market share, they frequently lower their prices to gain a competitive advantage.

In light of these findings, it is imperative to consider a suite of managerial recommendations. Firstly, a paramount focus should be on cost efficiency to navigate the rapid price decline in the generic market. This entails optimization of the supply chain, and a concerted effort to curtail operational expenses to ensure profitability in an environment characterized by lower price points. Secondly, a strategic emphasis on brand positioning is vital to counter the challenges posed by generic competition. This entails reinforcing the brand's value proposition, emphasizing unique qualities such as trustworthiness, patient support programs, and proven efficacy to maintain demand at a higher price point. Additionally, a proactive generics strategy should be developed, potentially involving the introduction of authorized generics to capture market share and exert influence over the rate of price decline. A reassessment of market access strategies is essential, including diversification of the product portfolio.

## References


Agbejule, A., Rapo, J., & Saarikoski, L. (2021). Vertical and horizontal trust and team learning: The role of organizational climate. *International Journal of Managing Projects in Business, 14*(7), 1425. https://doi.org/10.1108/IJMPB-05-2020-0155

Ambrosini, V., & Altintas, G. (2019). Dynamic managerial capabilities. In *Oxford research encyclopedia of business and management*. Oxford University Press.

Barney, J. B. (1986). Organizational culture: Can it be a source of sustained competitive advantage? *The Academy of Management Review, 11*(3), 656–665. https://doi.org/10.2307/258317

Barney, J. (1991). Firm resources and sustained competitive advantage. *Journal of Management, 17*(1), 99–120.

Barney, J., Wright, M., & Ketchen, D. J., Jr. (2001). The resource-based view of the firm: Ten years after 1991. *Journal of Management, 27*(6), 625–641.

Baumol, W. J., Cyert, R. M., & March, J. G. (1964). A behavioral theory of the firm. *Journal of Marketing Research, 1*(1), 74. https://doi.org/10.2307/3150326

Butz, M. V., Sigaud, O., Pezzulo, G., & Baldassarre, G. (2007). Anticipations, brains, individual and social behavior: An introduction to anticipatory systems. In *Anticipatory behavior in adaptive learning systems: From psychological theories to artificial cognitive systems* (pp. 1–18). Springer. https://doi.org/10.1007/978-3-540-74262-3_1

Cepeda, G., & Vera, D. (2007). Dynamic capabilities and operational capabilities: A knowledge management perspective. *Journal of Business Research, 60*(5), 426. https://doi.org/10.1016/j.jbusres.2007.01.013

Cockburn, I. M., Henderson, R. M., & Stern, S. (2000). Untangling the origins of competitive advantage. *Strategic Management Journal, 21*(10–11), 1123. https://doi.org/10.1002/1097-0266(200010/11)21:10/11<1123::AID-SMJ130>3.0.CO;2-R

de Souza, E. M., & Forte, S. H. A. C. (2021). Exploring the relationship between managerial cognitive capabilities and dynamic managerial capabilities. *International Journal of Business Administration, 12*(5), 1. https://doi.org/10.5430/ijba.v12n5p1

Delgado, M., Porter, M. E., & Stern, S. (2014). Clusters, convergence, and economic performance. *Research Policy, 43*(10), 1785. https://doi.org/10.1016/j.respol.2014.05.007

Fiss, P. C. (2007). A set-theoretic approach to organizational configurations. *Academy of Management Review, 32*(4), 1180. https://doi.org/10.5465/amr.2007.26586092

Gary, S., Kunc, M., Morecroft, J., & Rockart, S. (2007). System dynamics and strategy: Accomplishments and future opportunities. In *Proceedings of the 2007 International Conference of the System Dynamics Society*.

Gavetti, G. (2011). *Toward a behavioral theory of strategy. Working paper*. Harvard Business School.

Gavetti, G. (2012). Perspective toward a behavioral theory of strategy. *Organization Science, 23*(1), 267. https://doi.org/10.1287/orsc.1110.0644

Helfat, C. E., & Peteraf, M. A. (2015). Managerial cognitive capabilities and the microfoundations of dynamic capabilities. *Strategic Management Journal, 36*(February), 831–850. https://doi.org/10.1002/smj.2247

Helfat, C. E., Finkelstein, S., Mitchell, W., Peteraf, M. A., Singh, H., Teece, D. J., & Winter, S. G. (2007). Dynamic capabilities: Understanding strategic change in organizations. *Strategic Management Journal, 18*(7).

Henderson, R. M., & Clark, K. B. (1990). Architectural innovation: The reconfiguration of existing product technologies and the failure of established firms. *Administrative Science Quarterly, 35*(1), 9. https://doi.org/10.2307/2393549

Kahneman, D., & Tversky, A. (1979). Prospect theory: An analysis of decision under risk. *Econometrica, 47*(2), 263–292. https://doi.org/10.1111/j.1536-7150.2011.00774.x

Kauffman, S. A. (1995). *At home in the universe: The search for laws of self-organization and complexity*. Oxford University Press.

Kazakov, R., & Kunc, M. (2016). Foreseeing the dynamics of strategy: An anticipatory systems perspective. *Systemic Practice and Action Research, 29*(1), 1–25. https://doi.org/10.1007/s11213-015-9349-0

Kristensen, T. B., Saabye, H., & Edmondson, A. (2022). Becoming a learning organization while enhancing performance: The case of LEGO. *International Journal of Operations and Production Management, 42*(13), 438. https://doi.org/10.1108/IJOPM-10-2021-0676

Kunc, M., & Morecroft, J. (2010). Managerial decision making and firm performance under a resource based paradigm. *Strategic Management Journal, 1182*(March), 1164–1182. https://doi.org/10.1002/smj.858

Leydesdorff, L., & Franse, S. (2009). The communication of meaning in social systems. *Systems Research and Behavioral Science, 26*(1), 109–117. https://doi.org/10.1002/sres.921

Lin, Y., & Wu, L. Y. (2014). Exploring the role of dynamic capabilities in firm performance under the resource-based view framework. *Journal of Business Research, 67*(3), 407. https://doi.org/10.1016/j.jbusres.2012.12.019

McKelvey, B. (1999). Avoiding complexity catastrophe in Coevolutionary pockets: Strategies for rugged landscapes. *Organization Science, 10*(3), 294. https://doi.org/10.1287/orsc.10.3.294

Meyer, G., & Szirbik, N. (2007). Anticipatory alignment mechanisms for behavioral learning in multi agent systems. In *Anticipatory behavior in adaptive learning systems* (pp. 325–344). Springer. https://doi.org/10.1007/978-3-540-74262-3_18

Miller, D. (1986). Configurations of strategy and structure: Towards a synthesis. *Strategic Management Journal, 7*(3), 233. https://doi.org/10.1002/smj.4250070305

Nelson, R., & Winter, S. G. (1982). The Schumpeterian tradeoff revisited. *American Economic Review, 72*(1).

Olsen, J. E., & Haslett, T. (2002). Strategic management in action. *Systemic Practice and Action Research, 15*(6). https://doi.org/10.1023/A:1021008619381

Peteraf, M. A. (1993). The cornerstones of competitive advantage: A resource-based view. *Strategic Management Journal, 14*(3), 179–191.

Pezzulo, G. (2008). Coordinating with the future: The anticipatory nature of representation. *Minds and Machines, 18*(2), 179–225. https://doi.org/10.1007/s11023-008-9095-5

Porter, M. E. (1998). Clusters and the new economics of competition. *Harvard Business Review, 76*(6), 77.

Rosen, R. (1985). Anticipatory systems: Philosophical, mathematical, and methodological foundations. In *IFSR international series on systems science and engineering* (Vol. 1). Springer. https://doi.org/10.1080/03081079.2012.726322

Sher, P. J., & Lee, V. C. (2004). Information technology as a facilitator for enhancing dynamic capabilities through knowledge management. *Information and Management, 41*(8), 933. https://doi.org/10.1016/j.im.2003.06.004

Simon, H. A. (1984). On the behavioral and rational foundations of economic dynamics. *Journal of Economic Behavior and Organization, 5*(1), 35–55. https://doi.org/10.1016/0167-2681(84)90025-8

Simon, H. A. (1991). Bounded rationality and organizational learning. *Organization Science, 2*(1), 125–134. https://doi.org/10.1287/orsc.2.1.125

Sirmon, D. G., Hitt, M. A., & Ireland, R. D. (2007). Managing firm resources in dynamic environments to create value: Looking inside the black box. *Academy of Management Review, 32*(1), 273–292.

Sterman, J. D. (2001). System dynamics modeling: Tools for learning in a complex world. *California Management Review, 43*(4), 8–25. https://doi.org/10.1111/j.1526-4637.2011.01127.x

Sterman, J. D. (2006). Learning from evidence in a complex world. *American Journal of Public Health, 96*(3), 505–514. https://doi.org/10.2105/AJPH.2005.066043

Teece, D. J. (2007). Explicating dynamic capabilities: The nature and microfoundations of (sustainable) enterprise performance. *Strategic Management Journal, 28*(13), 1319–1350.

Teece, D. J., Pisano, G., & Shuen, A. (1997). Dynamic capabilities and strategic management. *Strategic Management Journal, 18*(7), 509–533.

Ulrich, D., & Barney, J. B. (1984). Perspectives in organizations: Resource dependence, efficiency, and population. *Academy of Management Review, 9*(3), 471–481. https://doi.org/10.5465/AMR.1984.4279680

# Chapter 7
# Financial Markets and Price Bubbles

**Abstract** Financial systems can also be viewed as complex adaptive systems consisting of interacting resources and agents. Investor herding behaviour is a phenomenon where investors follow each other's decisions, leading to the concentration of investments in certain assets. This behaviour can have a significant impact on financial markets, as it can lead to price distortions and market bubbles, where the prices of a particular product or commodity rise rapidly and unsustainably, often followed by a decline.

Both investors and consumers herding behaviour can be influenced by a variety of factors, such as social media, advertising and word-of-mouth. This chapter explores the mechanisms that can lead to herding behaviour and price bubbles, applying the RAM methodological framework.

In such systems, agents can interact with each other and available resources in various ways. These interactions can create feedback loops that reinforce or modify the behaviour of agents and the level of resources, as well as enable or constrain the emergence of new patterns of system behaviour. Financial systems are also influenced by regulations, laws, norms, and expectations.

A complex adaptive systems perspective emphasizes the dynamic and emergent nature of financial systems, as well as the interplay between resources, agents and feedback loops.

## 7.1 Introduction

As defined in the SD and AB theory in relation to the resource agent mapping approach applied here, a 'resource' is as a stock which can accumulate or decrease through incoming and outgoing flows, and an 'agent' is an individual or an organization whose actions influence the incoming or outgoing flows of a resource, making that resource to increase or decrease (Sterman, 2001; Axtell et al., 1996). In financial or commodity products markets, the resource are money, which can accumulate or decrease through incoming and outgoing flows such as investments and



R. Kazakov et al., *Understanding and Managing Socioeconomic Systems Behaviour*, Contributions to Management Science,
https://doi.org/10.1007/978-3-031-57057-5_7

transactions, and traded products. The main agents are individuals who are buying or selling and whose actions influence the incoming or outgoing flows of money and commodity products, leading to an increase or decrease in the supply and demand (Barnett & Salomon, 2012).

By analyzing the interactions between these agents and the available financial resources, insights can be gained into how markets function. The interactions between resources and agents in that market can influence prices in several ways. For example, the quantity of a financial asset or goods available (resource) and the willingness of buyers and sellers to buy and sell (agents) can affect the price. If there is a high demand for a particular asset and a limited supply, the price of that asset may increase. Conversely, if there is a surplus of a particular asset and little demand, the price may decrease.

The perception of investors (agents) regarding the overall state of the economy, political stability, and other factors can influence their trading decisions (Cheng et al., 2019). Positive sentiment can lead to increased demand for assets and therefore higher prices. Negative sentiment can lead to decreased demand and lower prices. In some cases, agents can manipulate the market to influence prices. These are just a few examples of how the interactions between resources and agents can influence prices in financial and product markets. These markets are complex systems with many variables, resources, agents, and endogenous and exogenous factors that can affect price movements and system dynamics.

In markets like that, price can refer to the value assigned to an asset or a commodity product. This price is determined by the interaction of the supply and demand and reflects the buying and selling agents decision heuristics and the effects of the anticipated future market developments (Brounen et al., 2006).

For example, if an asset or a commodity performs well and is expected to continue doing so, investors may become more interested in buying its stock, increasing demand and driving up the price. Conversely, if market indicators suggest a downturn in the asset's or the product's value, investors can follow their risk-averse heuristic, reducing demand and driving down the stock's price.

## 7.2 Investor's Herding Behaviour and Price Bubbles

Investor herding behaviour is a phenomenon where investors follow each other's decisions, often without any fundamental analysis, leading to the concentration of investments in certain assets or securities. This behaviour can have a significant impact on financial markets, as it can lead to price distortions and market bubbles.

Investors herding behaviour can lead to price bubbles, where the prices of a particular product or asset class rise rapidly and unsustainably, often followed by a decline. A product price bubble can have significant economic consequences, affecting market stability and investor confidence. Several studies have explored the link between investors' herding behaviour and product price bubbles.

For instance, Scharfstein and Stein (1990) and Grinblatt and Titman (1995) analyzed the impact of herding behaviour on asset prices in financial markets. They found that investors tend to herd when they face uncertainty about market conditions or the quality and access of information. This herding behaviour can lead to price bubbles, where asset prices rise above their fundamental value, creating a speculative market. Similarly, Brunnermeier (2001), Cont and Bouchaud (2000), Grinblatt et al. (1995), Lux (1995), and Welch (2000) analyzed the role of herding behaviour in stock market bubbles. They found that herding behaviour can lead to stock price bubbles, where the prices of certain stocks rise rapidly and unsustainably. This can lead to a misallocation of resources, as investors may invest in overpriced assets instead of focusing on other investment opportunities.

## 7.3 Price Bubbles Due to Consumer Herding Behaviour

Consumer herding behaviour can be influenced by a variety of factors, such as social media, advertising, and word of mouth. Consumer herding behaviour can lead to price bubbles, where product prices rise above their fundamental value, creating a speculative market. Social media can exacerbate herding behaviour, as consumers tend to follow the opinions and actions of others, leading to a reinforcing cycle of buying and selling. Advertising can also influence consumer herding behaviour and lead to price bubbles (Almudhaf, 2017; Blanchard, 1979; Holt, 2009; Lux, 1995; Phillips, 2016; Schaller & van Norden, 2005). This can have significant economic consequences, affecting market stability and consumer welfare.

For example, a number of cryptocurrencies have been subject to significant price bubbles in recent years, with prices rising rapidly and unsustainably before crashing back down. Here are some examples:

1. Bitcoin price bubble of 2013: In late 2013, the price of bitcoin rose from around \$13 to over \$1000 in just a few months, creating a massive price bubble. The bubble burst in early 2014, with the price falling back down to around \$200 (Li et al., 2019).
2. Ethereum price bubble of 2017: In 2017, the price of Ethereum, another popular cryptocurrency, rose from around \$10 in January to over \$1400 in December, creating a massive price bubble. The bubble burst in early 2018, with the price falling back down to around \$300 (Caferra et al., 2021).
3. Cryptocurrency price bubble of 2021: In early 2021, the prices of many cryptocurrencies, including Bitcoin, Ethereum, and Dogecoin, rose rapidly and unsustainably, creating a massive price bubble. For instance, the price of bitcoin rose from around \$10,000 in September 2020 to over \$64,000 in April 2021, before crashing back down to around \$30,000 in May 2021 (Corbet et al., 2018; López-Cabarcos et al., 2021; Shu & Zhu, 2020).

These price bubbles were likely caused by a combination of factors, including investor herding behaviour, hype, and speculation. As more investors piled into the market, the prices of these cryptocurrencies rose rapidly, leading to a self-reinforcing cycle of buying and selling. However, as the market became saturated and more investors began to sell, the prices of these cryptocurrencies crashed back down, leading to significant losses for many investors.

Agrifood commodities, such as wheat, soybeans, and coffee, have also experienced price bubbles in the past. Here are some examples (https://www.macrotrends.net):

1. Wheat price bubble of 2008: In 2008, the price of wheat rose to over $13 per bushel, creating a massive price bubble. The bubble burst in the following years, with the price falling back down to around $4 per bushel by the end of 2010.
2. Soybean price bubble of 2012: In 2012, the price of soybeans rose to over $17 per bushel, creating a massive price bubble. The bubble burst in the following years, with the price falling back down to around $9 per bushel by the end of 2015.
3. Coffee price bubble of 2011: In 2011, the price of coffee rose to over $3 per pound, creating a massive price bubble. The bubble burst in the following years, with the price falling back down to around $1 per pound by the end of 2013.

## 7.4 Garlic Example for Price Bubble

An interesting example of a price bubble is known as the 'garlic bubble' or the 'white gold bubble', which occurred in China in the early 2010s, increasing by 605% to $1200 per ton from March 2009 through February 2010. In 2009, the price of garlic in China was around 0.6 yuan per km. However, by 2011, the price had risen to over 10 yuan per km, creating a massive price bubble. Some reports even suggest that the price of garlic increased by as much as 900% during this period (https://www.theguardian.com/world/2010/jul/30/garlic-chinese-commodity-bubble).

The reasons for the garlic bubble are varied, but it is believed to have been driven by a combination of factors, including speculation, herding, and bad weather. In particular, a severe drought in 2010 reduced garlic production, leading to a shortage of supply and higher prices. This shortage, combined with speculators and investors looking to make a quick profit, led to the price bubble (https://money.cnn.com/2010/03/23/news/international/china_garlic_bubble.fortune/index.htm).

The garlic bubble eventually burst in 2012, with the price of garlic falling back down to around 2–3 yuan per km. Many investors were left with significant losses as a result of the price crash. The garlic bubble is an interesting example of how even seemingly mundane commodities like garlic can experience price bubbles under certain market conditions. It also highlights the potential risks of investing in speculative markets, particularly those that are subject to supply and demand imbalances and other external factors.

## 7.5 Housing Market Bubble

In the case of the housing market bubble, the resource are the stocks of houses, and the agents are the buyers, sellers, real estate agents, lenders, and investors who are involved in the market. Demand from buyers, lending by banks, and speculation by investors, is interconnected with supply of new houses, buying rates, and interest rates (Kwoun et al., 2013; Nneji et al., 2013).

As demand for houses increases, prices start to rise, leading to a feedback loop where rising prices attract more buyers and investors rushing to enter the market, leading to further price increases. This positive feedback loop can continue until prices reach unsustainable levels and the bubble bursts (Holt, 2009).

## 7.6 Dot-Com Bubble

Similarly, in the case of the dot-com bubble (Crain, 2014; Herwarth Kohn & Valls Pereira, 2017; Lusyana & Sherif, 2016), the resource were technology stocks, and the agents were the investors, venture capitalists, and companies involved in the tech industry. Demand from investors, IPOs by tech companies, and the promise of future earnings, affected on the increased competition, overvaluation of companies, and eventual market correction. In principle, the interactions between resources and agents can create a feedback loop that can lead to rapid and unsustainable price increases. Understanding these interactions can help us identify and prevent price bubbles and their market effects.

The following Fig. 7.1 provides a general causal loop diagram for a consumer price bubble, involving increasing demand due to marketing influence, which in turn generates an increasing product price. The higher price increases revenues and marketing budget allocation, leading to a reinforcing positive feedback loop.

A causal loop diagram (CLD) visualizes how different variables within a system influence one another, often by indicating causal relationships with arrows and employing positive (+) and negative (−) signs to represent the nature (reinforcing or balancing) of feedback loops.

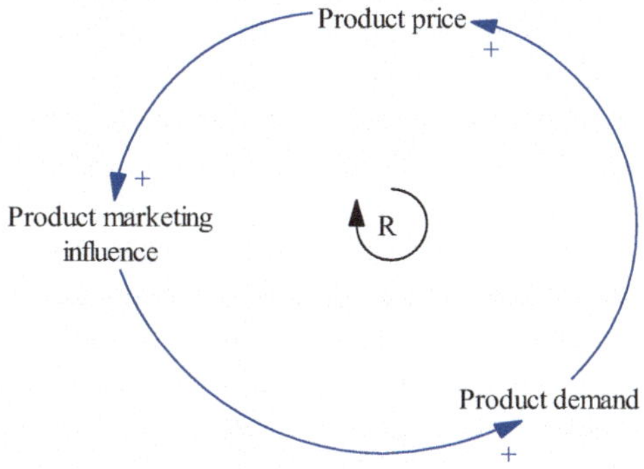


**Fig. 7.1** General CLD for consumer product price bubble

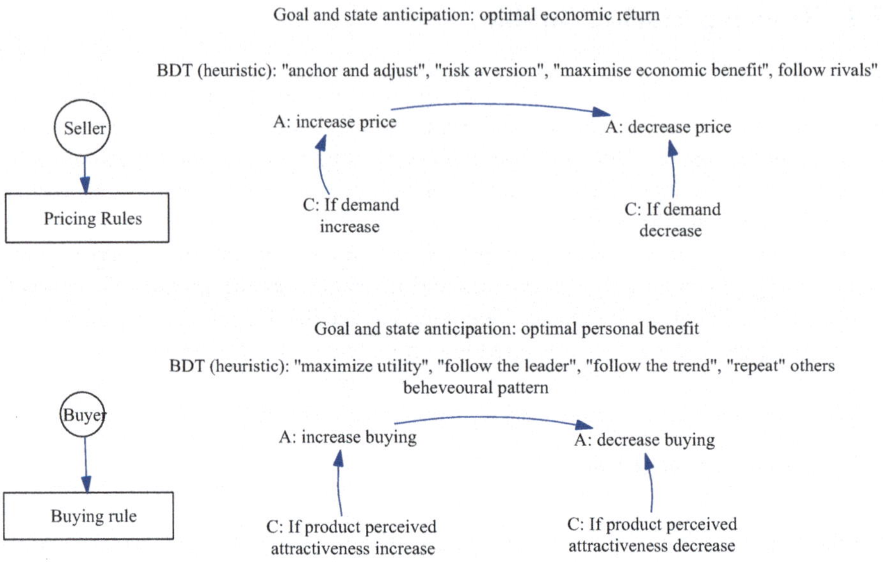


**Fig. 7.2** A seller agent and a buyer agent behaviour maps representing their behavioural decision patterns

The system as presented creates a reinforcing loop that, in a simplified scenario, promotes a continuous increase in demand and price driven by marketing. However, in a real-world application, various factors, including market saturation, consumer price sensitivity, and external economic factors, could introduce balancing loops that moderate or counteract these effects. Expanding on this example of a price bubble process a seller agent can be included holding a behavioural heuristic decision protocol regarding product price and a buyer agent also following a behavioural decision protocol.

The seller agent (Fig. 7.2) can follow several decision heuristics, including ‘anchor and adjustment’, where he sets the price of the product based on a starting point and adjusts it based on changes in demand; ‘maximize economic benefit’, where he seeks to maximize his profits; ‘risk aversion’, where he is cautious about taking on too much risk; and ‘follow rivals’, where he adjusts his price based on the prices of his competitors. These decision heuristics and the seller agent's price decision protocol create a feedback loop in which an increase in demand leads to an increase in price, which in turn leads to an increase in profit, reinforcing the seller agent's decision to raise the price even further.

The buyer agent (Fig. 7.3), on the other hand, is following decision heuristics that include ‘maximize utility’, where he seeks to get the most value for his money; ‘follow the trend’, where he is influenced by the behaviour of others; and ‘follow the leader’, where he looks to others for guidance on what to buy. These heuristics and the buyer agent's behaviour create another feedback loop, in which an increase in product price leads and increase in product attractiveness, lending to an increase in

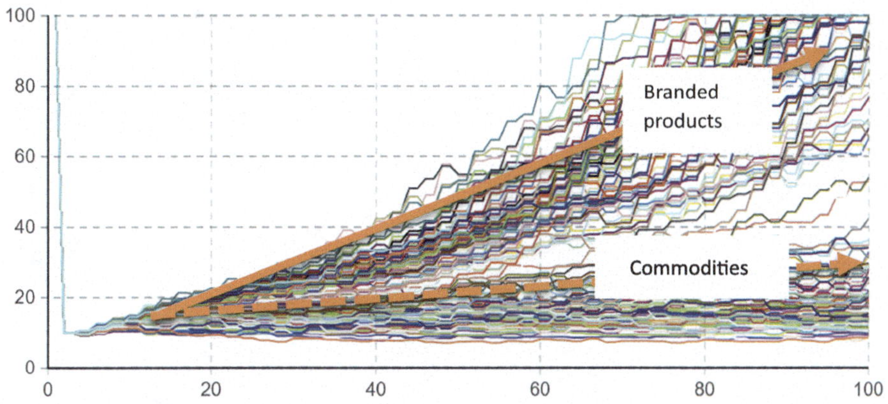


**Fig. 7.3** Simulated experiment example of the agent's behaviour, leading to price bubbles

buying, which in turn reinforces the perception that the product is becoming more attractive, leading to further buying.

Together these feedback loops can create a price bubble in which the price of the product becomes disconnected from its underlying value, as buyers continue to purchase the product at increasingly high prices and sellers continue to raise the price in response to the high demand. Eventually, the bubble may burst as buyers begin to realize that the price of the product is not sustainable and stop buying, leading to a decrease in demand and a subsequent decrease in price.

The system diagram may also include other variables that contribute to the feedback loops, such as external factors like changes in the economy or market conditions, or internal factors like changes in the seller agent's production costs or changes in the buyer agent's financial situation. By further mapping out these variables and the feedback loops they create, potential points of intervention to prevent or mitigate the effects of a price bubble can be found.

However, an increasing demand due to herding and then decreasing due to higher supply then demand can lead to a balancing feedback loop (Fig. 7.4).

Figure 7.4 introduces a crucial balancing feedback loop to the system, which often happens in real-world scenarios, where increased demand leads businesses to ramp up production, sometimes resulting in oversupply if the demand stabilizes or decreases. The oversupply of a product triggers a balancing loop. To avoid having too much inventory, organizations might lower the product's price to encourage sales, especially for products that can expire or become outdated. Lowering the price can stimulate more demand, creating another reinforcing loop. However, this can lead to lower profits due to the reduced price.

Looking at the whole system, there are two primary loops. The first is the reinforcing loop where product marketing influences demand, which affects the price. This loop can drive growth and expansion. The second loop is activated when oversupply occurs. It involves demand, oversupply, and decreased price. This loop acts as a counterbalance, preventing excessive price increases and demand, providing stability.

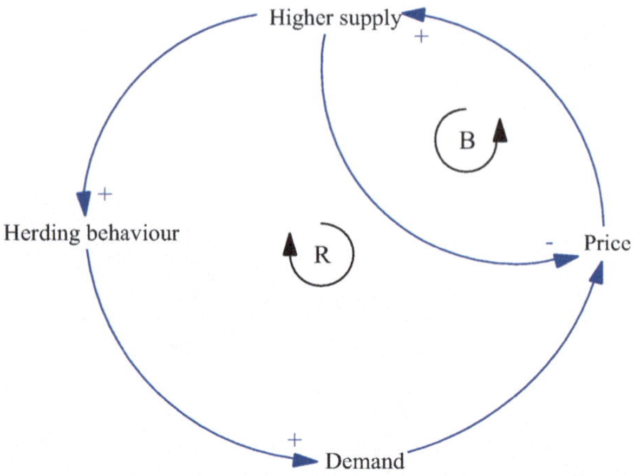


**Fig. 7.4** A general CLD involving a balancing feedback loop, demonstrating the behavioural mechanisms for price increases and price declines

In summary, the system has a delicate balance between reinforcing and balancing loops as demonstrated in this simple diagram (Fig. 7.4). This balance can lead to rapid growth followed by stabilization, often exhibiting a cycle boom and bust nature. However, external factors and timing can cause fluctuations in price and demand.

Further explanation of buying agents behaviour, in relation to financial markets, leading to price bubble and price decline, is provided using agent states diagram (Fig. 7.5), which includes an agent being at a state of a potential investor, then going to a state of active buyer due to product marketing and network communication, and then going to a state of selling and eventually returning to the first state due to certain given conditions.

- State 1: Potential buyer—At this state, the investor is interested in the product but has not made any purchasing decisions yet. They may have some awareness of the product through product-related communication on the market.
- State 2: Active buyer—At this state, the agent has made a decision to purchase the product due to increased demand or product attractiveness. They may be influenced by following the trend or the leader behavioural decision heuristics.
- State 3: Selling—At this state, the investor has decided to sell the product due to high prices and fear of market collapse. They may be influenced by the decision heuristics of ''risk aversion'.
- Return to State 1—After selling the product, the investor may return to the state of a potential buyer depending on certain conditions such as market developments, product attractiveness, supply and demand.

It is important to note that these states are influenced not only by the decision heuristics of the agents but also by external factors such as market conditions, available information, and competition. These external factors and how they interact with the agents' decision heuristics can be further included in the agent behaviour analysis, in relation to any specific research objectives.

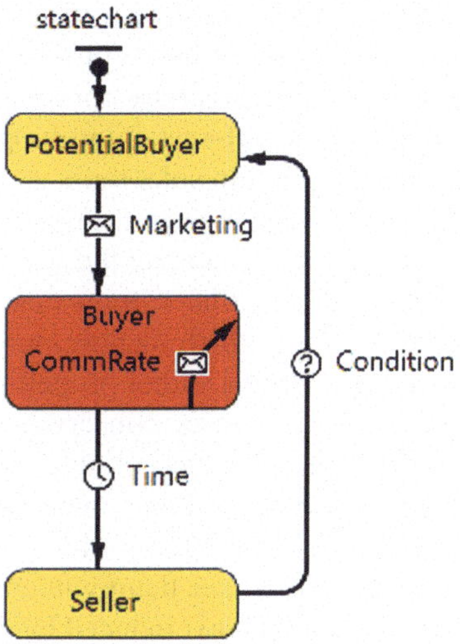


**Fig. 7.5** Investor agent state chart

This investor behavioural routine is circular and encompasses three primary states: potential buyer, active buyer, and seller.

Potential buyers are characterized by their interest in the market without a firm commitment to invest. They are in the early stages of exploring investment opportunities. Their decision-making is influenced by various factors, including marketing efforts, messages from investor networks, ongoing market trends, and external economic conditions. Transition triggers to the next state of active buyer can include perceiving an uptick in product demand, receiving positive messages from fellow investors, identifying a promising investment opportunity or other.

Active buyers are fully committed investors who actively participate in the market. They have made investments and are actively monitoring their assets. Their decisions are shaped by behavioural heuristics like trend-following or leader-following strategies, prevailing product demand trends, and their perceptions of profitability. Transition triggers to the next state of selling can include achieving a personal or market-wide profit threshold, encountering negative market signals, or observing changes in economic or product-related performance.

In the third state, investors are primarily focused on liquidating their investments. They may decide to exit the market due to various factors. Their selling decisions are influenced by factors such as price peaks, market volatility, risk aversion, and concerns about financial loss or a market collapse. Transition triggers to the first state of potential buyer, occur when investors complete the sale, prompting them to reconsider the market, evaluate different investment opportunities, or respond to altered market conditions.

Comprehending the states of investor behaviour and the feedback loops that govern them is essential in understanding the dynamics of financial markets from the perspective of complex socio-economic adaptive systems. In the world of investing, feedback loops can serve as critical mechanisms that either perpetuate or moderate an investor's behaviour. For instance, a reinforcing loop might be activated when an investor sees profits from a cycle of buying and selling. This success can boost their confidence, encouraging them to re-enter the market as a potential buyer, thereby continuing this cycle. Essentially, each profitable investment fuels a self-sustaining loop of increased confidence and subsequent investments. On the flip side, there is also a balancing loop. If an investor experiences a loss or even perceives a missed opportunity, this can result in decreased confidence, possibly causing them to hesitate or exit the market altogether. This forms a balancing feedback loop that works to moderate excessive risk-taking. Both types of loops illustrate how emotional and psychological factors can influence an investor's actions, either propelling them into a cycle of increasing risk or cautioning them into a more conservative stance.

When it comes to possible system weaknesses, overconfidence stands out as a major concern. Another factor is herd mentality, where investors follow market trends or leading figures without conducting their own detailed analysis. This kind of behaviour makes them vulnerable to collective market mistakes, including bubbles that could burst induced by their collective herding behaviour.

In terms of factors that could affect changes in investment states, external market elements such as economic shifts, regulatory changes, or impactful global events can have sudden and unexpected influences. These factors have the potential to cause rapid transitions between different states of investment. Additionally, mental biases and heuristics play an important role in investors decision-making pattern. For instance, anchoring—where an investor relies too heavily on a single piece of information—can skew perception and their decisions. Similarly, a bias towards loss aversion could disproportionately influence choices, leading investors to exit their market in order to avoid risks.

Simplified behavioural routines, especially when practiced by numerous investors, can indeed lead to financial market instability or even failure. This is largely due to the interconnectedness of individual actors within the financial market system and the cumulative impact of their actions on market dynamics.

Here is how this simple behavioural routine, along with other factors, could contribute to financial market failures:

1. **Herding behaviour and bubbles**
   If a large number of investors move through the agent states described above in a synchronized manner, buying when others buy and selling when others sell, it can lead to herd behaviour effects, which often inflates asset prices beyond their intrinsic value, creating bubbles. When these bubbles burst (due to an eventual recognition of overvaluation or other external shocks), it can lead to widespread market declines and potential financial crises.
2. **Collective selling and market crashes**
   The transition from 'active buyer' to 'seller' can be dramatically accelerated and amplified if large numbers of investors decide to sell off assets due to perceived risks or actual market downturns. This mass selling can exacerbate market declines, creating a downward spiral where falling prices induce further selling, potentially leading to market crashes.

3. **Mismatch of supply and demand**
   The cyclic transitions between buying and selling, if misaligned with actual economic fundamentals, can create scenarios where asset prices are either unduly depressed or inflated. This mismatch between supply and demand for assets distorts price discovery mechanisms, leading to misallocations of capital and potentially precipitating financial instabilities.

Several factors can contribute to market failure, each posing unique challenges to the stability of financial systems. First, lack of transparency and information asymmetry can lead to a skewed playing field, where investors make uninformed decisions or engage in manipulative trading practices (Barkley Rosser Jr, 2003; Stiglitz, 2002; Akerlof, 1970, 1989). Then there is the issue of leverage and overexposure to risk. Using borrowed funds to amplify investment gains can backfire dramatically, especially if market trends reverse. Over-leveraging can trigger large-scale liquidations, causing asset prices to plummet and shaking the very foundations of financial systems. Regulatory and systemic failures can exacerbate these problems. Whether it is inadequate oversight that fails to curb risky behaviours or infrastructural flaws in trading platforms and settlement processes, these systemic issues can precipitate larger market failures.

External shocks, such as geopolitical crises, pandemics, or policy shifts, pose another set of challenges. When these unexpected events occur, they can rattle financial markets, particularly if investors are unprepared or overly exposed to affected sectors. Financial innovations and complex instruments like derivatives bring their own set of risks. These novel financial products, if not well-understood and managed, can introduce systemic risks that result in widespread market instability. Finally, the rise of speculative and non-fundamental trading adds another layer of volatility. When trading is driven more by the pursuit of quick profits than by economic fundamentals, it can make financial markets increasingly susceptible to both sudden crashes and wild surges. Together, these factors create a complex web of vulnerabilities that can lead to market failure. A seemingly straightforward investor behavioural routine, when practiced ubiquitously, can indeed contribute significantly to financial market dynamics, potentially even initiating market failures or crises when combined with other risk factors and vulnerabilities within the system (Devenow & Welch, 1996; Welch, 2000).

Misallocation of capital is another issue that can be triggered by misleading information or artificial price movements. When investors direct their resources based on false premises, it can severely hamper the efficient distribution of capital across the economy, causing both short-term disruptions and long-term inefficiencies.

Maintaining financial market stability and governance is a multifaceted endeavour that demands comprehensive measures on multiple fronts. Among the most crucial of these is regulatory intervention. The importance of robust regulatory frameworks cannot be overstated, as they act as the first line of defence in maintaining the integrity of financial systems. Effective oversight is instrumental in curbing corrupt practices that can distort market functioning. With robust regulations, there is a greater likelihood that markets will function with the transparency and fairness

(Baker & Ricciardi, 2014; Behavioral Finance: What Everyone Needs to Know, 2020; Trehan & Sinha, 2019). These frameworks are pivotal for identifying and penalizing unlawful activities, thereby disincentivizing individuals and organizations from engaging in such behaviour in the first place.

While the simplistic three-state investor routine provides a basic framework for understanding individual investor behaviours, the effects of a herding behaviour can produce additional complexities and risks into the system. The interactions between individual investor behaviours in and among organizational practices can create a convoluted web of follow-the-herd-related actions and investor routines, leading to amplified responses and potential systemic instabilities (Demirer et al., 2010). Addressing and mitigating these challenges necessitates a multidimensional approach that emphasizes transparent practices, regulatory adherence, and informed investing at both the individual and organizational levels.

## 7.7 Financial Markets and Non-Fungible Tokens (NFT)

NFTs have emerged as a disruptive technology with the potential to revolutionize various industries, from art and music and other (Chandra, 2022; Colicev, 2023; Pinto-Gutiérrez et al., 2022). While their impact on the environment and lack of regulation remains a concern, the versatility and potential of NFTs suggest that they are here to stay.

Non-fungible tokens (NFTs) have become a popular topic in the world of art, collectibles, and cryptocurrency (Helman & Tur-Sinai, 2023; Taherdoost, 2023). One of the earliest mentions of NFTs can be traced back to the creation of the Coloured Coins protocol in 2012, which allowed users to create digital tokens representing physical assets. However, it was not until the emergence of the Ethereum blockchain in 2015 that the concept of NFTs as we know them today began to take shape. The ERC-721 standard, introduced by the CryptoKitties game in 2018, enabled the creation of unique, non-interchangeable digital assets, laying the foundation for the NFT boom.

The use of NFTs has since expanded beyond the realm of gaming to art, music, and other forms of digital content. In March 2021, digital artist Beeple sold an NFT artwork titled 'Everydays: The First 5000 Days' for a staggering $69 million at Christie's auction house. This marked a turning point in the art world, as it signalled the acceptance of digital art as a legitimate form of artistic expression and paved the way for other artists to monetize their work through NFTs.

The use of NFTs has also opened up new opportunities for musicians to engage with their fans and offer unique experiences, such as exclusive access to concerts or backstage passes. Additionally, the lack of regulation in the NFT market has led to issues of fraud and copyright infringement, with some artists and creators having their work plagiarized and sold as NFTs without their consent.

Non-fungible token (NFT) markets can be analyzed from a systems perspective as having a complex adaptive system resource-agent characteristics. A complex adaptive system is a system composed of a large number of interacting elements, which can adapt and learn from their environment and achieve emergent behaviours. In the context of NFT markets, the interacting elements can be seen as agents, who are the market participants, including buyers, sellers, artists, collectors, and platforms, and resources which are the traded NFT products and the exchanged financial flows, creating a network of transactions.

The behaviour of the NFT markets can be analyzed also in terms of feedback loops and non-linear relationships. Feedback loops occur when changes in one element of the system affect the behaviour of other elements, which in turn feedback to influence the original element. For example, an increase in the price of an NFT may lead to increased demand from investors and collectors, which in turn can increase the perceived value of the NFT, leading to further price increases. Non-linear relationships occur when changes in one element of the system do not have a proportional effect on other elements. For example, a small change in the reputation of an artist may lead to a large change in the price of their NFTs, as collectors are more willing to pay a premium for NFTs created by highly regarded artists.

NFTs allow for the creation and ownership of one-of-a-kind digital assets that can be bought, sold, and traded in a decentralized and transparent manner. This has opened up new opportunities for artists, musicians, and other creators to monetize their digital content in ways that were not possible before. NFTs are also being used to create new forms of online communities and social networks, where members can buy and trade unique digital assets as a way of engaging with each other. The NFT market has exploded in recent years, with sales of NFTs reaching record highs in 2021. Some of the most expensive NFT sales to date have included digital art pieces, virtual real estate, and unique collectibles. This has led to a surge of interest in the NFT market, with investors and collectors alike looking to capitalize on the potential financial and cultural value of these unique digital assets.

While the NFT market is still relatively new and evolving, it has already had a significant impact on the broader cryptocurrency and blockchain ecosystem. As more artists, musicians, and other creators begin to embrace NFTs as a means of monetizing their digital content, the market is likely to continue to grow and mature, creating new opportunities and challenges along the way (Dowling, 2022; Wilson et al., 2022).

However, there have been several instances of price bubbles in the NFT market, with some NFTs selling for exorbitant amounts of money before crashing in value (Bao & Roubaud, 2021; Kraizberg, 2023). One of the most notable examples of an NFT price bubble was the sale of a digital artwork titled ‘Everydays: The First 5000 Days’ by the artist Beeple. The artwork was sold at a Christie's auction for a record-breaking $69 million in March 2021. This sale was seen as a watershed moment for the NFT market, as it demonstrated that digital art could be sold for significant sums of money. However, in the months following the sale, the NFT market experienced a significant price correction, with many NFTs losing a significant portion of their value. Some industry experts have suggested that this was due in part to overspeculation and investor hype, which have made prices to increase to unsustainable levels.

Another example of an NFT price bubble was the sale of CryptoPunks, a series of 10,000 unique 8-bit characters that were created in 2017. While the initial sale price of CryptoPunks was relatively low, with some characters selling for as little as $10, the value of these NFTs has since skyrocketed, with some characters selling for millions of dollars. This surge in value has been attributed to increased demand for NFTs and the unique and collectible nature of the CryptoPunks characters.

Sure, the Bored Ape Yacht Club (BAYC) is a popular NFT collection that features 10,000 unique digital ape NFTs. Each NFT represents ownership of a unique Bored Ape character and grants access to exclusive membership benefits. The BAYC collection was launched in April 2021 and quickly gained popularity among collectors, with some of the rarest apes selling for millions of dollars.

In September 2021, a new NFT project called Bored Ape Kennel Club (BAKC) was launched, featuring a collection of 10,000 unique digital dog NFTs. The project was created by the same team behind BAYC and followed a similar format, with each NFT granting ownership of a unique digital dog character and access to exclusive membership benefits. The BAKC collection was well-received by collectors and some of the rarest dogs sold for several hundred thousand dollars.

These examples show that NFT market price bubbles are a real risk in this space, particularly as hype, herding behaviour and speculation can drive prices to unsustainable levels (Borri et al., 2022; Horky et al., 2022a, 2022b; Lommers et al., 2022).

In the NFT market, herding behaviour has been observed in several ways. For example, when a particular NFT gains a significant amount of attention and interest, other investors become willing to rush to buy similar NFTs in the hopes of capitalizing on the trend. This can lead to a surge in demand and prices, even if the underlying value of the NFTs is not actually justified by market fundamentals. Additionally, social media and online communities can also contribute to the herding behaviour in the NFT market. As NFTs become more popular and mainstream, online communities dedicated to the buying and selling of these assets have emerged. These communities can create a sense of hype and urgency around particular NFTs, leading to a surge in demand and prices.

Ultimately, herding behaviour phenomenon can contribute to the formation of price bubbles in the NFT market, as investors may be more focused on following the actions of others rather than making independent and informed investment decisions.

## 7.8 Resource Agent Mapping (RAM) and Analysis of the NFT Markets

Using a RAM on Fig. 7.6, the stocks refer to the available NFTs for sale on the market, while the stock of NFTs bought refers to the number of NFTs owned by investors. The price of NFTs is determined by the market demand and supply of NFTs and is influenced by factors such as the popularity of the artist, the rarity of the NFT, and the current market trends.

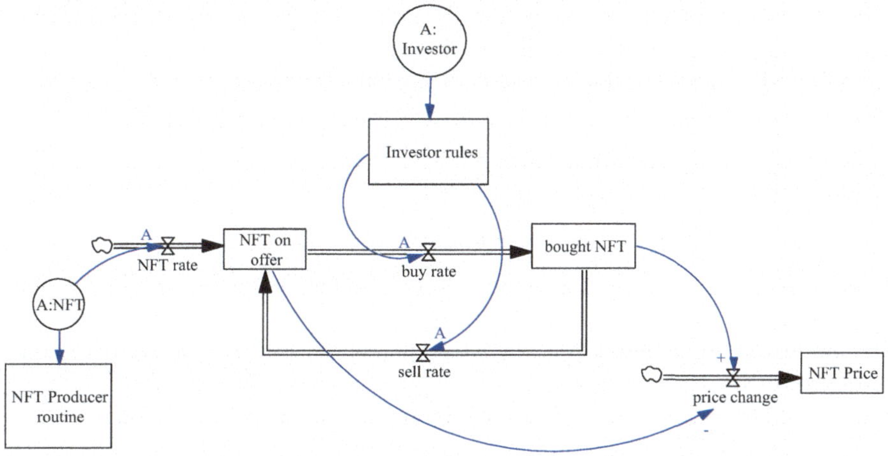


**Fig. 7.6** A simple RAM for the NFT market, involving traded NFTs, NFT price and NFT producer (artist) and buyer (investor) agents

The agent decision rules and activities influencing the stocks and flows in the NFT market could include the marketing communication strategies used by NFT sellers to increase demand, the popularity of the artists and art pieces associated with the NFTs, and the overall sentiment of the market. Similar to the example of the price bubble and decline, if there is a sudden surge in demand for NFTs due to market hype or social media buzz, the stock of NFTs bought may increase rapidly, leading to a potential price bubble. Conversely, if there is a sudden decrease in demand for NFTs, following an increase in NFTs supply, the price may decline rapidly, leading to a potential price downturn (Ali et al., 2023).

NFT producer agents may produce more NFTs if there is a higher demand for them, as indicated by increased sales or interest in the NFT market. Conversely, if demand decreases, the producer may decrease production to avoid an oversupply of NFTs. This decision-making process is driven by the behavioural heuristics of 'follow the trend' and 'follow the leader', where the producer seeks to align their production strategy with the overall market trend and market leaders.

On the other hand, an investor agent in the NFT market seeks to maximize their utility by using the heuristic of 'anchor and adjustment'. The investor may increase buying of NFT products if the product attractiveness and price increase, holding onto the NFT if the trend continues upward. However, if the trend starts to reverse and the NFT product becomes less attractive, the investors may adjust their behaviour and start selling the NFT product to avoid further losses.

An agent states diagram for an NFT investment market would be similar to the one described earlier for a price bubble and decline. In this case, an investor may start in a state of not owning any NFTs, and then move to a state of actively buying and selling NFTs based on marketing communication and network messaging. The decision-making processes of both the NFT producer and investor agents are influenced by market trends and the behaviour of other market participants. The stocks of NFTs on offer, NFTs bought, and NFT prices are all interconnected and constantly changing based on the decisions of the agents involved in the market.

In this NFT market example, we can identify the following stocks:

- Stock of NFTs on offer (number of NFTs available for purchase)
- Stock of NFTs bought (number of NFTs purchased by investors)
- Stock of NFT price (market price of NFTs)

We can also identify the following flows:

- Flow of NFT production (rate of NFTs produced by NFT producer agent per unit of time)
- Flow of NFT purchases (rate of NFTs purchased by investor agent per unit of time)
- Flow of NFT sales (rate of NFTs sold by investor agent per unit of time)

The following agent rules can be observed:

- NFT producer agent:
  - Decision heuristics: follow the trend, follow the leader
  - Decision protocol: increase production if demand increases, decrease production if demand decreases
- Investor agent:
  - Decision heuristics: maximize utility, follow the trend, follow the leader, anchor, and adjustment
  - Decision protocol: buy NFTs if the product attractiveness and price increase, hold NFTs if the trend goes up, sell NFTs if the trend reverts to selling and the NFT product becomes less attractive.

The interaction of these stocks, flows, and agent rules can lead to the emergence of patterns in the NFT market, such as price bubbles or crashes, depending on the level of demand and supply of NFTs and the decisions made by the NFT producer and investor agents (Figs. 7.7 and 7.8).

Figure 7.9 illustrates a striking boom-and-bust cycle of an NFT (non-fungible token) asset in the financial market. Initially, a combination of product attractiveness and rising prices, perhaps driven by exclusive content or successful marketing, catalyzed a bullish trend that piqued the interest of investor agents. Guided by decision heuristics like 'follow the trend' and 'follow the leader', investors surged into the market, further inflating prices in a feedback loop of escalating demand and value. However, as prices soared unsustainably, inevitably, a tipping point was reached. Investors, now adhering to heuristics such as 'maximize utility', 'risk aversion' and protocols to 'sell NFTs if the trend reverts', hastened to exit, plummeting the prices drastically and manifesting a price bust after the initial boom.

Figure 7.10 brings forth the supply and demand imbalances in the NFT market. Initially, an overwhelming demand for a particular NFT or series thereof sees the quantity of NFTs bought significantly outpacing those on offer, dictated by investor

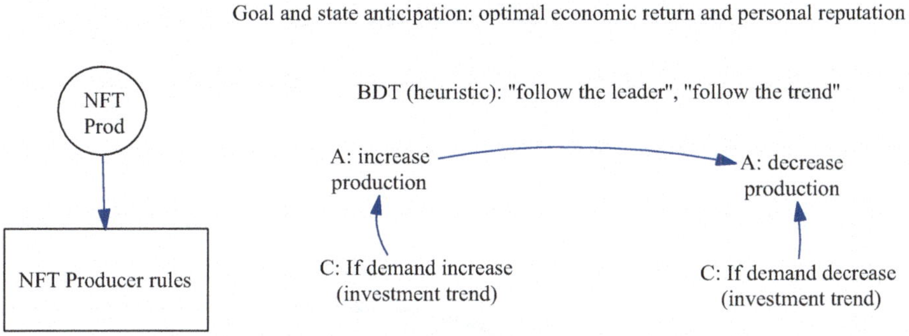


**Fig. 7.7** Agent behaviour map (AbM) for an NFT producer agent

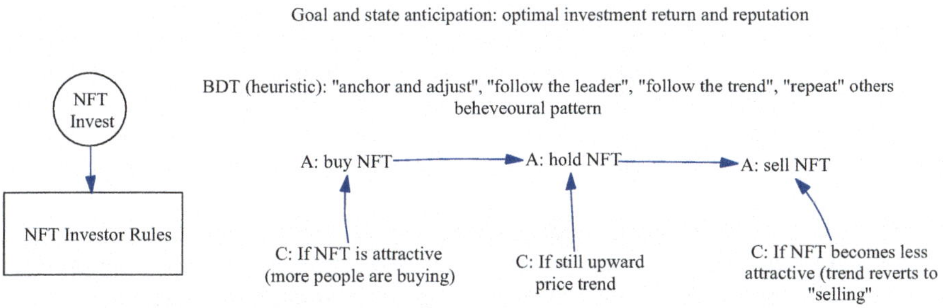


**Fig. 7.8** AbM for an NFT investor agent

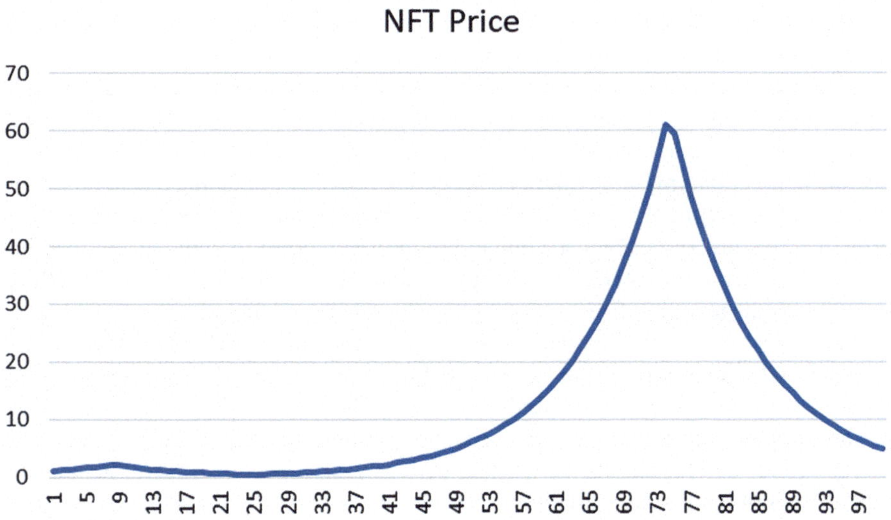


**Fig. 7.9** NFT price boom and bust illustration, resulting from agent interactions on the market as described in previous paragraphs

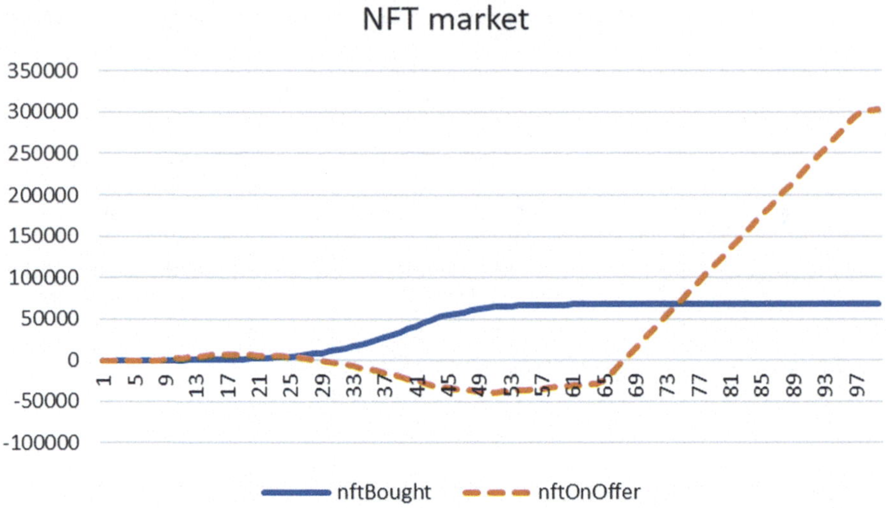


**Fig. 7.10** NFT market output plot exhibiting resource stock levels of NFTs bought and NFTs on offer

protocols to 'buy NFTs if the product attractiveness and price increase'. NFT producer agents, adhering to their own heuristics and protocols of increasing production in response to heightened demand, subsequently amplify their output.

However, this leads to an inadvertent oversaturation of the market. After a certain temporal lag, the oversupply becomes evident, inversely dwarfing demand and leading to a surplus of NFTs on offer, as opposed to those being bought. Investors, sensing the shift and adopting a sell-off strategy as per their decision protocols, intensify the disbalance between available supply and active demand (Fig. 7.11).

Figure 7.11 reveals how investor states can impact on market supply and demand, particularly focusing on how herding behaviour—where investors follow the crowd rather than their independent analysis—shapes these dynamics. At the outset, a decline in potential investors might be observed, possibly indicating a general group move away from initial interest in the asset. Following this, a surge and subsequent drop in active investors suggest a quick, group-driven boost in demand (or 'overdemand') and then a retreat, due to oversupply and increase in numbers of the selling investor agents resulting from oversupply outnumbering demand.

In essence, the graph illustrates how herding behaviour can drive cycles of overdemand and oversupply in the market, as investors collectively rush towards and then away from assets, significantly impacting their availability and value. This straightforward exploration underscores the continual push and pull observed in market trends and highlights the herding behavioural impact of investor actions on market stability and asset valuation.

Figures above prove that just like any other asset or investment, NFT prices can be influenced by a variety of factors, including supply and demand, market trends, investor sentiment, and overall economic conditions. If demand for a particular NFT

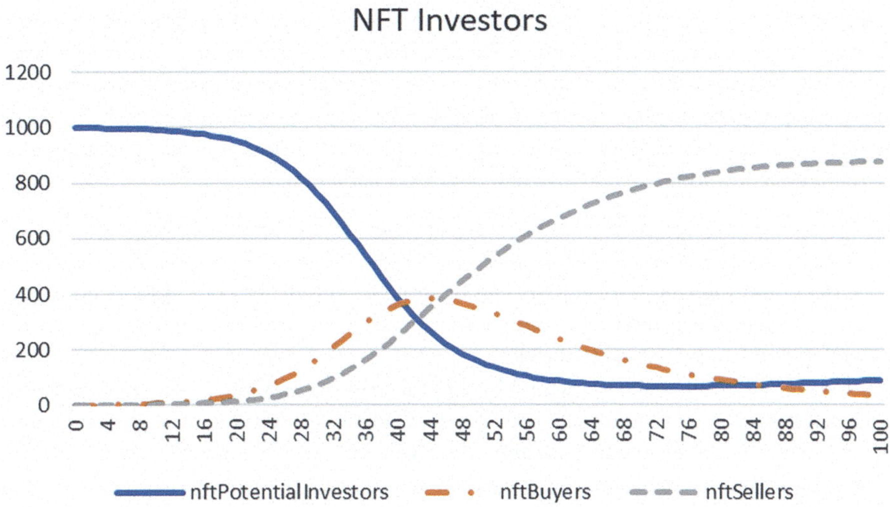


**Fig. 7.11** NFT investors plot exhibiting the evolution of the three investor states of potential investors, active investors, and selling investor agents

product exceeds supply, its price may rise rapidly as buyers compete for a limited number of available items. This can lead to a price bubble as investors and speculators jump on board, driving up prices even further. However, if demand suddenly drops, because a large number of NFT products come on the market, the price of the NFT may start to decline. This can cause a chain reaction as investors who had purchased the NFT product as an investment start to sell their holdings, leading to further price declines.

As noted before, there have been examples of NFTs experiencing price bubbles and subsequent declines in the market (Boido & Aliano, 2023), like CryptoKitties craze in late 2017, which was one of the earliest instances of NFTs gaining mainstream attention. The NFTs, which were unique digital collectible cats, gained popularity among investors and collectors, and at one point, some of the rarest CryptoKitties sold for over $100,000. However, the hype eventually decreased and the prices of the NFTs began to decline. Another example is the recent market for NFTs based on digital art, which experienced a significant surge in popularity and prices in early 2021, resulting in the sale of an NFT artwork by Beeple for a record-breaking $69 million. However, in the following months, the market experienced a decline in demand and prices for NFTs, with some artworks selling for a fraction of their earlier prices. These examples highlight the potential for NFTs to experience price bubbles and subsequent declines, similar to other markets and assets.

In regard to NFT marketplaces regulation, they need to comply with existing financial regulations, such as anti-money laundering (AML) and know-your-customer (KYC) rules. However, there is not yet a comprehensive regulatory framework specifically for NFTs in most jurisdictions, and the lack of regulation can lead to potential risks for investors, such as fraud, market manipulation, and lack of transparency. As the market continues to evolve and attract greater attention, it is likely that regulators will begin to develop more specific rules and guidance for NFT market participants. Although there is no uniform global regulatory framework governing the market, some general regulatory principles have been proposed to address NFT market inefficiencies, which could be factored in an extended RAM and scenario simulation exploration in support of public regulation development and efficient policy decision making:

1. Consumer protection: NFT market regulations should aim to protect consumers from fraud, misrepresentation, and other types of misconduct by NFT issuers, sellers, and intermediaries. This can be done by requiring NFT issuers and sellers to disclose relevant information about their NFTs, such as their origin, ownership rights, and associated risks.
2. AML/KYC compliance: Anti-Money Laundering (AML) and Know-Your-Customer (KYC) compliance measures are necessary to prevent money laundering and illegal financing through the NFT market. These measures can be implemented by requiring NFT issuers, sellers, and intermediaries to verify the identity of their customers and report suspicious activities to the relevant authorities.
3. Standardization and interoperability: To promote liquidity and efficiency in the NFT market, standards for NFT metadata, smart contracts, and other technical specifications should be developed.
4. Market stability: Regulations should aim to prevent market manipulation, insider trading, and other activities that can harm market stability and confidence, through disclosure requirements, trading restrictions, and surveillance systems.
5. Taxation: NFTs are considered to be assets and subject to taxation in many jurisdictions. Regulations should clarify the tax treatment of NFT transactions and ensure that NFT market participants comply with relevant tax laws.

Navigating through the landscape of non-fungible tokens (NFTs) requires an understanding of their inherent characteristics and interrelated resource agent interactions in the surrounding market, producing a complex system (Bao & Roubaud, 2022), adapting to supply and demand fluctuations, as well as the perceived value of the underlying assets.

## References

Ali, O., Momin, M., Shrestha, A., Das, R., Alhajj, F., & Dwivedi, Y. K. (2023). A review of the key challenges of nonfungible tokens. *Technological Forecasting and Social Change, 187*, 122248.

Akerlof, G. A. (1970). The market for lemons: Qualitative uncertainty and the market mechanism. *Quarterly Journal of Economics, 84*(3), 488–500. https://doi.org/10.2307/1879431

Akerlof, G. A. (1989). The economics of illusion. *Economics and Politics, 1*(1), 1–15. https://doi.org/10.1111/j.1468-0343.1989.tb00002.x

Almudhaf, F. (2017). Speculative bubbles and irrational exuberance in African stock markets. *Journal of Behavioral and Experimental Finance, 13*. https://doi.org/10.1016/j.jbef.2016.11.002

Axtell, R., Axelrod, R., Epstein, J. M., & Cohen, M. D. (1996). Aligning simulation models: A case study and results. *Computational & Mathematical Organization Theory, 1*(2), 123–141. https://doi.org/10.1007/BF01299065

Baker, H. K., & Ricciardi, V. (Eds.). (2014). *Investor behavior: The psychology of financial planning and investing* (Vol. 26).

Bao, H., & Roubaud, D. (2021). Recent development in Fintech: Non-fungible token. *FinTech, 1*(1). https://doi.org/10.3390/fintech1010003

Bao, H., & Roubaud, D. (2022). Non-fungible token: A systematic review and research agenda. *Journal of Risk and Financial Management, 15*(5) MDPI. https://doi.org/10.3390/jrfm15050215

Barkley Rosser, J., Jr. (2003). A Nobel for asymmetric information: The economic contributions of George Akerlof , Michael Spence and Joseph Stiglitz. *Review of Political Economy, 15*(1), 3–22. https://doi.org/10.1080/0953825022000033099

Barnett, M. L., & Salomon, R. M. (2012). Does it pay to be really good? Addressing the shape of the relationship between social and financial performance. *Strategic Management Journal, 33*(11). https://doi.org/10.1002/smj.1980

Behavioral Finance: What Everyone Needs to Know. (2020). *Quantitative Finance, 20*(9). https://doi.org/10.1080/14697688.2020.1809697

Blanchard, O. J. (1979). Speculative bubbles, crashes and rational expectations. *Economics Letters, 3*(4). https://doi.org/10.1016/0165-1765(79)90017-X

Boido, C., & Aliano, M. (2023). Digital art and non-fungible-token: Bubble or revolution? *Finance Research Letters, 52*. https://doi.org/10.1016/j.frl.2022.103380

Borri, N., Liu, Y., & Tsyvinski, A. (2022). The economics of non-fungible tokens. *SSRN Electronic Journal*. https://doi.org/10.2139/ssrn.4052045

Brounen, D., de Jong, A., & Koedijk, K. (2006). Capital structure policies in Europe: Survey evidence. *Journal of Banking and Finance, 30*(5). https://doi.org/10.1016/j.jbankfin.2005.02.010

Brunnermeier, M. K. (2001). Asset pricing under asymmetric information: Bubbles, crashes, technical analysis and herding. *Analysis, 1*(609), 233. https://doi.org/10.1093/0198296983.001.0001

Caferra, R., Tedeschi, G., & Morone, A. (2021). Bitcoin: Bubble that bursts or gold that glitters? *Economics Letters, 205*. https://doi.org/10.1016/j.econlet.2021.109942

Chandra, Y. (2022). Non-fungible token-enabled entrepreneurship: A conceptual framework. *Journal of Business Venturing Insights, 18*. https://doi.org/10.1016/j.jbvi.2022.e00323

Cheng, S., Massa, M., & Zhang, H. (2019). The unexpected activeness of passive investors: A worldwide analysis of ETFs. *Review of Asset Pricing Studies, 9*(2). https://doi.org/10.1093/rapstu/ray011

Colicev, A. (2023). How can non-fungible tokens bring value to brands. *International Journal of Research in Marketing, 40*(1). https://doi.org/10.1016/j.ijresmar.2022.07.003

Cont, R., & Bouchaud, J. P. (2000). Herd behavior and aggregate fluctuations in financial markets. *Macroeconomic Dynamics, 4*(2). https://doi.org/10.1017/s1365100500015029

Corbet, S., Lucey, B., & Yarovaya, L. (2018). Datestamping the Bitcoin and Ethereum bubbles. *Finance Research Letters, 26*. https://doi.org/10.1016/j.frl.2017.12.006

Crain, M. (2014). Financial markets and online advertising: Reevaluating the dotcom investment bubble. *Information Communication and Society, 17*(3). https://doi.org/10.1080/1369118X.2013.869615

Demirer, R., Kutan, A. M., & Chen, C. D. (2010). Do investors herd in emerging stock markets?: Evidence from the Taiwanese market. *Journal of Economic Behavior and Organization, 76*(2). https://doi.org/10.1016/j.jebo.2010.06.013

Devenow, A., & Welch, I. (1996). Rational herding in financial economics. *European Economic Review, 40*(3–5). https://doi.org/10.1016/0014-2921(95)00073-9

Dowling, M. (2022). Is non-fungible token pricing driven by cryptocurrencies? *Finance Research Letters, 44*. https://doi.org/10.1016/j.frl.2021.102097

Grinblatt, B. M., Titman, S., & Wermers, R. (1995). Momentum investment strategies, portfolio performance, and herding: A study of mutual fund behavior. *American Economic Review, 85*(5).

Grinblatt, M., & Sheridan Titman, R. W. (1995). Momentum investment strategies, portfolio performance, and herding.pdf. *American Economic Review, 85*(5).

Helman, L., & Tur-Sinai, O. (2023). Bracing scarcity: Can NFTs save digital art? *SSRN Electronic Journal*. https://doi.org/10.2139/ssrn.4378570

Herwarth Kohn, M. B., & Valls Pereira, P. L. (2017). Speculative bubbles and contagion: Analysis of volatility's clusters during the DotCom bubble based on the dynamic conditional correlation model. *Cogent Economics and Finance, 5*(1). https://doi.org/10.1080/23322039.2017.1411453

Holt, J. (2009). A summary of the primary causes of the housing bubble and the resulting credit crisis: A non-technical paper. *The Journal of Business Inquiry, 8*(1).

Horky, F., Rachel, C., & Fidrmuc, J. (2022a). Price determinants of non-fungible tokens in the digital art market. *Finance Research Letters, 48*. https://doi.org/10.1016/j.frl.2022.103007

Horky, F., Rachel, C., & Fidrmuc, J. (2022b). Price dynamics of non-fungible tokens: The case of the digital arts market. *SSRN Electronic Journal*. https://doi.org/10.2139/ssrn.4080372

Kraizberg, E. (2023). Non-fungible tokens: A bubble or the end of an era of intellectual property rights. *Financial Innovations, 9*(1). https://doi.org/10.1186/s40854-022-00428-4

Kwoun, M. J., Lee, S. H., Kim, J. H., & Kim, J. J. (2013). Dynamic cycles of unsold new housing stocks, investment in housing, and housing supply-demand. *Mathematical and Computer Modelling, 57*(9–10), 2094–2105. https://doi.org/10.1016/j.mcm.2011.08.005

Li, Z. Z., Tao, R., Su, C. W., & Lobonţ, O. R. (2019). Does Bitcoin bubble burst? *Quality and Quantity, 53*(1). https://doi.org/10.1007/s11135-018-0728-3

Lommers, K., Kim, J., & Baioumy, M. (2022). Market Making in NFTs. *SSRN Electronic Journal*. https://doi.org/10.2139/ssrn.4226987

López-Cabarcos, M. Á., Pérez-Pico, A. M., Piñeiro-Chousa, J., & Šević, A. (2021). Bitcoin volatility, stock market and investor sentiment. Are they connected? *Finance Research Letters, 38*. https://doi.org/10.1016/j.frl.2019.101399

Lusyana, D., & Sherif, M. (2016). Do mergers create value for high-tech firms? The hounds of dotcom bubble. *Journal of High Technology Management Research, 27*(2). https://doi.org/10.1016/j.hitech.2016.10.009

Lux, T. (1995). Herd behaviour, bubbles and crashes. *The Economic Journal, 105*(431). https://doi.org/10.2307/2235156

Nneji, O., Brooks, C., & Ward, C. (2013). Intrinsic and rational speculative bubbles in the U.S. housing market: 1960-2011. *Journal of Real Estate Research, 35*(2). https://doi.org/10.1080/10835547.2013.12091360

Phillips, P. C. B. (2016). Modeling speculative bubbles with diverse investor expectations. *Research in Economics, 70*(3). https://doi.org/10.1016/j.rie.2016.01.002

Pinto-Gutiérrez, C., Gaitán, S., Jaramillo, D., & Velasquez, S. (2022). The NFT hype: What draws attention to non-fungible tokens? *Mathematics, 10*(3). https://doi.org/10.3390/math10030335

Schaller, H., & van Norden, S. (2005). Fads or Bubbles? *SSRN Electronic Journal*. https://doi.org/10.2139/ssrn.57941

Scharfstein, D. S., & Stein, J. C. (1990). Herd behavior and investment. *American Economic Review, 80*(3).

Shu, M., & Zhu, W. (2020). Real-time prediction of Bitcoin bubble crashes. *Physica A: Statistical Mechanics and its Applications, 548*. https://doi.org/10.1016/j.physa.2020.124477

Sterman, J. (2001). System dynamics modeling. *California Management Review, 3*, 163p. https://doi.org/10.1007/978-1-4419-9416-5

Stiglitz, J. E. (2002). Information and the change in the paradigm in economics. *American Economic Review, 92*(3), 460–501. https://doi.org/10.1257/00028280260136363

Taherdoost, H. (2023). Non-fungible tokens (NFT): A systematic review. *Information (Switzerland), 14*(1). https://doi.org/10.3390/info14010026

Trehan, B., & Sinha, A. (2019). Investigating investors' herd behavior. *Amity Business Journal*.

Welch, I. (2000). Herding among security analysts. *Journal of Financial Economics, 58*(3). https://doi.org/10.1016/S0304-405X(00)00076-3

Wilson, K. B., Karg, A., & Ghaderi, H. (2022). Prospecting non-fungible tokens in the digital economy: Stakeholders and ecosystem, risk and opportunity. *Business Horizons, 65*(5). https://doi.org/10.1016/j.bushor.2021.10.007

# Chapter 8
# Art and Culture and Ideological Systems

**Abstract** Art, cultural and ideological systems can also be interpreted as being complex adaptive socioeconomic systems, consisting of interacting resources and agents. In this context, resources include artefacts, ideas, beliefs, values and norms, while agents include individuals, groups, institutions and organizations that create, hold and disseminate ideas and beliefs.

In an ideological system, agents can have heterogeneous goals, beliefs and behaviours and interact with each other through communication, persuasion, socialization and mobilization. These interactions can create feedback loops that reinforce or modify their behaviour and the level of used resources. Examples for ideological systems can include political campaigns and referendums, which can influence public opinions and social groups behaviour.

Art and culture-related systems consist of resources like art, literature, music, language, symbols and other cultural artefacts, while agents include artists, groups, institutions and organizations that produce and consume these artefacts. These systems are influenced by social, economic and institutional factors.

This chapter provides examples of RAM framework applications for the understanding of the behaviour of these systems and demonstrates how using hybrid simulation modelling can further provide means for experimentation and decision-making support.

## 8.1 Ideological Systems and Adoption and Diffusion of Ideas

Understanding ideological systems means looking at how we accept and spread ideas and beliefs, especially through the lens of system resources and how different players (agents) in the system interact. Simply put, we can take beliefs and ideas as stocks of resources in a market, in order to analyze how ideas are important resources that impact, and are impacted by, different players or groups in a social setting.

Ideological market systems consist of ideas and beliefs which are shared, discussed, and adopted in a way that is similar to how typical markets work. Here,



R. Kazakov et al., *Understanding and Managing Socioeconomic Systems Behaviour*, Contributions to Management Science,
https://doi.org/10.1007/978-3-031-57057-5_8

ideas viewed as resources are moved around within a social system, driven by various players like policy-makers, cultural groups, and media. These players, each with their own goals, work together or 'against' each other in this marketplace, constantly shaping and reshaping the paths through which beliefs are accepted and spread across the community.

The resources (ideas and beliefs) and the agents (different societal players) within the system interact with each other. Agents, carrying their own goals and strategies, use different methods to spread certain ideas. In parallel, the ideas diffusion influences the behaviour of different agents in the system.

Watts, D. J., and Dodds, P. S. (2007). *Influentials, Networks, and Public Opinion Formation. Journal of Consumer Research, 34(4), 441–458,* (n.d.) simulated the spread of opinions on a political issue among a population of individuals with varying degrees of influence. They found that small changes in the distribution of influence among individuals could lead to significantly different outcomes in terms of the overall adoption of different opinions. Such simulation studies can help us to better understand the complex processes involved in the adoption and diffusion of ideas or ideologies and to identify the key factors that influence these processes.

Referendum campaigns in any country can provide a good example for simulation exploration and insight analysis.

Ostendorf (2018) examines main social, cultural, and economic factors that influenced voting behaviour in referendum campaigns. The authors draw on a range of data sources, including surveys, focus groups, and election results, to build a comprehensive picture of the factors that shaped public opinion in the run-up to the referendum. They argue that a complex mix of factors, including cultural identity, political disaffection, and economic insecurity, contributed to the decision to 'against' the EU.

Clarke et al. (2016) used an aggregate-level data to analyse the relationship between voting patterns and a range of demographic, economic, and attitudinal factors. One specific area of research is focused on the role of the media. Media plays a significant role in shaping public opinion about an issue, with both traditional and social media providing a platform for 'pro-' and 'anti-' campaign voices. Another area of research has examined the role of emotions and opposing perceptions referendum campaigns, providing behavioural decision heuristics insights (Kahneman & Tversky, 1996).

The literature on political campaigns and voting behaviour highlights the complex interplay of various factors, resources, and agents that shaped 'pro-' and 'anti-' voting attitudes. The role of the media, emotions, identity, and political engagement all play significant roles in shaping the outcomes of any campaign, and have important implications for understanding the dynamics of political campaigning more broadly (Rita et al., 2023).

In the above regard, the following key 'resources' and 'agents' related to ideological propaganda can be pointed out:

- Resources: Information or content that can be communicated and disseminated through various channels, such as media outlets or social networks.

- Agents: Individuals or organizations that actively disseminate or receive ideological messages, as well as those who control the means of dissemination.

In this complex socio-economic system, the resources (ideological content, related information, etc.) are disseminated by agents through various channels (e.g. news media, social media, educational institutions), with the goal of influencing the beliefs and attitudes of the receiving agents. Incoming flows can represent the rate of increase in acquisition of new ideological content by agents, while the outgoing flows can represent the rate of dissemination of existing content by agents. Agents can also influence the content itself by providing feedback or input to those who control the means of dissemination, creating a feedback loop. Additionally, agents can influence each other through social networks and interpersonal communication, creating a network effect.

It is important to note that this system can be influenced by various factors, such as government regulation, corporate interests, and individual biases. These factors can impact the content being disseminated, as well as the behaviour of the agents who are receiving and disseminating that content. Important agents in the system are government officials and politicians, political parties, interest groups (e.g. business associations, trade unions, environmental organizations), media outlets, individual citizens and activists, and other.

Main interactions between the above agents are connected to information flows from government officials and politicians, political parties, and interest groups in the form of speeches, press releases, and advertising campaigns aimed at influencing public opinion, feedback from individual citizens and activists, media outlets, and leaders and organizations in response to the campaign messages, incoming and outgoing flows of financial resources between various agents in order to fund campaign activities such as advertising and public events, the votes individual citizens during the actual referendum.

The above complex adaptive system involves also positive feedback loops that may occur if an agent's campaign message gains popularity and support, leading to more resources and public support, balancing feedback loops that may occur if an agent's campaign message is poorly received or if the agent is associated with a scandal or controversy, leading to a decrease in public support and other resources.

Other factors can include an increase in public attention and involvement in the campaign, leading to more outgoing and incoming resource flows and potentially more feedback loops, anticipated changes in government leadership or economic policies, leading to shifts in power and influence within the system, shift of influence of certain agents or interest groups depending on the anticipated outcome of their campaign efforts and their ability to adapt to changing public opinion.

In addition to the resources mentioned earlier, several other resources play an important role in voting campaigns, like social media that can spread misleading or false information, political parties campaigning for ‘pro-’ and ‘anti-’ voting choices and traditional media that can reinforce true or misleading information in interviews and news articles. All of these resources had varying degrees of influence in relation to the voting outcome.

During such campaigns, 'pro-' and 'anti-' actors can navigate public opinion through a variety of tactics. Firstly, both sides can use targeted advertising on social media platforms to reach specific demographics with tailored messages. This allowed them to present their arguments to the most receptive audiences. Secondly, both campaigns can use prominent and influential figures to endorse their positions. These included politicians, celebrities, business leaders, and other public figures. By associating their positions with these respected individuals, the campaigns aimed to sway public opinion. Thirdly, both campaigns can engage in public events and debates, such as town hall meetings and public rallies, to get closer to potential voters and present their arguments in person.

Finally, both 'pro-' and 'anti-' campaigns can use a variety of media channels, including traditional print and broadcast media as well as social media, to disseminate their messages and engage with voters. They also can utilize polling and focus group data to track public opinion and adjust their messages and tactics accordingly.

## 8.2 Exploring Voting Agents Behaviour Using Agent Behaviour Maps

We can think of any referendum campaign as a flow of potential voters entering into two separate stocks: the "potential voter 'against'" stock and the "potential voter 'pro'" stock, influenced by agents' decision rules, as illustrated on Figs. 8.1 and 8.2. The flow is influenced by two other variables: the "'against' campaign effectiveness and the "'pro' campaign effectiveness." The effectiveness of each campaign increases or decreases the flow of potential voters entering each stock.

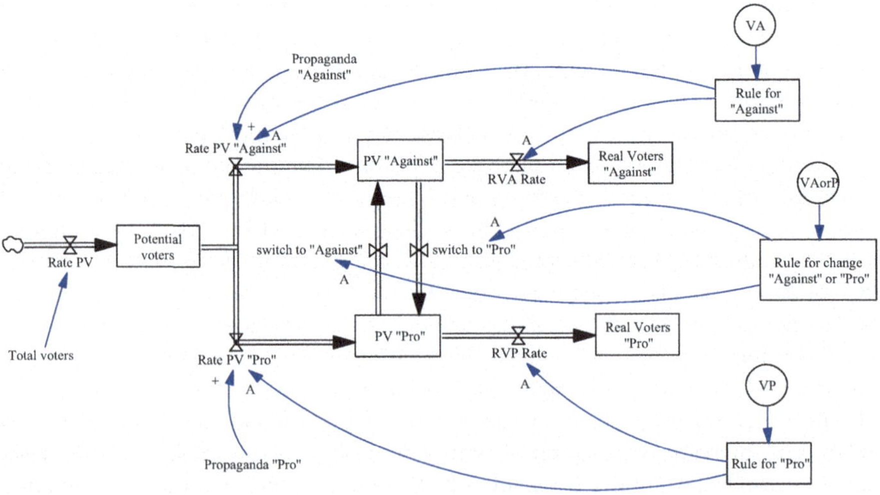


**Fig. 8.1** Resource agent map (RAM) for a national referendum campaign system

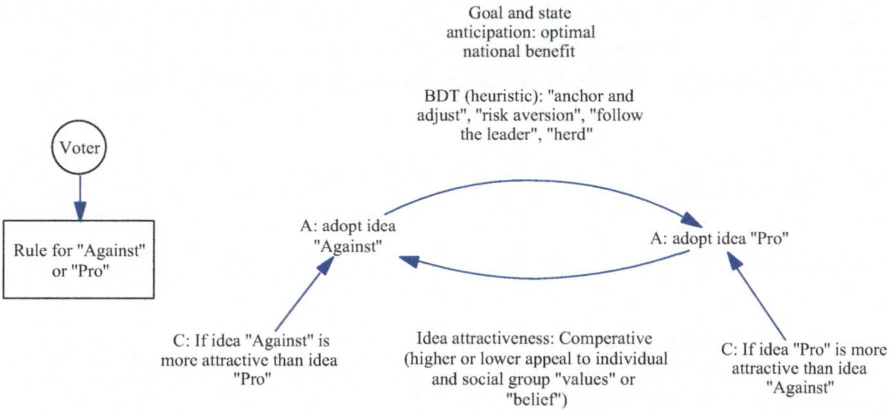


**Fig. 8.2** Agent behaviour map (AbM) for voter agent, describing agent's decision rules and their related conditions

Once the potential voters enter one of the two stocks, they become part of the 'real voter' stock. However, the potential voters stocks are not fixed—they can change as voters can switch their allegiance based on the intensity of the campaigning and the effectiveness of the messages. This is represented by the switching flows between the "potential voter 'against'" stock and the "potential voter 'pro'" stock, influenced by the communication effectiveness and agents rules for switching between the two.

In this representation, the real voters rates are functions of the intensity and effectiveness of the campaigning, as such campaigning is likely to result in more voters and the voters rules to act in favour of the adoption of 'against' or 'pro'. This joint agent-based and system dynamics approach combines the individual decision-making of agents with the feedback dynamics of resource stocks and their inflow and outflow rates. In this hybrid approach, agents are represented as decision-making entities with their own rules and preferences, while stock and flow variables represent the resource dynamics of the system. The decision-making of agents influences the evolution of the stock and flow variables, and the levels of these variables in turn feeds back to influence the decision-making of the agents.

The simulation of this hybrid approach involves creating resource agent maps (RAM) that describe the decision rules and activities of agents, the resources and feedback loops that govern the system dynamics, and the interactions between these components. The simulation model can then be implemented using a suitable simulation modelling software that can generate outputs that represent the evolution of the system over time.

Analyzing this dynamic through the system's resources and agents' behaviour perspective, the changing levels of decided and undecided voters are affected through the continuous interaction and feedback loops between campaign strategies, messaging efficacy, prevailing societal narratives, and heuristic-guided voter behaviour. The transitions through various phases of the campaign reveal the elastic and volatile nature of public voting disposition, affirming the substantial impact of timely, resonant, and strategically aligned messaging in attracting a heuristic-decision-making electorate, aligned around a main goal or anticipated result.

Here are the agents and the resources in the above-described system:

**Agents**
- Potential voters
- Campaign managers
- IF-THEN condition: idea attractiveness (higher or lower appeal to individual and social group 'values' or 'belief')

**Stocks**
- Number of potential voters.
- Number of voters who support 'against'
- Number of voters who support 'pro'

**Flows**
- Conversion rate from potential voter to supporter of 'against' campaign
- Conversion rate from potential voter to supporter of 'pro' campaign
- Rate of new potential voters entering the system
- Rate of voters changing their support from 'against' to 'pro'
- Rate of voters changing their support from 'pro' to 'against'

Campaign effectiveness could be incorporated by adding a variable representing the effectiveness of each campaign message in converting potential voters to supporters of either 'against' or 'pro', through influencing upon agents voting IF-THEN condition to action pattern by trying to increase the level of attractiveness of each of the two opposing ideas. This variable could be influenced by factors such as the clarity and persuasiveness of the message, the credibility and likability of the messenger, the reach and frequency of the message, and the resonance and relevance of the message to the target audience.

Agents voting behaviour, particularly within the context of a campaign for contrasting ideologies, and the systemic interplay of various agents and resources introduces a multifaceted and complex environment. Herein, agents such as potential voters, campaign managers, and actual voters interact with resources, chiefly campaign-related information regarding the ideas being promoted for a vote, and the actual voting decision they undertake.

Agents voting behaviour is further represented through states in this hybrid resource agent system (Fig. 8.3). The system is a political campaign for a national referendum, and the agents are the potential voters who can be influenced by campaign messages through various communication channels.

The states of the agents in this simulation are 'potential voter', "potential voter 'pro'", and "potential voter 'against'.". The agents can move between these states based on the effectiveness of the marketing messages they receive, the effects of inter-agent communication, and their decision rules.

The simulation experiments can be used to test the effectiveness of different campaign strategies and to study the dynamics of the voters adopting or not one or another voting behaviour. For example, by adjusting the campaign effectiveness on becoming a potential voter 'against' or 'pro', we can model the impact on the initial attitudes of the population on the outcome of the campaign (Bello & Rolfe, 2014; Rita et al., 2023;

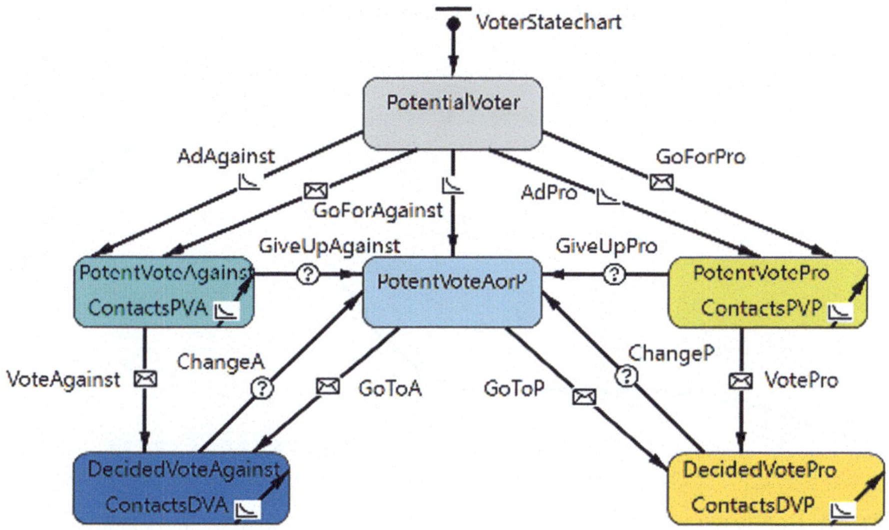


**Fig. 8.3** (Redraw) Agent state chart mapping voters' behaviour during voting campaigns

Santoro & Beck, 2016). By adjusting the factors influencing on switching between potential voter 'against' or 'pro', we can model the impact of events or messages that change people's attitudes. By adjusting the intensity of the campaign and the competition messages, we can model the impact of different communication strategies.

Figure 8.4 describes the complex behavioural decision heuristic behaviour of voters in the campaign where several discernible phenomena are observed.

When the decided voters for 'pro' increase, outperforming voters for 'against' during an initial phase, it might hint towards an effective campaign 'pro' strategy or a widely resonating message with the electorate. This might be attributed to the 'follow the leader' heuristic if a prominent figure or even 'follow the herd' if early adopters significantly sway public opinion in favour of 'pro'. The 'pro' campaign messaging, possibly leveraging a mix of risk aversion and anchoring tactics, appears to resonate more compellingly with the voting populace during this phase. It is possible that 'against' campaign might be encountering issues at this stage or is less compelling in comparison.

The subsequent decline of decided voters for 'pro' and the rise for 'against' indicate a shift in public sentiment or perception, which could be triggered by several factors: unveiling of new information, effective counter-campaigning for 'against', or a potential decrease in effectiveness in the campaign for 'pro'. This shift might invoke the anchor and adjust heuristic as voters recalibrate their positions in light of new data or changing circumstances. If campaign for 'against' successfully undermines the credibility or attractiveness of campaign 'pro' propositions or showcases a more resonant ideology, the voter's 'IF-THEN' decision-making rules would have been successfully navigated in their favour.

The initial increase in potential voters either for 'pro' or 'against', followed by a decrease, reflects a period of uncertainty or exploration, wherein voters are possibly gathering information, being exposed to campaigns, or deliberating their alignment

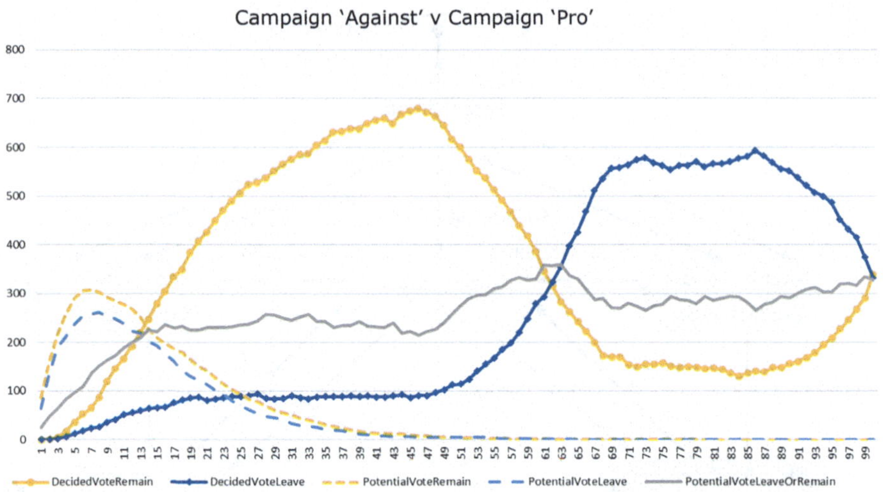


**Fig. 8.4** Decision to vote 'pro', decision to vote 'against', potential voter 'pro', potential voter 'against', potential voter 'pro' or 'against' (not decided)

based on personal and social values. The decrease indicates decision consolidation, as the undecided voters begins to affiliate with one ideology over the other, possibly due to intensified campaign efforts, emerging social consensus, or evolving societal narratives.

The relatively stable pool of undecided voters, wavering with minor fluctuations, is indicative of a segment of the public that 'pro's undecided or unconvinced by either campaign, possibly due to a disconnect with their personal or social values or scepticism towards the proposed ideologies. These individuals potentially represent a segment that either abstains from voting due to indecision or makes a last-minute decision based on late-breaking information or prevailing social winds, thereby introducing a level of unpredictability into the campaign outcomes.

Another simulation experiment included a stochastic parameter connected to the effectiveness levels of both 'pro' and 'against' campaigns (Fig. 8.5). The simulation results exhibit a behaviour for both voting categories, very similar to actual data related to opinion polls conducted for a period of a few months before the real referendum vote (Fig. 8.6), and analyzed in a study by Hobolt and Wittrock (2011), and Tilley and Hobolt (2023).

The experimental results through using resource agent simulations can help us to further understand agents' behaviour, particularly that of voters, through using the lens of behavioural decision theory (BDT) heuristics. A number of decision patterns play an important role, shaping voters behaviour evolution:

1. **Anchor and adjust**: Voters could fixate (anchor) on the initial information, whether it is the potential economic boon or fallout of a decision, and then inadequately adjust their views in light of subsequent information.

2. **Risk aversion**: A clear tendency could emerge to avoid options that are framed as risky or uncertain, thereby leaning towards options that promise stability or align with the status quo.
3. **Follow the leader**: Observably, voters might align their choices with those advocated by prominent figures or experts, presuming an informed basis behind their endorsements.
4. **Follow the herd**: Herd behaviour suggests that voters may also look to the majority's inclination, adhering to collective wisdom or seeking solace in conformity.

Incorporating these heuristics into the voting system reveals interesting dynamics:

- **Amplification of perceptions**: Biased or partially informed viewpoints might be amplified as voters lean on cognitive shortcuts and societal influences rather than detailed evaluation.
- **Polarization**: Potential polarization between voter bases may arise, fortified by mutually reinforcing 'follow the leader' and 'follow the herd' dynamics, perpetuating ideological dichotomies.
- **Misinformation vulnerability**: The electorate's susceptibility to initial information, especially if it is misleading, is highlighted by anchoring, wherein subsequent, possibly corrective, information might be undervalued.
- **Stability vs. change**: A collective lean towards stability may be observed due to risk aversion, possibly impeding progressive decisions that entail inherent risks.

Campaign managers can not only disseminate objective information but also navigate the heuristics that subtly, yet substantively, influence voters perceptions and choice. Understanding that voter decisions are often less a reflection of logical processing and more a product of heuristic decision rules, helps illuminate the complex landscape of voters' behaviour, especially in the context of ideological market

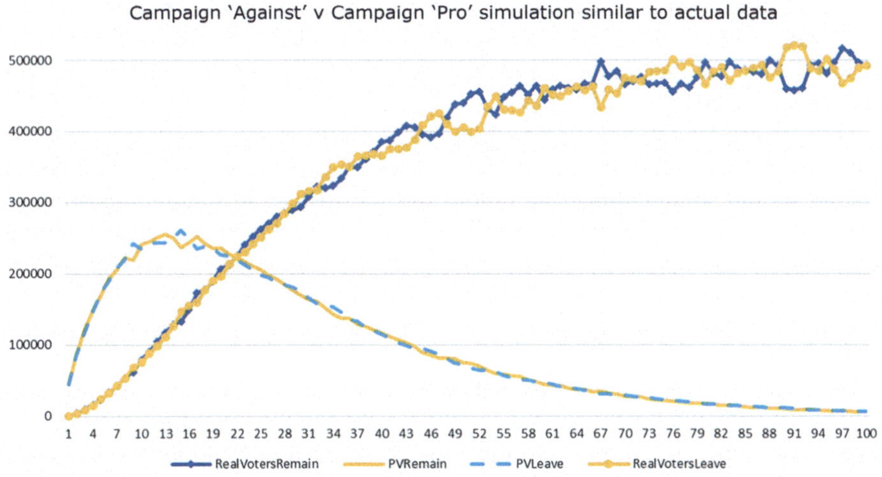


**Fig. 8.5** SD output of voting campaign, including propaganda effectiveness, contact rate, and word-of-mouth effects

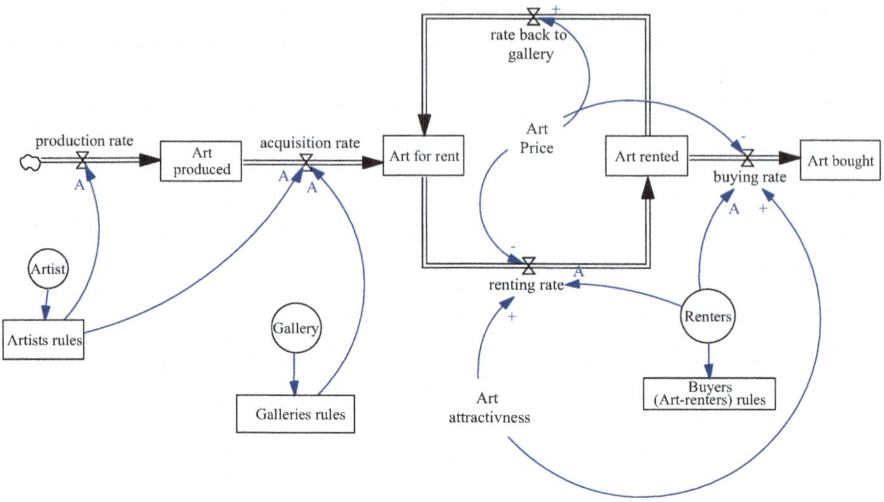


**Fig. 8.6** A RAM of the art renting market involving main resource stocks, their flows, and main agent and their behaviour rules

systems. The multi-faceted interplay between resources, agents, and decision heuristics can further become a focus of more experimental analysis, to include additional important factors and to provide more fine-tuned insights into the mechanisms driving adoption and diffusion of ideas within voting contexts.

## 8.3 Art Renting Market

The art renting market is a relatively new and emerging market that has gained popularity in recent years. This market allows individuals and businesses to rent artworks for a temporary period, rather than buying them outright (Khangeldieva, 2015).

There is growing trend of art renting, particularly in the corporate world. Art rental companies such are becoming increasingly popular among businesses looking to add some culture and colour to their offices without committing to purchasing expensive artwork. Similarly, the art rental market is expanding beyond just corporate clients and is becoming popular among individual collectors and art enthusiasts as well. The lower cost of renting art compared to buying it outright becomes a major draw for many attracted to art people (Huang et al., 2023).

However, there are challenges and opportunities that come with the art renting market. There is potential for it to grow and become a more mainstream alternative to buying art, but also there are challenges of building a sustainable business model in a market that relies heavily on subjective tastes and preferences.

Art renting allows individuals to constantly change and update their collection without having to worry about the financial burden of purchasing and maintaining artwork, and enjoying the flexibility and convenience that comes with renting art. Art renting also allows individuals to experiment with different styles and mediums, and can also be a more cost-effective way of owning art.

Art rental markets can also be analyzed from the perspective of complex socio-economic systems, in which the interactions of artists, collectors, and galleries create emergent behaviours and feedback loops. Feedback loops can occur when changes in one element of the system affect the behaviour of other elements, which in turn feedback to influence the original element. For example, an increase in the number of collectors using rental platforms may lead to an increase in demand for rental artworks, which in turn can lead to increased demand from artists to have their work represented on these platforms (Klamer & Petrova, 2007; van Haaften-Schick & Whitaker, 2022).

Understanding the dynamics of art rental markets from this perspective can help artists, collectors, galleries, and rental platforms to better navigate the complex and rapidly evolving landscape of art rentals, and potentially unlock new opportunities for the creation and exchange of artwork (Bialynicka-Birula, 2018; Huang et al., 2023).

Here is a system analysis of the art rental market using the concepts for a 'resource' and an 'agent' according to the resource agent mapping approach:

**Main Resources**

- Artwork inventory: A stock of artwork pieces that can accumulate or decrease over time through incoming and outgoing flows
- Art materials for production
- Information about contemporary and classical art available on the art renting market

**Agents**

- Artists: Individuals who create artwork.
- Art renters: Individuals or organizations that rent artwork pieces, influencing the outgoing flow of rented artwork pieces and the incoming flow of rental fees and newly created artworks.
- Art owners or art galleries: Individuals or organizations that own the artwork inventory available for rent, influencing the incoming flow of rental fees and the outgoing flow of artwork pieces.

**Interactions**

- Incoming flows: Art renters pay rental fees to art owners and art galleries to rent artwork pieces from the inventory.
- Outgoing flows: Art owners release artwork pieces from the inventory to art renters in exchange for rental fees.
- Feedback loops: The demand for certain types of artwork pieces may increase or decrease over time, affecting their rental prices and the frequency of their rental, including the rate of supply and demand of artworks.

The factors that influence the price of renting art products can vary depending on the specific market and context (Grant, 2010). However, some common factors that may impact the price of renting art include:

1. Artist popularity and demand: The popularity and demand for specific artists and their work can significantly impact the price of renting their art pieces. Established artists with a strong following are likely to have higher rental prices compared to emerging artists.
2. Art medium and quality: The medium and quality of the artwork can also impact rental prices. For example, a high-quality original painting is likely to be more expensive to rent than a print or reproduction.
3. Rental duration: The length of time the art piece will be rented can also impact the price. Longer rental periods may come with discounted prices compared to shorter rental periods.
4. Artwork size: Larger artwork pieces may be more expensive to rent compared to smaller pieces, as they may require more resources and space to transport and install.
5. Availability and location: The availability of art pieces and location can also impact rental prices. Art pieces that are in high demand or in limited supply may have higher rental prices. Additionally, art pieces that are rented for display in high-traffic areas, such as museums or galleries, may have higher rental prices compared to those rented for private events.

As art rental market can be influenced by various factors, rental prices may fluctuate based on the supply and demand of specific artists and art pieces, as well as the specific context of the rental agreement.

It is possible for any market to reach a point of a price bubble, including the art rental market. In the art rental market, the value of artworks is subjective and can be influenced by factors such as trends, popularity, and scarcity. If there is a sudden increase in demand for a particular artist or style, it could lead to a rise in prices that is not necessarily supported by the fundamental value of the artworks. This could potentially lead to a price bubble if the demand for artworks continues to rise without a corresponding increase in their underlying value. However, it is important to note that the art rental market is relatively niche, and its size and liquidity are not comparable to larger markets such as stocks or real estate, which are more prone to price bubbles.

There are behavioural decision heuristics (Kahneman, 2003; Kahneman & Tversky, 1979) that are related to reputation on the art renting market. Such heuristics could lead potential renters to overvalue the reputation of a well-known artist or art rental company that is easily recognizable, while undervaluing lesser-known artists or companies.

A decision heuristic (Bobadilla Suarez, 2017) that is applicable to reputation in the art renting market is the tendency to judge someone or something positively based on available information. In the context of the art renting market, a company or artist that is well-known for producing high-quality artwork may benefit from the halo effect, as potential renters may assume that all of their artwork is of a high standard.

Another heuristic that is relevant to reputation on the art renting market is the 'confirmation bias' (Charness & Dave, 2017). This is the tendency to seek out information that confirms one's pre-existing beliefs or biases, while ignoring information that contradicts them. In the context of the art renting market, this could lead potential renters to focus on positive reviews or endorsements of a particular artist or rental company, while ignoring negative reviews or information about their reputation. Behavioural decision heuristics related to reputation can play a significant role in shaping prices and demand in the art renting market, as potential renters rely on their perceptions of an artist or rental company's reputation to inform their decision making.

Reputation connection to social status of the art renters can influence the perceived value of the artwork and the decision-making process of potential renters. Renters may be more inclined to rent an artwork from a reputable artist or gallery, as it can enhance their own social status and reputation, as individuals may want to rent artwork that aligns with their personal image or the image they wish to project to others.

However, it is important to note that other factors such as the quality and uniqueness of the artwork, the rental price, and the rental agreement terms may also play a significant role in the decision-making process. Ultimately, the importance of reputation and social status may vary depending on the individual renter and their specific motivations for renting artwork.

Simulation modelling is a common method used in economics to study market dynamics and can be applied to various markets, including the art rental market. One possible way to simulate the art rental market is by developing an agent-based model, where agents (e.g. renters, art dealers, galleries) are modelled with certain decision rules and interact with each other in a simulated market environment. For example, agents could be programmed to consider factors such as the reputation of the artist or gallery, the rental price, and the uniqueness of the artwork when making rental decisions.

The model could be calibrated using real-world data on art rental transactions and then used to explore how changes in various factors (e.g. economic conditions, art market trends and other) may impact the art rental market. This type of simulation modelling can provide insights into market behaviour and potentially inform strategy decisions related to the art rental market.

However, it is important to remind that simulation modelling is a complex process that requires careful consideration of the assumptions made and data used, and its results should be interpreted in relation to research objectives and system boundaries.

Figure 8.7 presents a simple agent interaction map (AiM) and Figure 8.8 presents a simple resource agent map (RAM) for the renting market. The price for renting a piece of art (painting, sculpture, graphics print, or other) is a function of art supply and art renting demand, including art attractiveness level and time delay for art renters' reaction to changes in the art rental prices (Fig. 8.9).

**Main Resource Stocks in the Art Renting System**

- Stock of art produced: This stock represents the total amount of artwork produced by artists at a given time. The rate of change of this stock depends on the production rate of artists.
- Stock of artwork acquired in galleries and offered for rent: This stock represents the artwork that galleries have acquired from artists and are offering for rent to potential renters. The rate of change of this stock depends on the acquisition rate of galleries and the rental rate of renters.
- Stock of artwork rented: This stock represents the artwork that has been rented by renters from art galleries. The rate of change of this stock depends on the rental rate of renters and the return rate of rented artwork.

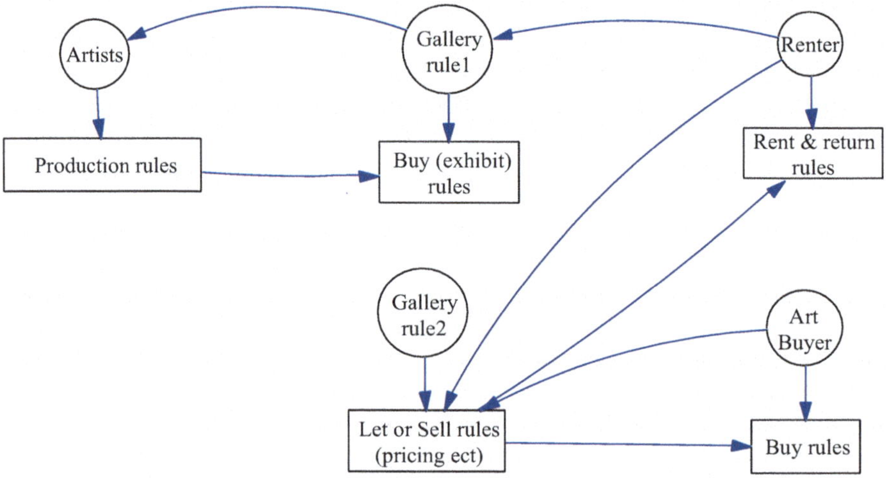


**Fig. 8.7** Agent Interaction map (AiM) involving main agents in the art renting system and their decision rules

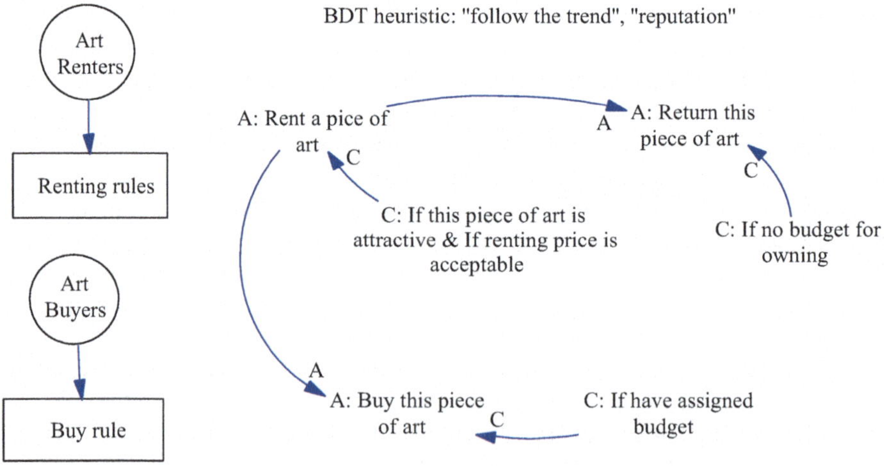


**Fig. 8.8** Agent behaviour map (AbM) involving decision rues of art renters and art buyers

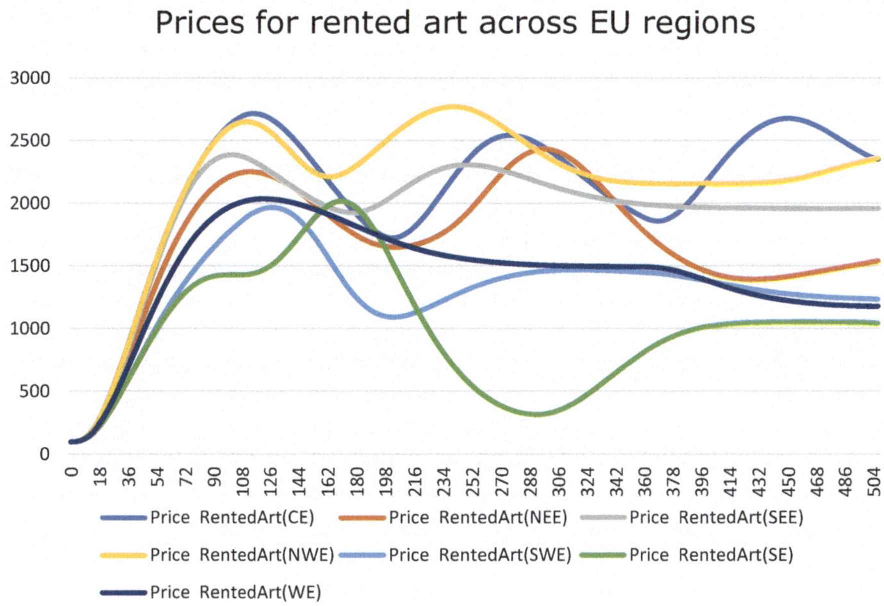


**Fig. 8.9** Prices of rented artwork and their evolution across different EU regions

- Stock of art returned: This stock represents the artwork that has been returned by renters to art galleries. The level of change of this stock depends on the return rate of rented artwork.
- Stock of art bought: This stock represents the artwork that has been bought by buyers from artists or art galleries. The rate of change of this stock depends on the buying rate of buyers.

**Main Agents**

- Artists agents: These agents produce artwork and supply it to galleries. The production rate of artists influences the rate of change of the stock of art produced.
- Galleries agents: These agents acquire artwork from artists and offer it for rent to potential renters. The acquisition rate of galleries influences the rate of change of the stock of artwork acquired in galleries and offered for rent. The rental rate of galleries influences the rate of change of the stock of artwork rented. The return rate of rented artwork is influenced by the ability of galleries to manage the rental process and the quality of the artwork.
- Renters agents: These agents rent artwork from galleries and return it after a certain period of time. The rental rate of renters influences the rate of change of the stock of artwork rented. The return rate of rented artwork influences the rate of change of the stock of art returned. The buying rate of renters influences the rate of change of the stock of art bought.

In this system, the rate of change of each resource stock depends on the decision pattern of the different agents and the resource flows they influence. For example, if galleries are acquiring artwork at a faster rate than renters are renting it, the stock of artwork acquired in galleries and offered for rent will increase, while the stock of artwork rented will decrease. If artists are producing artwork at a slower rate than buyers are buying it, the stock of art produced will decrease, while the stock of art bought will increase.

This resource agent systems approach can be used to simulate the dynamics of the art rental market and to study the effects of different policies or decisions on the stocks and flows of artwork resources.

If some renters agents decide to become buyers, this would lead to a decrease in the stock of artwork available for rent and an increase in the stock of artwork bought. This could potentially lead to an increase in the price of artwork, as the demand for artwork for purchase increases and the supply of artwork for rent decreases. It could also lead to a decrease in the rental income of galleries, as they have less artwork available for rent. The artists agents may benefit from this shift, as the increased demand for artwork for purchase may lead to higher prices for their artwork. However, it could also lead to a decrease in the demand for their artwork to be rented, as renters agents shift towards becoming buyers agents. This shift in behaviour could have significant impacts on the dynamics of the art market.

If the rental market for artwork includes different regions within a country, or a group of countries, then there may be additional factors that can influence the dynamics of the system. For example, the demand for certain types of artworks may vary depending on the region or country, which can affect the stock of artwork produced and acquired in galleries. The rates of acquisition, rental, and return may also vary depending on the region or country, as well as the availability of galleries and renters agents.

In addition, there may be regulatory and legal differences across different regions or countries that can affect the behaviour of artists, galleries, and renters agents. For instance, there may be different tax laws or regulations regarding the ownership and rental of artwork. These differences can influence the flow of artwork between different regions or countries and can affect the overall stock of artwork resources produced, acquired, rented, and bought.

Furthermore, cultural and social factors can also play an important role in the dynamics of the system. Different regions or countries may have different preferences and tastes in art, which can influence the demand for certain types of artworks. This can affect the behaviour of artists, galleries, and renters agents in terms of the types of artworks produced, acquired, rented, and bought. The dynamics of the rental market for artwork can be influenced by a range of factors, including regulatory and legal differences, cultural and social factors, and economic conditions across different regions or countries. A hybrid resource-agent simulation approach can be useful for understanding and exploring the complex interactions between these factors and their impact on the system.

In the presented simulation modelling structure, main influencing variables regarding the price of rented art are 'attractiveness' and 'reaction time to price change'.. 'Attractiveness' refers to how appealing an artwork is to potential renters. This can be influenced by various factors such as the artist's reputation, the quality of the artwork, rarity, and cultural significance. If an artwork is highly attractive, it may command a higher rental price than a less attractive one.

'Reaction time to price change' refers to how quickly renters respond to changes in the rental price of an artwork. If renters are slow to react to price changes, the rental market may be slow to adjust to changes in supply and demand, leading to potential imbalances in the market. Conversely, if renters are quick to react to price changes, the market may be more efficient in balancing supply and demand.

Together, these two variables can create a dynamic interplay between resources and agents in the rental market for art. For example, if an artwork is highly attractive, renters may be willing to pay a higher rental price for it. However, if the rental price is too high, some renters may choose to rent a less attractive artwork instead. This may lead to a decrease in demand for the highly attractive artwork, resulting in a decrease in its rental price. Similarly, if renters are slow to react to a decrease in the rental price of an artwork, the market may 'pro' oversupplied for some time, leading to a surplus of rental art inventory. Conversely, if renters are quick to react to a decrease in rental price, the market may adjust more quickly to changes in demand, leading to a more efficient allocation of rental artwork inventory.

There are several other important influencing variables that could affect the art rental market:

1. Quality of artwork: The quality of the artwork can influence the rental price. The higher the quality of the artwork, the higher the rental price can be.
2. Artist popularity: The popularity of the artist can also influence the rental price. The more popular the artist, the higher the rental price can be.
3. Economic conditions: Economic conditions can influence the rental market. In times of economic growth, the demand for art rental can increase, leading to higher rental prices. Conversely, in times of economic downturn, the demand for art rental can decrease, leading to lower rental prices.
4. Supply and demand: The supply and demand of artwork can also influence rental prices. If there is high demand for a particular piece of art and limited supply, the rental price can increase. On the other hand, if there is low demand for a piece of art and a high supply, the rental price can decrease.
5. Location: The location of the rental market can also play a role in determining rental prices. For example, if the rental market is located in a wealthy area with high demand for luxury goods, rental prices may be higher compared to a rental market in a less affluent area.
6. Art market trends: The current trends in the art market can also influence rental prices. For example, if a particular style of art becomes popular, the demand for that style of art can increase, leading to higher rental prices.

There might be other factors like some general constraints that may influence a person's decision to rent a piece of artwork:

- Budget: One of the primary constraints for art renters is budget. The rental fee for artwork can vary greatly depending on the size, artist, style, and condition of the piece. Art renters may have a budget in mind and look for pieces within that range.

- Location: The location of the art rental company or gallery may also be a constraint for some renters. They may want to rent artwork from a location that is easily accessible or convenient for them.
- Aesthetics: Renters may have specific preferences in terms of the style, medium, and genre of artwork they are interested in renting. They may also consider the overall look and feel of the piece, as well as how it complements their existing decor.
- Purpose: The purpose for which the art will be rented can also be a constraint. Some renters may be looking for artwork to display in their home, while others may be interested in renting pieces for a special event or exhibition.
- Duration: The length of time the artwork will be rented for is also a constraint. Some art rental companies may have minimum or maximum rental periods that renters need to adhere to.
- Availability: Renters may also be constrained by the availability of the artwork they are interested in. Some pieces may be in high demand and therefore difficult to rent, while others may only be available for a limited time.

Figures 8.10 and 8.11 provide simulated examples regarding renting artwork prices and their evolution, artworks which are rented and those which are available for rent, including their distribution among different locations. The geographic locations included in the simulation are Central Europe (CE), North East Europe (NEE), South East Europe (SEE), North West Europe (NWE), South West Europe (SWE), South Europe (SE), and West Europe (WE).

The market simulation for the art renting model contains variables like available budget for renting, artwork and renters' location, rental duration time, available and rented artwork, and others.

The decision-making process of an art renter can influence the stock and flows of artwork produced, stored in galleries, rented, and returned or eventually bought in several ways:

1. Art production: The demand for certain styles or genres of artwork by art renters can influence the production of artwork by artists. If certain styles or genres of artwork are in high demand for rental, artists may be more likely to produce more of those types of artworks to meet that demand.
2. Gallery acquisition and storage of artwork: The decision-making process of art renters can also influence the stock of artwork stored in galleries. If certain artists and artworks are in high demand, galleries may would like to acquire more of those types of artworks.
3. Rental: The decision-making process of art renters can influence the flows of artwork that is rented.
4. Sales: Finally, the decision-making process of art renters can influence the eventual sale of artwork. If a renter becomes attached to a rented piece of artwork and have the budget to purchase it, that artwork may be taken out of the rental pool

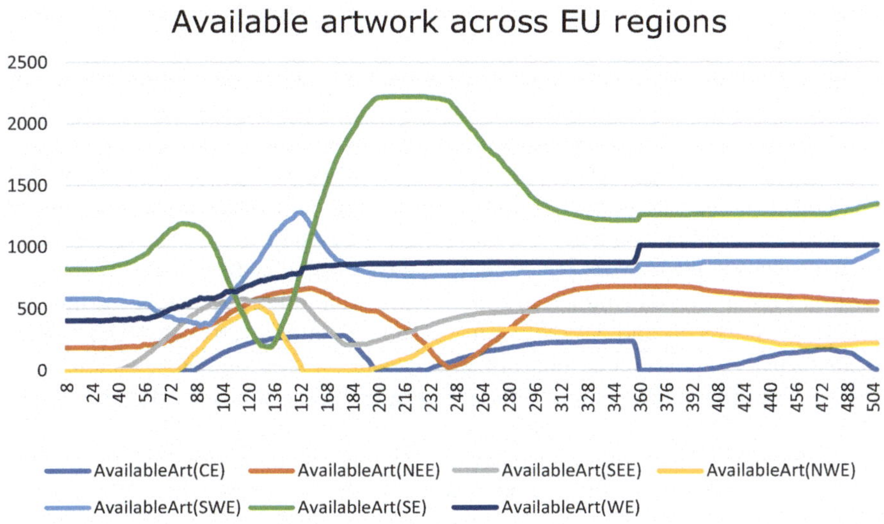


**Fig. 8.10** Available artwork for rent across different EU regions

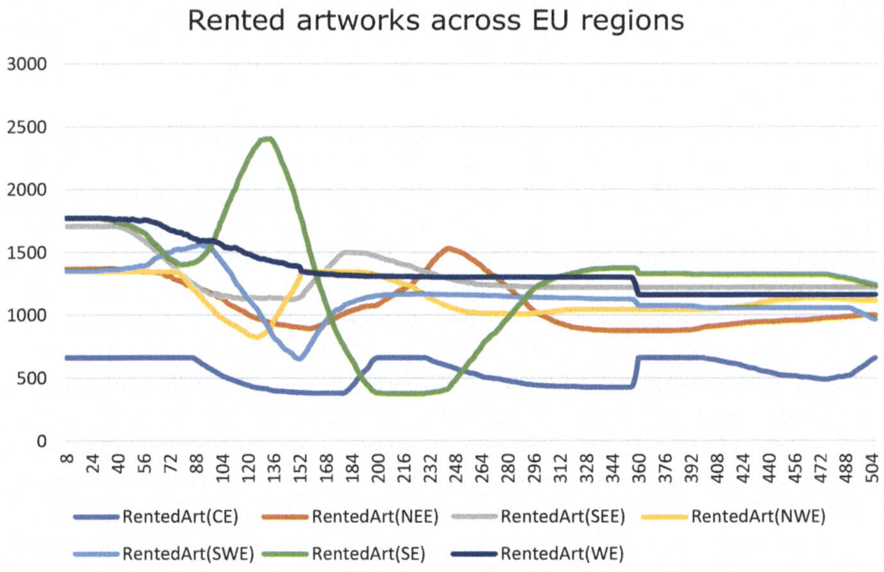


**Fig. 8.11** Rented artwork across different EU regions

and become part of a private collection, reducing the stock of available artwork for rental.

The decision-making process of art renters and art galleries can have a significant impact on the stock and flows of artwork produced, stored, rented, and eventually bought by galleries, artists, and collectors. By analysing the resource flows and agents behaviour, decision makers can better understand the specifics of this interesting market.

Figure 8.9 above exhibits the prices for rented art and their evolution across different EU regions. For example, the highest prices appeared in Central and North West Europe and the lowest are in South Europe, South West and West Europe.

This price dynamics follows the dynamics of artworks being offered on the market as exhibited on Fig. 8.10 (supply stocks of art resources) and rented artworks (demand for renting) as exhibited on Fig. 8.11, including other factors like renting agents' reaction to changes in the artwork prices, renters' location, and budgetary constraints.

The art rental market simulation experiments exhibit the outcome of the interactions (Figs. 8.9, 8.10 and 8.11) between system resources (artworks) and system agents (artists, renters, rental platforms or agencies, collectors, and potential customers). The three output graphs reflect over time the variations in art rental prices, volume of rented artworks, and available artworks for rental, providing insights for market demand, availability of resources, and price modulation analysis.

Figure 8.9 provides results on fluctuations in the art rental prices. These price evolutions could be attributed to various factors within the system, such as the scarcity or abundance of available artworks, prevailing demand, and the perceived value of artworks which might be influenced by artists' reputation. Agents, particularly artists and agencies, might inflate prices during periods of heightened demand (e.g. during prominent art exhibitions or cultural festivals), leveraging on the 'scarcity' heuristic, where the perceived value of artworks is elevated due to limited availability or elevated demand.

Figure 8.10 is illustrating available artworks for rent, which might oscillate based on seasonal artist production, inflow of new artists into the rental market, and the temporal dynamics of rented artworks (i.e. pieces being rented out and then re-entering the availability pool). The availability might also be impacted by external markets (art sales, exhibitions) and the internal dynamics of rental platforms, such as their purchasing, commissioning, and stocking policies. It might also be influenced by artists' production heuristics and strategies, which could be governed by their perceptions of market demand, economic viability, and creative inclinations.

Figure 8.11 exhibits the volume of rented artworks, which might mirror several market developments: changes in cultural consumption patterns, economic conditions, and social dynamics. For instance, an uptick in rented artworks could signify a prospering economy, an escalating appreciation or trend towards art consumption, or just an effective promotional strategy from rental platforms. Conversely, a downturn might reflect an economic recession, a shift in recreational or aesthetic preferences, or potentially more attractive alternative investment or consumption avenues for potential renters. Here, the 'follow the trend' heuristic might be in play, as renters may incline towards or divert from art rentals based on prevailing market or social trends.

Collectively, the combined output exhibited on these three figures represents the complexities of the art rental market from a system's perspective, taking account of the resource agent interrelations over time. Fluctuations in rental prices might directly impact the volume of rented and available artworks, governed by renter's response to price modulations and their consequent rental decisions. Furthermore, the volume of rented artworks and available art pieces for rent can have indirect countereffects through influencing rental prices and shaping artists' and agencies' stocking and pricing strategies.

These dynamics in the system are shaped and reshaped by the interrelations between market agents and resources, including economic, social, cultural, and individual factors. Using resource agent simulation approach therefore can support decision making and provide insights for exploring future trajectories and devising adaptive strategies the art rental market.

## References


Bello, J., & Rolfe, M. (2014). Is influence mightier than selection? Forging agreement in political discussion networks during a campaign. *Social Networks, 36*(1). https://doi.org/10.1016/j.socnet.2013.06.001

Bialynicka-Birula, J. (2018). Changes in the global art market. *Oeconomia Copernicana, 9*(4). https://doi.org/10.24136/oc.2018.034

Bobadilla Suarez, S. (2017). The interaction between task goals and the representation of choice options in decision-making. *Doctoral Thesis*, UCL (University College London).

Charness, G., & Dave, C. (2017). Confirmation bias with motivated beliefs. *Games and Economic Behavior, 104*. https://doi.org/10.1016/j.geb.2017.02.015

Clarke, H., Goodwin, M., & Whiteley, P. (2016). Leave was always in the Lead: Why the polls got the referendum result wrong. British Politics and Policy Blog, London School of Economics and Political Science, July 2016.

Grant, D. (2010). *The business of being an artist*. Simon and Schuster.

Hobolt, S. B., & Wittrock, J. (2011). The second-order election model revisited: An experimental test of vote choices in European Parliament elections. *Electoral Studies, 30*(1). https://doi.org/10.1016/j.electstud.2010.09.020

Huang, D. C., Liu, L. C., Deng, Y. Y., & Chen, C. L. (2023). An artwork rental system based on Blockchain technology. *Symmetry, 15*(2). https://doi.org/10.3390/sym15020341

Kahneman, D. (2003). A perspective on judgment and choice: Mapping bounded rationality. *American Psychologist, 58*(9), 697–720. https://doi.org/10.1037/0003-066X.58.9.697

Kahneman, D., & Tversky, A. (1979). Prospect theory: An analysis of decision under risk Daniel Kahneman; Amos Tversky. *Econometrica, 47*(2), 263–292. https://doi.org/10.1111/j.1536-7150.2011.00774.x

Kahneman, D., & Tversky, A. (1996). On the reality of cognitive illusions. *Psychological Review, 103*, 582–591. https://doi.org/10.1037/0033-295X.103.3.582

Khangeldieva, I. G. (2015). Traditional form in the non-traditional context, or the instruments of renting and leasing in fine arts. *Brukenthal Acta Musei, 10*(2).

Klamer, A., & Petrova, L. (2007). Financing the arts: The consequences of interaction among artists, financial support, and creativity motivation. *Journal of Arts Management Law and Society, 37*(3). https://doi.org/10.3200/JAML.37.3.245-256

Ostendorf, A. (2018). Brexit: Why Britain voted to leave the European Union. *Zeitschrift Für Außen- Und Sicherheitspolitik, 11*(2). https://doi.org/10.1007/s12399-018-0695-8

Rita, P., António, N., & Afonso, A. P. (2023). Social media discourse and voting decisions influence: Sentiment analysis in tweets during an electoral period. *Social Network Analysis and Mining, 13*(1). https://doi.org/10.1007/s13278-023-01048-1

Santoro, L. R., & Beck, P. A. (2016). Social networks and vote choice. The Oxford handbook of political networks, June.

Tilley, J., & Hobolt, S. B. (2023). Brexit as an identity: Political identities and policy norms. *Political Science and Politics, 56*(4). https://doi.org/10.1017/S1049096523000367

van Haaften-Schick, L., & Whitaker, A. (2022). From the Artist's contract to the blockchain ledger: New forms of artists' funding using equity and resale royalties. *Journal of Cultural Economics, 46*(2). https://doi.org/10.1007/s10824-022-09445-8

Watts, D. J., & Dodds, P. S. (2007). Influentials, networks, and public opinion formation. *Journal of Consumer Research, 34*(4), 441–458.

# Chapter 9
# Education Systems Efficiency and Social Networks

**Abstract** Interactions between resources and agents in education systems have effect on the system efficiency and quality. This chapter provides exploration of the counterproductive effects of a national regulation focused on budgeting schools based on the number of students enrolled, rather than on learning outcomes. The example shows that this can lead to decreased quality and integrity of the education processes and learning outcomes.

With respect to the factors and their effects on the education system integrity and quality, social networks play an important role too. The use of social networks in education can have both pros and cons. They can increase student engagement by providing a platform for collaboration and discussion. Also, social networks can increase access to educational resources beyond the traditional classroom, enabling students to learn from a diverse range of sources.

However, social networks can be a source of distraction, potentially reducing student focus and productivity. Social networks can be subject to bias and misinformation, which can influence student perceptions and attitudes. Also, they can raise concerns around student privacy and security and can be used as a platform for cyberbullying.

## 9.1 Introduction

Education has long been considered a key factor in economic development. Many countries invest heavily in education with the belief that a better-educated population will lead to a more productive workforce, greater innovation, and overall economic growth. However, despite these investments, some national education systems still fail to achieve their desired outcomes, and this can have negative impacts on economic development.

Several studies have explored the link between education and economic development, highlighting the role of education in developing human capital, increasing



R. Kazakov et al., *Understanding and Managing Socioeconomic Systems Behaviour*, Contributions to Management Science,
https://doi.org/10.1007/978-3-031-57057-5_9

productivity, and promoting innovation and economic development (Hanushek & Kimko, 2000; Hanushek & Wößmann, 2007; Goczek et al., 2021).

However, if the education system is inefficient, it can hinder economic development. Inefficient education systems can result in inadequate learning outcomes, low educational attainment levels, and inadequate human capital development. These factors can, in turn, result in a less-productive workforce, a lack of innovation, and decreased economic growth. A study by Hanushek and Woessmann (2021) found that differences in educational quality across countries can explain a substantial portion of the differences in economic growth rates.

Furthermore, inefficient education systems can exacerbate inequality and social exclusion. Poor-quality education may limit opportunities for disadvantaged groups, leading to a lack of social mobility and increased poverty. This, in turn, can lead to political instability and social unrest, which can further hinder economic development.

In conclusion, an inefficient national education system can have significant negative impacts on economic development. Investing in education is important, but it is equally important to ensure that the education system is efficient and effective in achieving its desired outcomes. Addressing the regulation causes of inefficiencies, such as inefficient budgeting rules, inadequate infrastructure, and insufficient performance criteria, is crucial for achieving better learning outcomes, higher levels of educational attainment, and ultimately, greater economic growth.

Key for the sustainability of the economic system is the sustainable education system, which ensures that the needed qualified individuals are adequately educated in order to support long term economic efficiency and high productivity in a country.

In an inefficient regulatory framework and institutional budgeting defined by the principle of 'quantity' rather than 'quality', and the lack of controlling mechanism regarding the latter, the system produces larger proportion of professionals with lower expertise than the proportion of the 'genuine' experts, this way eroding the overall economic efficiency and output (Carnoy, 1999; Maria Sandi, 1991).

Other important factors like favouritism, plagiarism, and compromised knowledge evaluation system, resulting in equalization between the higher performing and lower performing students further contribute to the overall inefficiency and undermine the national economic sustainability.

Both the inefficient educational and unsustainable economic systems lead to higher rate of demotivation among the genuinely skilled experts, higher demand for quality education abroad, and higher level of professional immigration, leaving even higher percentage of lower performing specialists in the country and higher level of economic unsustainability in the future.

## 9.2 Inefficient Educational Regulatory Framework

A national public education system, as represented on the resource agent map on Fig. 9.1, includes a stock for school ranking, a variable for higher marks and grading, a stock for the number of students, a stock for students' true expertise, a stock

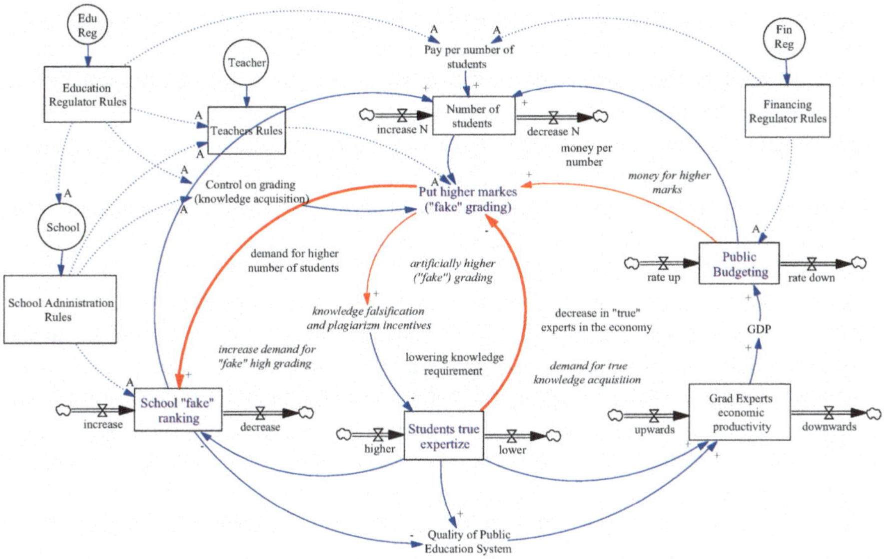


**Fig. 9.1** RAM of an inefficient national education system

of public budgeting, a stock for graduate experts' economic productivity. There are also agents like school administrators, education regulators, and financial regulators, which all have rules aligned to the inefficient principle of budgeting for the quantity (number of schools, rankings, number of students at school, number of higher marks) rather than quality of education and true expertise.

The stock of school ranking represents the perceived ranking of schools within the national education system. It can be influenced by factors such as funding, teacher qualifications, student test scores, and various incentives. However, it may not accurately reflect the quality of education being provided by each school, since this stock is encouraging a focus on quantity rather than on quality.

The variable for marks and grading represents the grades and test scores given to students within the education system. It can be influenced by factors such as teacher biases, the pressure to improve school rankings, and cheating, and the level of plagiarism tolerance. However, it may not accurately reflect the true expertise of students.

The stock of the number of students represents the number of students enrolled in the education system. It can be influenced by factors such as population growth, school funding, and rankings.

The stock of students' true expertise represents the actual knowledge and skills that students acquire through their education. It can be influenced by factors such as teaching quality, curriculum design, and student motivation.

The stock of public budgeting represents the amount of public funding allocated to the national education system. It can be influenced by factors such as regulation priorities, economic conditions, and competing demands for public resources.

The stock of graduate experts' economic productivity represents the economic productivity of graduates from the national education system. It can be influenced by factors such as the quality of education received, the level of efficient public budgeting, and the quality of the education system.

There are several agents groups involved in the national education system, including school administrators, education regulators, and financial regulators. Each of these agent's groups has different rules and decision-making heuristics that influence the stocks and flows within the system (Kahneman & Tversky, 1982; Vevere & Mons, 2020).

School administrators are primarily concerned with improving their school's ranking and increasing enrolment. They may prioritize activities such as public funding acquisition, advertising, and improving student scores to achieve these goals.

Education regulators are responsible for setting standards and monitoring compliance within the education system. They may prioritize activities such as developing curricula, assessing school performance, and implementing policies to increase knowledge transfer and education efficiency.

Financial regulators oversee the allocation of public funds to the education system. They may prioritize activities such as developing effective criteria regarding public funding, conducting audits, enforcing accountability measures, and ensuring that public funds are being used efficiently.

However, these agents may be influenced by incentives that prioritize quantity over quality. For example, school administrators may be incentivized to increase enrolment and improve test scores to receive more funding, even if this does not result in better education outcomes for students. Education regulators may be incentivized to show improvements in school rankings or test scores to demonstrate their effectiveness, even if these improvements are not genuine, because financial regulators allocate more funds to schools with higher enrolments or better rankings (no matter true or false), even if these schools are not providing high-quality education.

The stocks and flows within a national education system are influenced by a complex set of factors, including funding, rankings, scores, and true student expertise. The agents involved in the system may be incentivized to prioritize quantity over quality, which can lead to inefficiencies and a lack of true expertise among students.

## 9.3 Need for a Change

The system described on Fig. 9.1 highlights a departure from educational integrity and quality due to the systemic counter-effective rules and incentives in place. These inefficiencies are connected to practices that deviate from the intended purpose of education, which is the development of student knowledge and critical thinking skills.

The map indicates that teachers are incentivized to inflate grades because their compensation is tied to student performance and school rankings. This creates a situation where the actual assessment of student abilities is compromised in favour of better apparent performance. As a result, educational standards are at risk as the drive for higher rankings and student numbers leads to 'false' grading—grades that do not accurately reflect student learning or capabilities.

This grade inflation has a cascading effect on student competence. Graduates may leave the education system with high grades but without the corresponding expertise and knowledge. This discrepancy can result in a workforce that lacks genuine qualifications, undermining the economy's need for skilled professionals and experts. This leads to a decrease in the number of true experts contributing to the economy, which would adversely affect national productivity and economic competitiveness.

Additionally, the map outlines a problematic feedback loop involving education regulators, who adjust public funding based on student numbers, potentially encouraging the perpetuation of these corrupt practices. If funding is linked to the same performance metrics that could be manipulated, it can lead to a decline in the quality of public education. Such regulatory policies do not address the underlying issues of grade inflation and may inadvertently finance the maintenance of an inefficient system.

The interconnected nature of the system's agents: teachers, school administrators, and regulators create a systemic issue where the 'compromised' educational quality is self-reinforcing. Without significant changes to this system, the cycle is likely to continue. The long-term consequences of such a system could be severe, with an education system that fails to produce a capable and innovative workforce, ultimately hampering the nation's economic growth and development.

To rectify these issues, systemic reforms are required. These should aim to realign incentives with the true value of education, ensuring that student learning and development are at the forefront of educational practices. Additionally, safeguards against the eventual manipulation of performance metrics need to be established to preserve the integrity of the education system.

The agent behaviour rule map depicted on Fig. 9.2 presents the decision-making routine for a 'teacher agent' within this inefficient system. The diagram is segmented into two primary decision paths based on whether cheating and plagiarism are allowed (A: Allow cheating and plagiarism) or not allowed (A: Do not allow cheating and plagiarism). The actions (A:) and conditions (C:) inform the agent-based rules that simulates the decisions of a teacher based on various incentives and pressures. Here is an analysis of the depicted rules:

1. Allow cheating and plagiarism path (left side)

    - Teachers allow such behaviour if there is no proper control on education quality.
    - If this will increase teacher's personal, financial, or school reputation benefit, through better apparent performance metrics.
    - Put higher (not real) marks, artificially inflating grades.
    - If this will increase school ranking score ('not real' reputation), resulting in a higher number of students, resulting in higher public financing. The condition

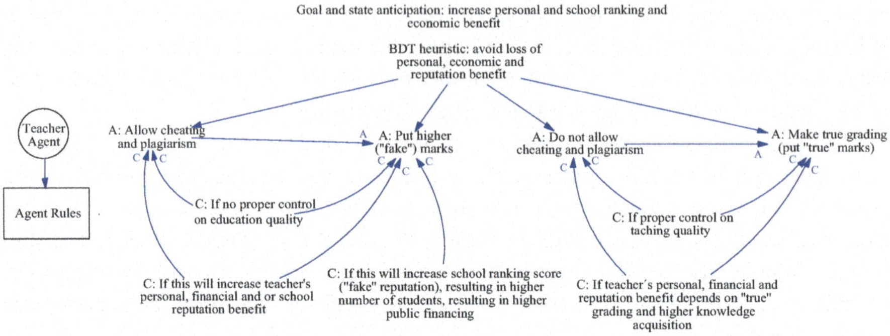


**Fig. 9.2** AbM for teachers

here implies a causal relationship between higher marks, improved school ranking, perceived reputation, increased student enrolment, and ultimately more public funding.

2. Do not allow cheating and plagiarism path (right side)

   - Do not allow cheating and plagiarism behaviour:
   - If proper control on teaching quality. This condition points to a commitment to high educational standards and integrity if there is proper control.
   - If teacher's personal, financial, and reputation benefit depends on 'true' grading and higher knowledge acquisition. The expected outcome is that genuine grading and actual learning will positively affect the teacher's personal and financial situation and authentic reputation.
   - Make true grading (put 'true' marks), honestly reflecting actual student performance.
   - If this is translated into better learning outcomes and enhance the teacher's personal, reputational, and financial benefits.

The rule map implies a decision-making process influenced by both ethical considerations and pragmatic outcomes. The 'if-then' structure indicates that the teacher agent's actions are contingent on certain conditions being met. This approach highlights the complexities of educational decision making, where actions are not only based on immediate consequences but also on broader implications for personal, financial, and institutional reputation.

The guiding goal and behavioural decision heuristics for the 'teacher agent' in the provided rule map appear to be centred around balancing personal, financial, and reputational benefits against the quality of education provided. The agent seems to weigh actions based on a heuristic that prioritizes decisions that could lead to personal gain or prevent loss. This can be seen in actions such as allowing cheating to inflate grades and subsequently improve school rankings and financial inflow.

Decisions are also influenced by the heuristic of maintaining or enhancing reputation. The agent assesses the potential impact of actions on the perceived quality and standing of the school and, by extension, its own reputation within the educational ecosystem.

The agent's behaviour reflects an approach, where actions are evaluated based on their outcomes, such as the potential increase in school rankings and the associated financial benefits. There is an underlying tension between the utilitarian goals and the ethical imperative of providing quality education. The agent is faced with the condition of maintaining educational integrity while also considering the potential benefits of actions that may compromise this integrity.

On the other side of the decision tree, if there is a proper control for not allowing cheating and ensuring true grading, the long-term benefits of genuine knowledge acquisition and the authentic development of student capabilities, can ensure sustainable personal and school reputation benefits.

Both paths include a risk aversion heuristic, where the agent aims to avoid actions that could lead to a loss of reputation or financial standing.

Figure 9.3 outlines a rule map for an 'education regulator agent'. This rule map is simpler than the previous one for the 'teacher agent' and presents the decision-making process concerning public funding adjustments based on student numbers.

The overarching goal stated here is 'equal access to public funding following the number of students at school'. This suggests a principle of equity in funding allocation, where funds are distributed based on the size of the students at school, likely to ensure that resources are matched to needs.

Main heuristic here is avoidance the funding of 'fake' schools, indicating a concern with ensuring that public funds are spent on legitimate educational activities, adjusting funding based on fluctuations in the student numbers: increasing funding if the student number at school increases and decreasing funding if the student number decreases.

The diagram conveys a simplified feedback loop where the regulator's actions are contingent on changes in student numbers, aiming to align funding with educational

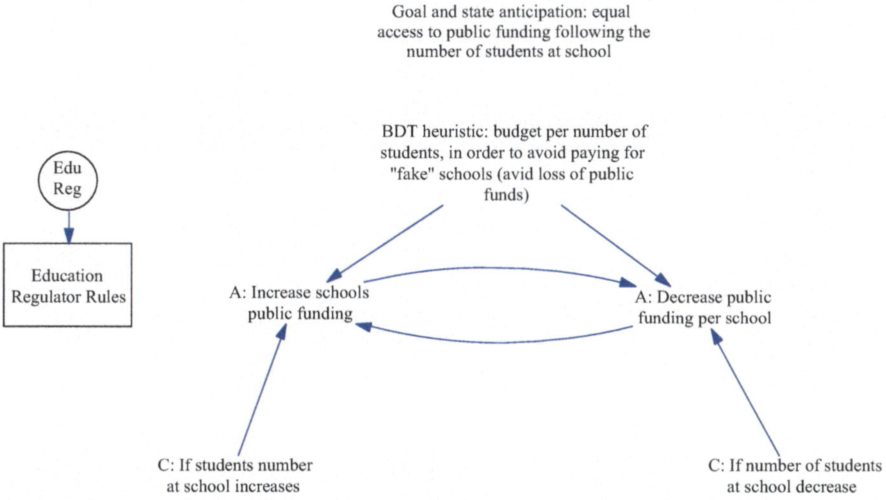


**Fig. 9.3** AbM for education regulators

demand. However, such approach to funding allocation takes account only of quantity and does not consider quality of education.

The agent behavioural rule map for school directors on Fig. 9.4 outlines a singular action and multiple conditions that influence this action.

The stated goal for the school is to achieve 'increased economic and reputational benefit by attracting a higher number of students each year'. This goal suggests that the school administration is focused on growth in both financial terms and prestige, with the latter perceived as a means to the former.

The BDT heuristic here includes 'follow competition' and 'avoid loss of budgeting and reputation'. This implies that the school administration is sensitive to the actions of other schools competing for public image and increasing funding.

School directors pay teachers' salary and bonus based on grades and school ranking (not on quality) which aims at increasing students number and of course the public funding. This makes teachers incentivised to inflate grades and the school's ranking. This reflects an inefficient results-oriented approach rather than one focused on the intrinsic quality of education.

Such behaviour could indeed have counterproductive effects. This incentive structure may inadvertently encourage behaviour that compromises educational integrity for the sake of perceived short-term gains. Teachers may prioritize grade outcomes over genuine learning, leading to grade inflation and a reduction in the rigor and quality of education. When rewards are tied to grades and rankings rather than the quality of teaching, teachers' incentives may become misaligned with educational best practices, focusing instead on whatever maximizes the metrics linked to their compensation.

Although inflated grades may boost school rankings and attract more students initially, in the long term, the students may be ill-prepared for further education or the workforce, potentially damaging the school's reputation and students' prospects.

Also, parents and students may lose trust in the school system. Students might not be adequately supported in their learning, which could hinder their intellectual

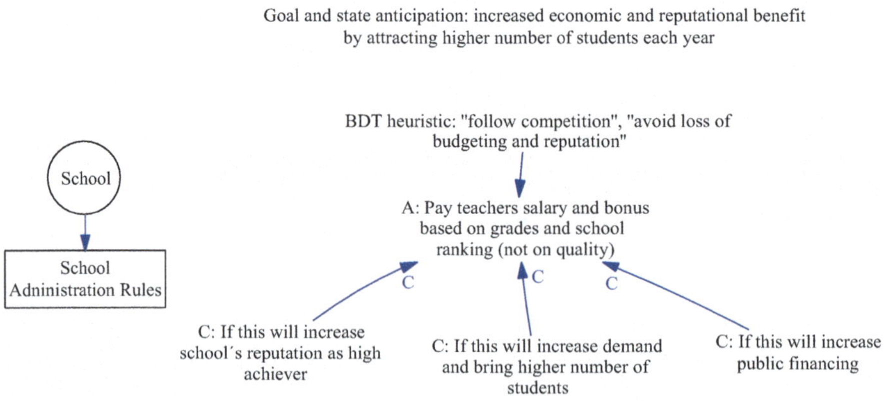


**Fig. 9.4** AbM for school administrators

growth, create tension between industrious learners and free riders. Teachers may be more likely to inflate grades rewarding students who are not performing well, widening the gap between high-performing and poor students.

This rule may ultimately undermine the very objectives it seeks to promote, such as school reputation and the provision of high-quality education. It highlights a common dilemma in performance management where the choice of metrics and rewards can have unintended consequences that are detrimental to the organization's long-term success and ethical standing.

The inefficient regulatory frame leads to a reinforcing feedback loop cycle, leading to increasing the number of low performing experts in the economic system. That kind of behaviour can keep going due to the lack of corrective internal controlling behaviour among teachers, lack of external regulatory control over true knowledge acquisition, that is, true grading, and a counterproductive 'pay per number' and 'pay per grade' award scheme.

Change can occur if external true knowledge control is implemented, that is, by 'pay per expertise' replacing the inefficient award scheme above and prioritizing demand for quality over demand for quantity. Plagiarism, favouritism, and agency related behaviour among educators and school administrators can certainly be factors that contribute to an inefficient education system. These issues can undermine the quality of education and limit opportunities for students, ultimately hindering economic development. Plagiarism also can result in inadequate learning outcomes and a lack of critical thinking skills among students, as students may simply copy and paste information rather than engaging with the material and developing their own ideas. This can lead to a less-productive workforce and decreased innovation, both of which are crucial for economic growth. Favouritism, related to inflating the results of poor performers and free riders, can lead to unequal treatment of students, exacerbating inequality and demotivating high performing students.

While all the above factors can contribute factors to an inefficient education system, there may be other factors at play as well, such as inadequate infrastructure, insufficient funding, and a lack of teacher training. Addressing these issues and promoting transparency, accountability, and ethical behaviour among educators and administrators is crucial for improving the quality and efficiency of national education systems.

When teachers tolerate plagiarism among students, it can have several negative effects on the students, the education system, and society as a whole. Here are some potential effects:

1. Diminished learning outcomes: Tolerating plagiarism deprives students of the opportunity to engage with the material and develop their own ideas. This can lead to a lack of critical thinking skills and a decreased ability to learn and apply new knowledge.
2. Reduced motivation: When students see that plagiarism is accepted or even encouraged by their teachers, it can reduce their motivation to learn and put effort into their assignments. This can lead to a lack of engagement in the classroom and reduced educational attainment levels.

3. Weakened academic integrity: Teachers who support plagiarism undermine the academic integrity of their institution and the broader education system. This can erode public trust in the education system and reduce the value of degrees and diplomas.
4. Negative impact on future careers: Plagiarism can negatively impact a student's future career prospects. If students do not develop the necessary skills and knowledge during their education, they may struggle in the workplace, leading to reduced productivity and economic growth.

If teachers are not holding students to high standards, this can result in a lower overall quality of education. This may benefit less industrious students who are not capable of meeting these standards, and create tension for more industrious students. If less industrious students are able to achieve similar outcomes as more industrious students without putting in the same level of effort, this can reduce the motivation of more industrious students to work hard and excel.

If less industrious students are being given similar opportunities and outcomes as more industrious students, this can perpetuate social and economic inequality. More industrious students may be denied opportunities based on merit, and this can lead to a society where success is determined by factors other than talent and effort.

The demotivation of more industrious students due to an inefficient education system can lead to a higher rate of migration to other countries where the education system is perceived to be better. When students are not engaged in their studies and not treated fairly by their teachers, they may lose interest in the national education system and seek out other opportunities elsewhere.

Furthermore, when parents of more industrious students see that their children are not being adequately educated and treated or given opportunities for growth and development, they may become disillusioned with the education system and seek out alternatives, such as private schools or even emigrating to another country.

Regulation can play an important role in ensuring the quality and effectiveness of the education system. By setting standards and enforcing compliance, regulations can help to prevent fraudulent practices and ensure that resources are being used effectively and efficiently.

However, if regulations are poorly designed or implemented, they can have unintended consequences that can contribute to inefficiencies and even fraud in teaching and administration practice. For example, as discussed in the previous paragraphs, if schools are budgeted based on quantity rather than quality of learning outcomes and results, this can incentivize schools to focus on enrolment numbers rather than educational outcomes. This can lead to manipulative or other inefficient practices in order to meet enrolment targets and secure funding, even if students are not receiving a high-quality education.

The role of the regulation in the education system must be carefully balanced to ensure that it promotes quality, while also preventing manipulation and inefficiencies. This requires ongoing monitoring and evaluation of regulatory policies and practices, as well as active engagement with stakeholders in the education community to ensure that regulations are meeting their intended objectives. For example, if there is insufficient oversight or accountability in the grading process, teachers or administrators may feel more comfortable manipulating grades in order to meet enrolment targets or other performance metrics. Similarly, if there is a lack of transparency or consistency in the grading process, it may be easier for teachers or administrators to engage in such practices.

Therefore, it is important for regulations to provide clear guidelines and standards for grading and assessment, and to establish mechanisms for oversight and accountability to ensure that grades are being assigned fairly and accurately. This can help to reduce the risk of fraudulent practices such as fake marking, and promote a more effective and efficient education system.

In regard to connections with the economic system, the effects of a poorly educated workforce can be significant. Education is an important driver of economic growth and development, as it helps to build the knowledge and skills needed for innovation, productivity, and competitiveness (Cai et al., 2020; Kong et al., 2022).

When specialists are poorly educated, they will not have the skills or knowledge needed to perform their jobs effectively. This can lead to lower productivity and quality of output, as well as higher rates of errors and inefficiencies. Poorly educated specialists may also be less innovative and creative, which can limit their ability to contribute to the development of new products, services, or processes.

In addition, a poorly educated workforce can limit the ability of firms and industries to compete in global markets. In today's knowledge-based economy, where the value of goods and services is increasingly tied to intellectual property and technological innovation, having a highly educated workforce is a critical advantage (Hanushek, 2016). Countries with better-educated populations tend to be more competitive and successful in global markets, while those with poorly educated populations may struggle to keep up.

Overall, investing in education is an important way to support economic growth and development. By providing people with the skills and knowledge needed to succeed in the workforce, education can help to increase productivity, innovation, and competitiveness, which can in turn drive economic growth and prosperity (Jahic & Pilav-Velic, 2021; Psacharopoulos & Patrinos, 2018; Sahnoun & Abdennadher, 2022).

Table 9.1 presents a brief comparison between several EU countries based on their education system quality and its links to their GDP. For example, Finland consistently ranks as one of the highest performing countries in education, with a well-funded and well-structured education system that prioritizes teacher training and equitable access to education. Finland's GDP per capita is also among the highest in Europe. Germany has a strong vocational education and training system that prepares students for specific careers and emphasizes practical experience. Germany's economy is also the largest in Europe, with a strong emphasis on manufacturing and exports. Sweden's education system places a strong emphasis on individualized learning and student-centred teaching, with a focus on creativity and innovation. Sweden has a high GDP per capita and a strong economy based on technology, research, and innovation.

On the opposite, Greece has struggled with an inefficient education system in recent years, with limited access to resources and inefficient regulation. This has

**Table 9.1** Education quality rankings and GDP per country

| Country | Education quality ranking | GDP per capita (EUR) |
|---|---|---|
| Finland | 1st out of 137 | €410,600 |
| Denmark | 2nd out of 137 | €510,500 |
| Sweden | 7th out of 137 | €51,300 |
| Belgium | 8th out of 137 | €46,700 |
| Germany | 11th out of 137 | €48,400 |
| Estonia | 13th out of 137 | €18,300 |
| Austria | 14th out of 137 | €54,700 |
| France | 15th out of 137 | €42,600 |
| United Kingdom | 18th out of 137 | €42,200 |
| Slovenia | 21st out of 137 | €27,600 |
| Ireland | 22nd out of 137 | €84,800 |
| Latvia | 24th out of 137 | €16,500 |
| Spain | 25th out of 137 | €31,300 |
| Portugal | 26th out of 137 | €24,1000 |
| Luxembourg | 210th out of 137 | €107,400 |
| Italy | 31st out of 137 | €36,400 |
| Czech Republic | 33rd out of 137 | €110,600 |
| Cyprus | 35th out of 137 | €30,100 |
| Poland | 36th out of 137 | €14,1000 |
| Lithuania | 37th out of 137 | €17,400 |
| Malta | 41st out of 137 | €28,400 |
| Hungary | 42nd out of 137 | €14,300 |
| Slovakia | 46th out of 137 | €17,700 |
| Greece | 410th out of 137 | €21,700 |
| Romania | 60th out of 137 | €11,500 |
| Bulgaria | 63rd out of 137 | €10,200 |

Source: Eurostat

been reflected in Greece's relatively low GDP per capita and struggling economy. Italy's education system has also been criticized for being overly bureaucratic and lacking in resources, which has contributed to high dropout rates and low achievement. Italy's economy is also struggling, with high unemployment and low growth rates. Spain's education system has undergone significant reforms in recent years, but still faces challenges in terms of resource allocation and equity. Spain's economy has also struggled in comparison with the first group of countries.

The national education system plays an important role in supplying the skilled workforce that is needed for the national economic system. The quality and accessibility of education, as well as the alignment of curriculum with employer needs, can impact the competitiveness and growth of the national economy.

There are several factors that can lead to an inefficient national education system. These include inadequate and insufficient funding leading to a lack of resources, outdated materials and equipment, and a shortage of qualified teachers. The quality of teachers can have a significant impact on the quality of education. Inefficient teacher training, low pay, and poor working conditions can lead to a lower morale and shortage of qualified teachers. An outdated curriculum that fails to keep pace with advances in technology, new research, and changes in society can result in graduates who lack the skills needed to compete in the global economy. Inequality in access to education can lead to disparities in academic performance, with some students receiving a subpar education due to factors such as income, race, ethnicity, or geographic location.

On the management side, a lack of accountability and oversight can lead to ineffective policies, wasteful spending, and poor outcomes for students. Too much bureaucracy can hinder the ability of schools and teachers to adapt to changing needs and requirements, leading to inefficiency and poor performance. A lack of integration between the education system and the national economic system can lead to graduates who lack the skills and knowledge needed to contribute to the country's economic growth and development. All these factors can lead to an inefficient national education system that fails to prepare students for the challenges of the modern world, negatively impacting not only the individuals but also the country's economic growth and development (Dickens et al., 2006). In regard to education quality, manipulative marking and compromised organizational morale are among the most important endogenous factors that can lead to an inefficient education system. These factors and their persistence are often supported by a counterproductive funding regulation, based on quantity rather than on quality. Such regulation provides incentives among schools, administrators, and teachers to compete for budgeting on the expense of the quality of the education practice.

## 9.4 The Role of Social Networks in the Education System

In respect to discussed system factors so far and their effects on the education system integrity and quality, social networks play an important role too.

The use of social networks in education can have both pros and cons when it comes to the quality of educational outcomes (Lim & Richardson, 2016). On one side, social networks can increase student engagement by providing a platform for collaboration, discussion, and peer feedback. Also, social networks can increase access to educational resources and expertise beyond the traditional classroom, enabling students to learn from a diverse range of sources. They can provide a flexible learning environment that allows students to learn at their own pace and on their own schedule, enabling personalized learning experiences and access to content and resources tailored to individual student needs and interests. In regard to teachers work, social networks can enable the development of innovative teaching methods and approaches that leverage the power of technology and social media.

However, social networks can be a source of distraction, potentially reducing student focus and productivity during class time. Social networks can be subject to bias and misinformation, which can influence student perceptions and attitudes towards certain topics and ideas. Also, they can raise concerns around student privacy and security, particularly when sensitive information is shared online, and can be used as a platform for cyberbullying, which can negatively impact student well-being and academic performance (Gok, 2016).

Another effect of the use of social networks can potentially lead to feelings of anxiety and insomnia, particularly if social media use is excessive or disruptive to sleep patterns (Tandon et al., 2020; Vernon et al., 2015). Research has found that excessive social media use can be associated with higher levels of anxiety, depression, and other mental health problems, particularly among younger populations. This may be due to a range of factors, such as social comparison, cyberbullying, and exposure to negative news and content. In addition, the blue light emitted by electronic devices such as smartphones and tablets can disrupt circadian rhythms and negatively impact sleep quality, leading to insomnia or other sleep-related problems.

The use of social networks also can potentially enhance the release of dopamine, which is a neurotransmitter associated with pleasure and reward (MACİT et al., 2018; Fareri et al., 2008). When we engage in activities that we find enjoyable or rewarding, such as receiving likes or positive feedback on social media, our brains release dopamine, which can reinforce the behaviour and motivate us to repeat it. Research has found that social media use can activate the same reward pathways in the brain as other pleasurable activities, such as eating or gambling. This may help to explain why social media can be so engaging and addictive for some people.

Educators and parents can take steps to mitigate the negative effects of social media use in education, such as setting limits on screen time, encouraging healthy sleep habits, promoting positive social interactions, and providing resources for mental health support. In addition, educators can also incorporate social media literacy and digital citizenship skills into their teaching, to help students navigate the online world responsibly and safely, promoting a balanced approach to social media use in education and by encouraging students to engage in offline activities that enhance their well-being and positive social connections (Vural, 2015).

In relation to learning, social networks can potentially support plagiarism and cheating. Social networks provide a platform for easy and quick access to vast amounts of information, including text, images, and videos. While this can be beneficial for learning and research, it also creates opportunities for plagiarism and cheating. Students can use social networks to copy and paste content from other sources or to purchase pre-written essays or papers. In addition, social networks can also be used to share answers to assignments or exams, or to communicate with others during assessments. The effects of social networks on plagiarism and cheating can vary depending on individual factors, such as academic integrity and personal values. In addition, educators can take steps to mitigate them using plagiarism detection software, and monitoring social media activity during assessments (Parks et al., 2018).

Another important influence of social networks is their effect on the learning attention span, which can vary depending on individual factors and the specific ways in which social networks are used. However, some research (Carstens et al., 2018; Paul et al., 2012) suggests that social networks can potentially have a negative impact on attention span, particularly if social media use is excessive or disruptive. Social networks are designed to be highly engaging and attention-grabbing, with features such as notifications, likes, and comments that can trigger a dopamine response and reinforce continued use. This can create a sense of 'digital distraction' that can make it difficult to focus on other tasks, such as studying or completing assignments. In addition, the constant flow of information and content on social networks can lead to 'information overload', which can make difficult to filter and process information effectively. This can result in a decreased ability to concentrate and retain information, which can negatively impact learning outcomes.

On the other side, social networks can have a positive effect on good mood through the sharing of cheerful and humorous content. Social networks provide a platform for people to connect and share content with others, including funny memes, videos, and jokes. This type of content can be entertaining and provide a source of humour and enjoyment, which can contribute to a positive mood. Furthermore, social networks can also provide opportunities for social support and connection, which can also have a positive impact on mood. Users can connect with others who share similar interests, experiences, and perspectives, and can receive emotional support and validation through likes, comments, and messages.

Social networks can have both positive and negative effects on group inclusion and exclusion, and these effects can in turn impact learning outcomes (Phillipson et al., 2017). On one side, social networks can enhance group inclusion by providing opportunities for collaboration and communication among students, particularly in online learning environments. Social networks can allow students to connect with each other outside of class, form study groups, and share resources and ideas. This can foster a sense of community and support, which can enhance motivation, engagement, and learning outcomes.

On the other, social networks can also contribute to group exclusion, particularly if they are used to create cliques or reinforce existing social hierarchies (Fox & Moreland, 2015) . This can lead to feelings of exclusion and isolation among certain students, which can negatively impact motivation, engagement, and learning outcomes. In addition, social networks can also perpetuate biases and stereotypes, which can contribute to group exclusion and undermine learning outcomes. For the above reasons, educators and instructional designers can take steps to promote a sense of community and inclusion in online learning environments, such as providing opportunities for collaborative learning, fostering respectful communication, and addressing biases and stereotypes.

## 9.5 Exploring System Effects Using Qualitative Modelling-Related Problem Structuring Approaches

Researchers can employ problem structuring approaches to explore important systems factors related to the effects of social networks on education. Using qualitative and quantitative simulation modelling, interactions among teachers and students and information flows can be modelled, accounting for the effects of social networks on the learning outcomes, including all the abovementioned interrelations.

A learning outcomes stock in such a simulation would represent the knowledge and skills of the students in the course, which would increase or decrease over time. The flow of knowledge and skills would be influenced by a number of factors, including the quality and frequency of interactions among students, the level of group inclusion or exclusion, and the quality of instructional design and support.

To simulate the effects of group inclusion and exclusion, a simulation study would account for the formation of cliques or subgroups. These groups would be formed based on shared interests, prior relationships, or other factors. The simulation model would track the interactions within and between these groups, and the impact of these interactions on learning outcomes.

The simulation structure would also account for the effects of instructional design and support on learning outcomes. For example, the simulation could include variables such as the quality of course materials and teachers engagement, the frequency of feedback and support from instructors, and the level of engagement and interaction required of students.

Such simulation modelling approach would provide insights into the complex interactions and feedback loops that occur in traditional classrooms while using social networks. By exploring the effects of group inclusion and exclusion, instructional design, teaching quality and support, and other factors on academic performance and student well-being, this simulation could help educators, policy-makers, and school administrators to gain insights and optimize their practices, and to facilitate learning outcomes, student well-being, and overall systems improvement.

An initial step in the modelling process is to draft a cognitive map of the system including important factors and variables and their interrelations (Fig. 9.5). Cognitive maps can be created following a conversational approach with students on their experience in relation to social networks effects on learning and education.

One of the most serious issues with the increasingly pervasive penetration of social networks into all spheres of life is that they can become powerful 'thieves' of a person's free time, which could be used for much more beneficial activities, related to learning and well-being. This is amplified by the need for communication between students, the easy access to social networks at any time of day or night, and the undeniable fact that this activity triggers the brain's reward system to release dopamine, the feel-good chemical, which everyone seeks at a subconscious level. The instinct, so deeply embedded in human perceptions, nudges one to steer clear of any discomfort, pain, and, if and when possible, any effort.

Adding to the known discovery from the study conducted by the University of Virginia and Harvard University (Wilson et al., 2010, 2014) that people would prefer physical pain over boredom due to having their mind disengaged, we can conclude that social networks have become extremely enticing due to providing means to engage people's minds with minimal effort (i.e., no special concentration required, allowing for multitasking, which in turn leads to other negative effects such as lower quality of study and work, more time spent on it), boredom is eliminated, dopamine is released into the brain, and this happens in an exceptionally short time. Besides, social networks often are not only a source of information but also provide entertainment through humour, and also appeal to the need for communication between

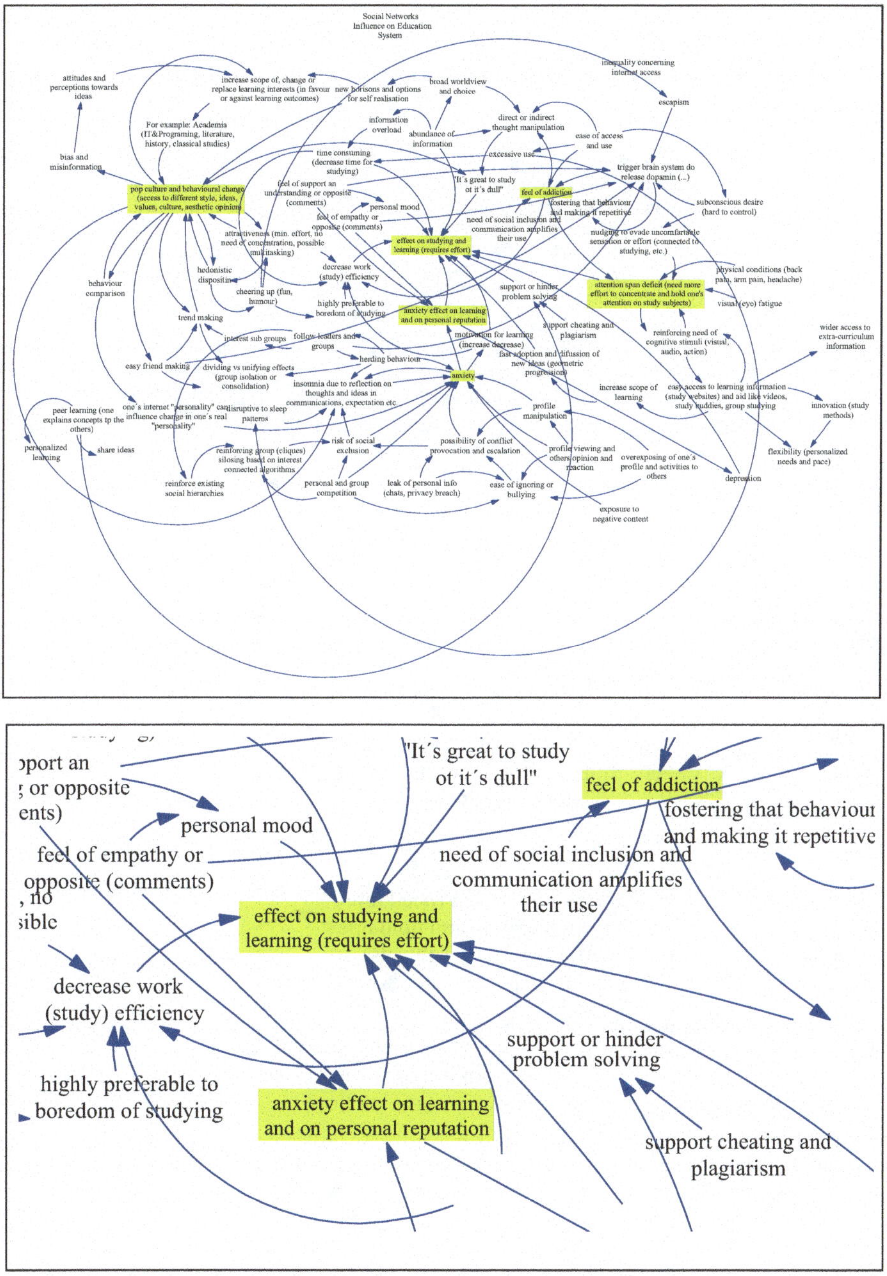


**(a)**

**Fig. 9.5** Cognitive map of social networks influence and effects on the educational system and study routines. (**a**) A map zoom-in on the studying and learning-related effects. (**b**) A map zoom-in on the ‘pop culture and behavioural change’-related effects. (**c**) A map zoom-in on the ‘attention span deficit’- related effects. (**d**) A map zoom-in on the ‘anxiety’-related effects

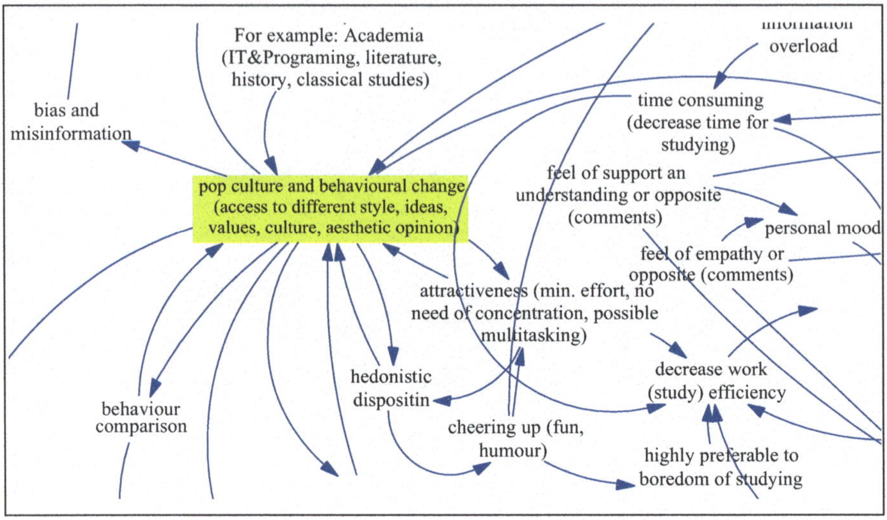


(b)

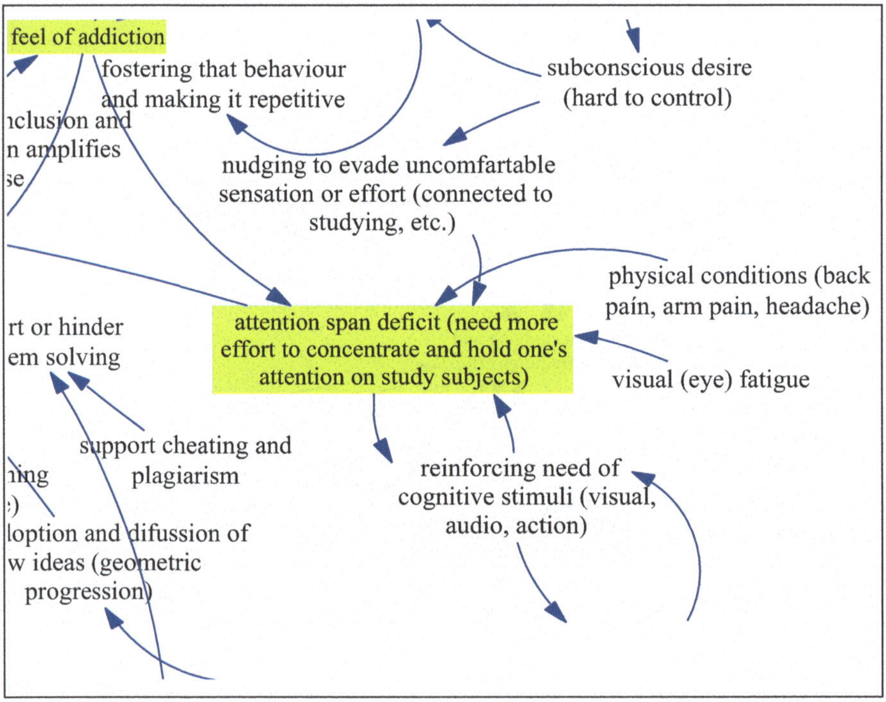


(c)

**Fig. 9.5** (continued)

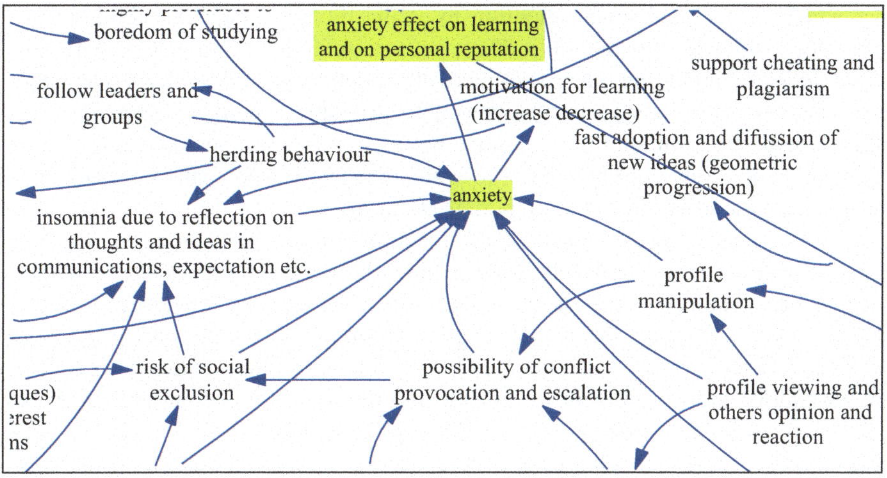


(d)

**Fig. 9.5** (continued)

people, where even shared feelings and the sensation of being understood and supported are achieved very easily.

The transience and easy accessibility of, for example, videos or texts that 'you can always stop and watch whenever you want'—inevitably and imperceptibly spirals into addiction. A person's interest in anything (from products to scientific fields, books, games, concepts, life philosophy) is nurtured, which leads (if the interest grows) to immersion and devoting more time to this interest than to education. This is also due to the enormous influence of social networks on pop culture and vice versa. It is an extremely important phenomenon, as it is foundational (although this may sound unnatural) to a person's life philosophy. The influence on a person's mental processes is not only exerted by influencers, but they are the most glaring example. The market strategy remains in the background—when people imitate others or simply follow their own desires and interests, the followers of these interests grow, and the notions themselves gain a broader scope of impact and build upon themselves, scaling up. The speed of this phenomenon is comparable to geometric progression due to the pervasiveness of social networks. However, this does not mean that a person cannot feel isolated even in a group, as the opposite also holds true. For more clarity, an example can be given with the social networks algorithms—they filter out what a particular person watches the most, likes or saves, or sends to others, or is sent to them. Hence, these algorithms lead to the narrowing of the range of topics, ideas, etc., that come to the forefront for a person, and accordingly to the formation of various subcultures in pop culture.

This, in turn, almost always divides people, instead of fulfilling the purpose of social networks, namely to unite. However, the expansion of the overwhelming information (speaking generally) is also observed constantly, with the tossing of new information and displacement of the old, and on the other hand, the removal of that which is not paid much attention to at the moment, happens continuously, simultaneously, and imperceptibly. Thus, people are divided into groups with 'different interests' including the type of media they consume, styles, ideas, and values they adhere to. This does not just happen on the principle of herd behavior, to be part of the crowd, the community. By giving voice to something, a person receives more information about it, making it easier to evaluate in every aspect, and the more fashionable it is, the more information there is about it.

When certain ideas are shown as true for a long time and by many people, one starts subconsciously to find truth in them, not only because 'others say so', but also because they themselves start to think that way. The opposite (stigmatization) also applies. This has always been the case, but through social networks, it finds an easier and faster expression. But because many, let us call them interests and ideas, are constantly and simultaneously thrown into this space, a person has easier and quicker access to many viewpoints and corresponding interests and ideas, aesthetic views. And because they change almost as imperceptibly and quickly as the algorithms change the main page, a person has the opportunity to scrutinize and evaluate many notions, to reject, accept, and consider them in incomparably less time, than the same would have taken a person before the age of digital media, which gives them a broader worldview and allows them to be true to oneself. Because, even though with influence (which can never be avoided), they now have the opportunity to choose from many more things, no matter that there will always be a group of people who will support them, as there will always be people who claim the opposite. This makes people accept much more openly and easily the truth about the opinion of others and not to take it so much into account, to be less influenced by the criticism of others.

But even if a person becomes strongly interested in something at the expense of their education, this is not inherently bad. Perhaps through more accessible information, one might understand what really interests them, in opposition to the traditional educational system, which is too limited in relation to taught subjects, methodologies, sub-disciplines. On another side, in the digital overload, one might reach a total lack of interest in everything, which can be mistaken for a state of depression or laziness. While this state can be caused by social networks, it can also be overcome through their use.

However, excessive use of social networks can lead to decreasing attention span. One feels harder to concentrate, meaning much more study related effort is required, which is why people turn even more to social media for support (may be consciously or unconsciously), for a feel of dopamine, resulting in a vicious cycle, and also to an eye fatigue. Time passes exceptionally quickly and imperceptibly in any social network. This could be a waste of time taking hours from the night, that are needed for a healthy sleep, which further adversely affects the learning process (Smith & Christakis, 2008).

Another effect is related to comparing oneself with others' activities with the presence of misinformation, leading to distressing feelings like worthlessness, envy (everyone pulling the other down so that they can be ahead or at least not fall behind), and the need for self-validation. The latter is achieved through, for example, multiple posts, changing one's lifestyle and personal information in order to match social norms, knowing that any part of this can be 'completely unintentionally' recorded and disclosed.

Through their profiles, one can manipulate others' opinions about a person and create an intended first impression, which not only can be untrue but burdens the profile holder to take account of the idea that everyone can see them (or if blocked, they can see and learn from someone else), thus increasing levels of anxiety. Different groups have different ways of perception and expression, and one never knows how something said or done will be received, being aware that one will always do and say something that will be perceived in an unfavourable way. A post that offends no one, but just does not follow the given unwritten rules within a social network group (which will change very often), can be harmful to a person's reputation. This applies even more so to group comments.

In addition, this is very easy for anyone to be thrown out of a social group, insulted, their personal information spread across a large part of the network. Because social networks are 'small worlds' and from one contact one can reach a person at the other end of the country, conversations never remain personal, as they can be recorded and photographed at any time and at the whim of any of the participants in them or even by people external to the group, and that too without owner's consent. This contributes to the feeling of anxiety and even to a feeling of paranoia and that one cannot rely on anyone or anything in the group. The feeling is that nothing remains personal, and an escape from this is merely impossible as in this overly large space of social networks, one can always meet with a contact of another contact. Communication misunderstandings and conflict situations are unavoidable, but without access to networks, one remains outside of the information field. An analogy can be made with a tribe—once rejected by the tribe or having chosen to leave it (the social network group, which here takes larger dimensions due to more easily accessible information), one no longer receives information about animal tracks for hunting, and does not have a 'pack' that can protect from others' attacks, even only because of its presence. So, there is a feeling of no choice, that one can always end up in a conflict situation and can be isolated unjustly, no matter which path of behaviour is taken. The question is to make it as slow and to a lesser extent possible, as social networks inevitably contribute to the acceleration and intensification of this conflict generation process. That is why many users live 'on pins and needles', and this way of going is too exhausting and having negative effects on the process of studying and learning at school.

Other education-related effects of social networks can be connected to the following:

- It is much easier to meet other people, start friendships that can become strong over time (or the opposite). One can easily understand who belongs to which social network group and weigh the chances of friendship or enmity, but on the other side this often can be also deceptive. This can support and hinder the education related integration process and inclusivity and contributes to the feeling of anxiety.

- Realising one's true interests can lead to genuine specialization. Easy and quick learning through videos, study buddies, easy to find information on every useful site, saves a lot of time and can be much more effective than traditional education.
- Opportunity for online education and practice, sometimes more effective, other times not.
- Easier connection and communication with friends, consequently more time together on the networks and feeling of more intimacy and empathy.
- Opportunity for escapism, networks as another world that can be freer or more limited one (as mentioned above).
- Intensified competition, which could be either a demotivating or a motivating factor.
- Easier reach for personal praise and showcasing of personal abilities, as social networks can be used as a platform for action, where more people can see one's contribution and can provide support, thus having motivating effects.
- When study information is provided by teachers only to the larger social group of students (including information about ways of learning, the lessons themselves, classes, etc.), students that are not included, would not have access to that information which will have effect on the quality of education. These students would not have access to all of the available information, to different teachers and students viewpoints and what to expect from the learning process and their engagement with school activities. For example, the choice of which specialisation to pursue would be more difficult, but at the same time one's choice would be less influenced by others' opinions and the subjective information.
- When there is a conflict situation, induced by the networks, students would not even want to go to school and attend classes, they would not have any desire to study or to listen to lessons in class.

All the above effects of social networks on the education system are presented in their complex interrelationships on the system cognitive map on Fig. 9.5.

Figure 9.5a presents a zoom-in of the cognitive map (Fig. 9.5) on the studying and learning objectives. It highlights a web of interconnected influences that affect a student's engagement and effectiveness in the learning process. The map suggests several key points:

- Personal mood is influenced by the feel of empathy and feel of support and understanding, which can significantly influence studying and learning. Positive personal mood may increase the efficiency of study, while a negative mood may decrease it. The need for social inclusion and communication amplifies certain behaviours. If a student feels that studying is seen positively by their social network, they may be more inclined to engage in it. Conversely, if the perception is negative, they may feel an aversion to studying or find it dull.
- The 'feel of addiction', also can impact study time and focus. This affects anxiety and both learning and personal reputation. Anxiety further can decrease work efficiency, making studying less preferable and more associated with boredom or effort. It can also stem from the pressure of maintaining a certain reputation within social networks.

- Social networks can either support or hinder problem solving, which is a crucial part of the learning process. Supportive networks may enhance a student's ability to tackle academic challenges, while unsupportive networks may lead to increased reliance on behaviours like cheating and plagiarism, especially when the latter becomes a behavioural norm.
- The cognitive map paints a complex picture of how social factors can significantly shape a student's learning experience. It emphasizes the importance of a supportive social environment and the potential for negative social influences to distract from or undermine educational endeavours. Furthermore, it shows the multifaceted nature of learning, which is not only cognitive but also emotional and social. Addressing these factors could be crucial in creating effective educational strategies and interventions to support students.

The zoomed-in section of the cognitive map on Fig. 9.5b focuses on the influence of pop culture and behavioural change on learning and studying behaviours (Ohiagu & Okorie, 2014). It illustrates the various ways that exposure to different styles, ideas, values, and aesthetic opinions within pop culture can impact a student's approach to education. This exposure can lead to changes in how individuals perceive and engage with academic material, possibly aligning or conflicting with traditional academic values.

However, bias and misinformation can arise from comparisons with pop culture behaviours. This can impact students by skewing their perceptions of what is normative or desirable behaviour in academic settings. A hedonistic disposition can reinforce the engagement with pop culture. This can make the effortful process of studying less attractive, particularly if pop culture celebrates minimal effort and multitasking.

Engagement with pop culture can be time consuming, reducing the time available for studying. Moreover, the vast amount of information available can lead to overload, potentially distracting students from their academic goals. Pop culture often promotes multitasking as an attractive way to operate, implying minimum effort with the possibility of more fun or engagement. This contrasts with the focused concentration typically required for effective studying.

Pop culture can have a significant impact on personal mood, providing cheer and humour, which can serve as a counterbalance to the boredom or monotony of studying. However, reliance on pop culture for mood enhancement can detract from the work (study) efficiency. Broader learning themes, including areas such as IT & programming, literature, history, and classical studies, potentially can have influences of pop culture. Changes in these areas may reflect broader cultural shifts. The influence of pop culture can modify the kind of support and understanding that students seek and receive (Lizardo, 2008; Rafique et al., 2022). For example, students might look for affirmation from their peers that aligns with the values and behaviours endorsed by pop culture. The interplay between the entertainment value of pop culture and the discipline required for academic success creates a dynamic tension that can affect educational outcomes.

Figure 9.5c of the cognitive map centres on the attention span and the various factors that can influence it in the context of studying and learning.

Repetitive social networks behaviours and engaging in certain activities can lead to a feel of 'addiction', affecting attention spans negatively. There are also subconscious predisposition that are hard to control, such as performing immediately gratifying activities rather than studying, to evade uncomfortable sensations or efforts associated with studying routines. This can be a significant contributor to an attention span deficit, as it encourages switching focus to less cognitively demanding tasks.

Physical discomfort, such as back pain, arm pain, headaches, or visual fatigue, is also a factor, emerging from the excessive engaging with social networks device applications that can significantly decrease the ability to focus and thus contribute to attention span deficit. This leads to a reinforcing need for cognitive stimuli, visual, audio, or action oriented, which further is contributing to the attention span deficit. This suggests that individuals may become accustomed to high levels of stimulation, making it difficult to focus on less stimulating tasks like studying.

In turn, the attention span deficit supports cheating and plagiarism, because these behaviours require less-sustained attention than genuine study and learning.

The cognitive map on Fig. 9.5d zooms in on the 'anxiety' and interrelated effects on various aspects of behaviour and learning, acting as both a product of various pressures and a catalyst for further challenges.

The map indicates that anxiety can either increase or decrease motivation and attention for learning. Anxiety is influenced also through herding behaviour, where individuals follow the actions of a group rather than making independent decisions. This could be due to the fear of social exclusion or the desire to be accepted, which can impact learning if the group's direction is not aligned with educational goals.

Anxiety can cause insomnia due to the over-reflection on thoughts, ideas, communications, and expectations. This can significantly impact an individual's ability to learn effectively due to decreased cognitive function from lack of sleep. The fear of being socially excluded can create anxiety, particularly in a learning environment where peer interaction and acceptance are important. This fear can lead to behaviour changes as individuals seek to conform to perceived group norms.

Anxiety could be related to situations where there's a possibility of conflict, provocation, and escalation, which can create a disruptive learning environment and potentially harm personal reputation. Anxiety can be exacerbated by the viewing of others' profiles and their opinions and reactions. This can lead to a constant state of comparison and heightened sensitivity to feedback, which can be counterproductive to learning. In an effort to manage or mitigate feelings of anxiety, especially those related to personal reputation, individuals may engage in profile manipulation. This refers to the alteration of one's online or public persona to influence others' perceptions. In addition, anxiety may lead to supporting cheating and plagiarism as coping mechanisms for dealing with the pressure to perform or achieve certain academic standards.

The 'anxiety effect on learning and on personal reputation' is being influenced by factors like 'anxiety', 'feel of empathy or opposite (comments)', 'feel of support and understanding or opposite (comments)'.

'Anxiety' can impact learning and personal reputation within the context of social networks influence on education and learning outcomes. 'Anxiety' factor can have a direct effect on a person's ability to learn. High levels of anxiety might lead to reduced concentration, memory problems, and difficulty grasping new concepts. 'Feel of empathy or opposite (comments)' factor is related to the emotional tone of comments and interactions on social networks, which can influence an individual's anxiety levels. Positive and empathetic comments might alleviate anxiety, while negative or hostile comments could exacerbate it. 'Feel of support and understanding or opposite (comments)' factor is similar to empathy, feeling supported and understood and can have a significant impact on anxiety levels. Positive interactions and supportive comments can create a sense of security, whereas negative or dismissive interactions might increase anxiety.

In addition, the following interrelations can be further explored. The emotional tone of comments can influence a person's perception of support and empathy. Positive and supportive comments might reduce anxiety, while negative comments might increase it. Anxiety can affect how a person interprets comments. Someone experiencing anxiety might be more sensitive to negative feedback and less receptive to positive comments. The collective effect of comments, whether empathetic and supportive or negative and dismissive, can shape an individual's overall experience on social networks, affecting their anxiety levels and, in turn, their learning process.

Although the map simplifies a complex emotional and psychological process, it provides a system perspective to understand how anxiety and social interactions might relate to learning outcomes.

Anxiety can be influenced by various factors related to online behaviour and interactions. For example, being exposed to negative or distressing content on social networks can increase anxiety levels and overall stress. Overthinking and reflecting on online interactions, combined with high expectations, can lead to insomnia and heightened anxiety. One's internet 'personality', which can influence change in one's real 'personality', is a behavioural factor which is related to how online behaviour and interactions can facilitate changes in real-world personality traits and generate anxiety over these changes. Another factor is related to personal and group competition. Competing for attention, recognition, or social status online can create anxiety and stress, especially in competitive environments. In addition, possibility of conflict provocation and escalation on social networks can create anxiety about confrontation and negative interactions. Other factors like profile manipulation, viewings and others' opinion, risk of social exclusion can produce concerns about how one's online identity is being manipulated or misrepresented, how others could react to one's profile changes and fear of online social groups tensions or exclusion. This can lead to anxiety and insecurity about one's social status and belonging.

In turn, the 'attention span deficit', or the difficulty in concentrating and maintaining focus, can be influenced by various factors related to online behaviour and cognitive processes. If individuals feel addicted to social media or online activities ('feel of addiction'), they might find it challenging to divert their attention away from these platforms, impacting their ability to focus on study subjects. The desire to avoid discomfort or effort can lead to distraction and reduced attention span, as individuals may turn to online activities to escape from tasks that require cognitive effort ('nudging to evade uncomfortable sensation or effort (connected to studying, etc.)').

'Physical conditions (back pain, arm pain, headache)' can divert attention away from studying and contribute to an attention span deficit. 'Reinforcing need of cognitive stimuli (visual, audio, action)', related to frequent exposure to highly stimulating content online can create a need for continuous cognitive stimulation, making it difficult to concentrate on less stimulating study subjects. 'Visual (eye) fatigue', related to prolonged use of screens and exposure to digital content can lead to visual discomfort, which can impact learning attention span and focus too.

The 'feel of addiction' and the 'reinforcing need of cognitive stimuli' can interact, as addictive behaviours can reinforce the need for constant cognitive engagement through online stimuli. 'Physical conditions' such as pain and discomfort can lead to a desire to escape or distract oneself, increasing the likelihood of seeking out online content. 'Visual (eye) fatigue' and 'physical conditions' can compound each other, further reducing the ability to focus and maintain attention.

The 'feel of addiction' represents how the perception of addiction to social networks can be influenced by various factors related to accessibility, social needs, and neurological processes. For example, 'ease of access and use' factor: the easier it is for individuals to access and use social networks, the more likely they might engage with them frequently, potentially contributing to a sense of addiction. The 'need for social inclusion and communication amplifies their use'. Social networks are mainly used to connect with others, and the desire for social interaction and inclusion can intensify the use of these platforms, possibly leading to addiction-like behaviours. Social networks and online interactions can trigger the release of dopamine, a neurotransmitter associated with pleasure and reward. This neurological response can contribute to addiction-like behaviours by reinforcing the desire to engage with these platforms repeatedly.

The ease of access and use can work synergistically with the neurological effects of dopamine release. Easy access encourages frequent engagement, while dopamine reinforces the pleasurable experience, potentially leading to addictive behaviours. The need for social inclusion and communication can enhance the psychological rewards derived from using social networks, further contributing to the sense of addiction. The neurological component, triggering dopamine release, can interact with both ease of access and social needs, making the platforms more appealing and reinforcing their use.

'Pop culture and behavioural change (access to different styles, ideas, values, culture, aesthetic opinion)' represent how exposure to pop culture and various online content can lead to behavioural change and influence individual perceptions of styles, ideas, values, and cultural aesthetics. 'Attractiveness (minimal effort, no need for concentration, possible multitasking)' factor is related to pop culture content, which often offers easy consumption, requiring minimal effort and allowing for multitasking. This accessibility can make it more appealing and contribute to its influence on behaviour. 'Behaviour comparison' factor is related to the process when individuals observe and compare behaviours and lifestyles depicted in pop culture content. This could potentially lead to behavioural changes and pop culture adoption to align with perceived norms.

'Academia (IT & Programming, literature, history, classical studies)' factor suggests that pop culture exposure can extend beyond entertainment and impact even academic interests, such as IT, programming, literature, history, and classical studies.

'Hedonistic disposition' factor is related to pop culture content which provides immediate gratification or pleasure, appealing to individuals with a hedonistic disposition to engage with and adopt elements of it into their behaviours. 'New horizons and options for self-realization' factor is associated with the exposure to different styles, ideas, and cultures through pop culture, which can expand individuals' horizons and offer new avenues for self-expression and personal growth. 'Trend-making' is connected to pop culture introducing new trends and concepts. Engaging with these trends can influence individuals' behaviours as they try to align with what is currently popular.

'Attractiveness' and 'hedonistic disposition' can interact, as content that provides instant gratification is likely to be more attractive to individuals seeking pleasure. "Behaviour comparison' and 'trend-making' can interact, as individuals might compare their behaviours to trends in pop culture and adjust their actions accordingly.

Exposure to academic subjects can lead to behavioural changes that extend beyond entertainment, shaping career interests and hobbies. Expanding or altering learning interests can lead to shifts in focus and motivation. If students find new interests, their engagement in learning may increase, enhancing learning outcomes. Conversely, changing interests might lead to disengagement and lower outcomes. Accessibility to learning resources and aids can enhance learning outcomes by providing students with diverse ways to understand concepts. Innovative study methods can improve students' engagement and comprehension, positively influencing learning outcomes. These methods might encourage active learning, collaboration, and creativity.

Group dynamics can impact learning outcomes. If isolation occurs, students might lack peer interaction and collaborative learning. On the other hand, group consolidation can lead to collective support and shared insights that enhance outcomes.

## 9.6 Exploring Feedback Loops and Resource Agent Interactions Within the System

Feedback loops play a crucial role in understanding how the main stocks and influencing variables interact within the system. Feedback loops describe the circular relationships where the changes in one variable influence changes in another, and these effects can create reinforcing or balancing dynamics.

For example, an increase in information overload can lead to lower learning outcomes, as students struggle to process excessive information. In turn, lower learning outcomes might prompt students to seek more information, potentially contributing to information overload. On the other side, increased engagement with pop culture might divert attention from learning, affecting learning outcomes. Low learning outcomes might lead to seeking entertainment in pop culture as an alternative, reinforcing the influence of pop culture.

High anxiety can contribute to a reduced attention span, making it harder to focus on studying. Decreased attention span due to anxiety can lead to lower learning outcomes, thus increasing anxiety related to academic performance. In addition, addictive behaviours can reduce attention span for studying, affecting learning outcomes. Reduced learning attention span might lead to seeking immediate gratification through social networks, reinforcing addictive behaviours.

High anxiety can lower self-esteem and confidence, negatively affecting learning outcomes. Poor learning outcomes can lead to feelings of inadequacy and anxiety, creating a reinforcing loop. Positive peer interactions and support can enhance learning outcomes. High learning outcomes might lead to more positive interactions and social support, reinforcing the positive learning environment.

Exposure to biased or false information can distort understanding, leading to lower learning outcomes. Lower learning outcomes might result in less critical thinking and a reduced ability to discern accurate information, reinforcing exposure to misinformation. On the other side, innovative study methods can enhance engagement and comprehension, leading to improved learning outcomes. Positive learning outcomes can encourage students to adopt innovative study methods, reinforcing effective learning practices.

These feedback loops illustrate how variables within the system interact with each other, either reinforcing certain trends or balancing out the effects. The dynamics of these loops can have significant implications for the overall impact of social networks on learning and education outcomes.

Figure 9.6 above represents how the system behaviour is influenced by agents and their behavioural routines. In this system, there are several main stocks, which represent accumulations of various societal and personal resources: 'anxiety', 'learning attention span', 'feel of addiction to social networks', 'pop culture and behavioural change', and 'learning outcomes'. These stocks of resources interact with each other through a complex web of feedback loops, within which agents' routines influence their levels over time through their associated rates of change.

Agents' routines can impact the 'anxiety' stock, through their intensity of use of social networks, attention span level, pop culture adoption, and time allocated for learning. The higher the tensions between social networks use, pop culture adoption, attention span levels and learning outcomes, the higher can go the level of anxiety. Agents' behaviours affect their 'learning attention span', which represents their ability to focus and learn for a period of time. Depending on agents level of use of abundant information and their anxiety levels, their learning attention span can decrease or increase, influencing their level of learning outcomes. Agents' behaviours contribute to the 'feel of addiction to social networks' stock. Agents who

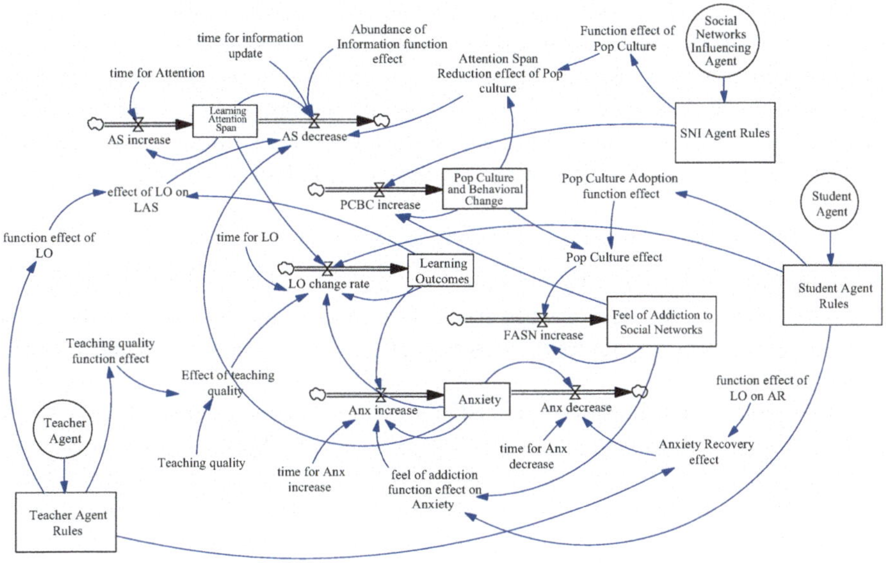


**Fig. 9.6** RAM of the social networks system effects

engage more with social networks contribute to an increase in this stock. Conversely, behavioural interventions aimed at reducing this addiction can contribute to decreasing this stock.

The 'pop culture and behavioural change' stock represents changes in societal norms and behaviours driven by pop culture. Agents' engagement with pop culture influences this stock positively or negatively. Higher engagement can lead to both positive and negative changes in behaviour, affecting other stocks like anxiety, learning outcomes, and addiction.

Agents' behaviours and their routines influence the 'learning outcomes', representing the overall educational achievements. Positive behaviours, including high learning attention spans and reduced anxiety, contribute to improving learning outcomes and vice versa.

Agents in this system are not passive; they interact with the stocks and with each other, shaping the dynamics of the entire system. Their behaviours create reinforcing loops that amplify trends, as well as balancing loops that counteract extreme behaviours. The agents' routines collectively contribute to the complex interactions among stocks, leading to dynamic changes in the system over time. To understand and manage this system effectively, policymakers and educators must consider how changes aiming at one stock or type of behavioural routine, can influence other stock and behavioural routines through feedback loops. Interventions aimed at improving learning outcomes or reducing anxiety, for instance, need to account for their potential impacts on other interconnected stocks and agents behavioural patterns. This perspective emphasizes the need for a holistic understanding of the system and the careful consideration of agents' behaviours and routines to achieve desired outcomes.

There are several behavioural decision heuristics that can influence the activity routines of the agents and subsequently impact the levels of the system stocks (Gilovich et al., 2002). Agents tend to imitate the behaviours of others, especially those they perceive as similar or influential. This can influence the adoption of behaviours related to 'pop culture and behavioural change', which in turn affects stocks like 'learning outcomes' and 'feel of addiction to social networks'.

Some of the main heuristics influencing agents behavioural routines include:

1. **Availability heuristic:** Agents may base their decisions on readily available information. This behavioural heuristic is amplified also by the 'abundance of information' stock, potentially influencing their learning attention span and anxiety levels.
2. **Anchoring and adjustment heuristic:** Agents often make decisions based on a reference point (anchor) and then adjust from there. This can influence agents' behaviour related to 'pop culture and behavioural change' and 'learning outcomes'. Agents may adjust their behaviours to manage the pop culture adoption in parallel with 'learning outcomes', thus affecting the levels of these stocks.
3. **Loss aversion heuristic:** Agents tend to avoid losses more than they seek gains. This can influence decisions related to 'feel of addiction to social networks'. If agents perceive that reducing their social network usage could lead to a loss of social connection, this might create tension, impacting the addiction stock.
4. **Confirmation bias:** Agents may seek information that confirms their existing beliefs and attitudes. This behaviour can be influenced by the 'abundance of information' stock, as agents may actively seek out information that aligns with their views, and can influence 'pop culture and behavioural change' stock, potentially reinforcing certain behaviours and attitudes.
5. **Temporal discounting heuristic:** Agents may prioritize immediate rewards over future benefits. This can affect the 'learning outcomes' stock, as agents might opt for short-term gratification (e.g. social media) over long-term investments in learning, influencing attention span and anxiety levels.
6. **Cognitive dissonance:** Agents experience discomfort when their actions contradict their beliefs. Agents may adjust their behaviours to align with their beliefs, potentially affecting stocks like 'feel of addiction to social networks' and 'pop culture and behavioural change'.

These heuristics represent simplified decision making algorithms that agents use to make decisions in complex environments (Kahneman & Tversky, 1979). They can significantly impact the dynamics of the system by shaping how agents engage with information, adopt behaviours, and interact with one another. Taking account of these heuristics can help for capturing more realistic agent behaviours and provide insights into how their decisions influence and are being influenced by the stocks and feedback loops in the system.

Agents and their activity routines are following a behavioural decision making protocol: IF certain condition is present, THEN the agent is doing a certain action. Here is an elaboration on the main agents, their activity routines, and decision-making protocol (Fig. 9.6).

**Main Agents**

1. **Students:** Students' behavioural routines are influenced by anxiety, learning attention span, motivation to learn, and addiction to social networks.
2. **Educators:** Teachers' behavioural routines may influence learning outcomes, motivation to learn, and anxiety through their teaching practices.
3. **Social influencers:** These agents' behavioural routines have influence on pop culture adoption and behavioural change, through influencing cultural and behavioural norms.

## 9.7 Creating Positive Change in the Education System

Changes in agents decisions and actions routines can create positive effects on the quality of the learning processes and education outcomes. For example, when students feeling of anxiety is high, they can be encouraged by the educators to engage in stress-reduction activities at school. If students' learning attention span is decreasing, then educators can use more inspirational content (e.g. interesting or motivational videos and other), in order to attract and hold students' attention on the taught subjects. In regard to issues related to addictive behaviour to social networks, educators can set designated time slots for social media usage.

If the quality of education outcomes is low, then teachers can incorporate interactive teaching methods in order to engage students more effectively. To cope with anxiety among students, schools can provide means for support and counselling resources.

Also, educators can incorporate real-world examples in lessons, which will increase the quality of education, positively affecting students' understanding and learning outcomes.

Designing lessons with relatable and practical applications will increase students' motivation to learn and actively engage in the education activities.

There can be opposition between the behavioural heuristics that influence social network interactions and those that influence teaching and learning outcomes. These oppositions arise due to the different goals, motivations, and cognitive biases that underlie these two sets of behaviours. Here are some potential oppositions that can be traced on the RAM on Fig. 9.6.

**Group Inclusion vs. Learning Goals**

- Social networks: Individuals on social networks might be driven by a desire for group inclusion, leading to conformity with popular trends or opinions.
- Teaching and learning: In the context of education, individuals' primary goal is often to achieve learning outcomes. This might involve adopting study techniques that are effective but not necessarily trendy or popular.

**Availability of Information vs. Evidence-Based Learning**

- Social networks: People on social networks often rely on the availability heuristic, where they make judgements based on the most easily available information. This can lead to the spread of misinformation and biased views.

- Teaching and learning: In education, evidence-based learning is important, where decisions are based on credible research and proven methods rather than what is most readily available or easily remembered.

**Social Herding vs. Individualized Learning**

- Social networks: The social herding heuristic can lead to the adoption of behaviours simply because others are doing it, even if it is not the best choice for an individual in respect to learning and education
- Teaching and learning: Effective education recognizes that each student has unique learning needs and preferences. Individualized learning strategies are designed to cater to these differences.

**Social Validation vs. Personal Motivation**

- Social networks: Individuals often seek social validation from their peers, which can lead to behaviours that are designed to elicit positive reactions from others.
- Teaching and learning: A focus on personal motivation involves striving for personal improvement and achievement, rather than seeking validation from others.

These oppositions highlight the potential challenges in aligning behaviours driven by social networks with behaviours that contribute to effective teaching and learning outcomes. Balancing these influences requires careful consideration of the motivations and biases driving each set of behaviours.

In turn, the social influencers might prioritize content and actions that are likely to attract more followers and increase their online popularity. They might align their content with current trends and popular topics to engage their audience and stay relevant. Also they might focus on creating visually appealing content, as visually stimulating content tends to attract more attention on social media platforms.

Each group employs behavioural heuristics which are associated with their personal goals and habits. For example, teachers might stick to traditional teaching methods, not realizing that students' anxiety levels affect their learning differently. Teachers may adjust teaching styles occasionally, but not consistently, to cater to students' attention spans. Teachers might cautiously incorporate pop culture references, fearing that it might dilute the academic focus. Teachers may tolerate plagiarism over original learning content, reinforcing demotivation and frustration among true learners. In addition, teachers may assign deliberately homework with timelines that inadvertently increase anxiety and can disrupt students' sleep patterns.

Because of inappropriate teaching behaviour, students might attempt to multitask while studying, frequently toggling between academic tasks and social media. Also, they could experience anxiety and demotivation due to competition associated teaching and learning methods, triggering an anti-dopamine response and dissatisfaction. As a counter response, students might engage in increased and even late-night interactions on social networks, contributing to insomnia related effects.

On the other side, influencers may share aspects of their lives selectively, concealing anxiety to maintain their image and attract higher number of followers. Influencers might share stories of their achievements, concealing struggles with anxiety. Influencers could incorporate trending pop culture elements to gain wider audience engagement. Influencers might schedule posts late at night, capitalizing on followers who are active during those hours.

These real behavioural patterns highlight how teachers, students, and social influencers might naturally react to specified phenomena, influenced by their individual inclinations, goals, habits, and limitations. It is important to recognize that individual behaviour can vary widely, and not all agents will conform strictly to these behavioural patterns. Increased reliance on social media can lead to decreased attention span, reduced study time, and increased anxiety due to information overload and comparison with others. In addition, the pressure to perform well academically, often showcased on social media, can exacerbate students' anxiety levels. Over-reliance on virtual interactions and reduced face-to-face communication due to social media use can provoke a feeling of social isolation. Engaging predominantly with content that aligns with existing beliefs can reinforce cognitive biases and hinder critical thinking.

On another perspective, social networks can provide quick access to educational resources, research, and news, enhancing students' knowledge and learning outcomes. Online communities and study groups on social media platforms can offer emotional support, collaboration, and opportunities for sharing insights. Well-designed educational content integrated with pop culture references can enhance engagement and make learning more relatable. Exposure to various viewpoints and cultures through social networks can broaden students' horizons and promote open-mindedness. Collaboration with peers on social platforms can encourage group learning, knowledge sharing, and the exchange of ideas. Constructive feedback and positive validation from peers and mentors on social media can boost motivation and self-esteem. Teachers and educators can use social networks to share teaching materials, strategies, and best practices, supporting the teaching and learning process. Discussions around anxiety on social media can raise awareness and encourage seeking support. Interaction with individuals from around the world on social networks can facilitate cross-cultural learning and understanding.

## References


Cai, Y., Ma, J., & Chen, Q. (2020). Higher education in innovation ecosystems. *Sustainability (Switzerland), 12*(11). https://doi.org/10.3390/su12114376

Carnoy, M. (1999). Globalization and educational reform: What planners need to know? *Fundamentals of Educational Planning*.

Carstens, D. S., Doss, S. K., Kies, S. C., & Bisk, N. M. (2018). Social media impact on attention span. *The Journal of Management and Engineering Integration, 11*(1).

Dickens, W. T., Sawhill, I. V., & Tebbs, J. (2006). *The effects of investing in early education on economic growth* (pp. 1–26). Brookings Institution.

Fareri, D. S., Martin, L. N., & Delgado, M. R. (2008). Reward-related processing in the human brain: Developmental considerations. *Development and Psychopathology, 20*(4). https://doi.org/10.1017/S0954579408000576

Fox, J., & Moreland, J. J. (2015). The dark side of social networking sites: An exploration of the relational and psychological stressors associated with Facebook use and affordances. *Computers in Human Behavior, 45*. https://doi.org/10.1016/j.chb.2014.11.083

Gilovich, T., Griffin, D., & Kahneman, D. (2002). Heuristics and biases: The psychology of intuitive judgment. *Academy of Management Review, 29*(4).

Goczek, Ł., Witkowska, E., & Witkowski, B. (2021). How does education quality affect economic growth? *Sustainability (Switzerland), 13*(11). https://doi.org/10.3390/su13116437

Gok, T. (2016). The effects of social networking sites on students' studying and habits. *International Journal of Research in Education and Science, 2*(1). https://doi.org/10.21890/ijres.10682

Hanushek, E. A. (2016). Will more higher education improve economic growth? *Oxford Review of Economic Policy, 32*(4). https://doi.org/10.1093/oxrep/grw025

Hanushek, E. A., & Kimko, D. D. (2000). Schooling, labor-force quality, and the growth of nations. *American Economic Review, 90*(5). https://doi.org/10.1257/aer.90.5.1184

Hanushek, E. A., & Woessmann, L. (2021). Schooling, cognitive skills, and the Latin American growth puzzle. *SSRN Electronic Journal*. https://doi.org/10.2139/ssrn.1515123

Hanushek, & Wößmann. (2007). Schooling, labor-force quality, and the growth of nations. *The American Economic Review, 90*(5).

Jahic, H., & Pilav-Velic, A. (2021). Measuring returns on Investment in Education: Lessons for sustainable and innovative education policy. *Interdisciplinary Description of Complex Systems, 19*(2). https://doi.org/10.7906/indecs.19.2.2

Kahneman, D., & Tversky, A. (1979). Prospect theory: An analysis of decision under risk Daniel Kahneman; Amos Tversky. *Econometrica, 47*(2), 263–292. https://doi.org/10.1111/j.1536-7150.2011.00774.x

Kahneman, D., & Tversky, A. (1982). The simulation heuristic. Judgment under Uncertainty: Heuristics and Biases, (pp. 201–208). https://doi.org/10.1093/oxfordhb/9780195376746.013.0038.

Kong, D., Zhang, B., & Zhang, J. (2022). Higher education and corporate innovation. *Journal of Corporate Finance, 72*. https://doi.org/10.1016/j.jcorpfin.2022.102165

Lim, J., & Richardson, J. C. (2016). Exploring the effects of students' social networking experience on social presence and perceptions of using SNSs for educational purposes. *Internet and Higher Education, 29*. https://doi.org/10.1016/j.iheduc.2015.12.001

Lizardo, O. (2008). The question of culture consumption and stratification revisited. *Sociologica, 2*(2).

Macit, H. B., Macit, G., & Güngör, O. (2018). A research on social media addiction and dopamine driven feedback. *Mehmet Akif Ersoy Üniversitesi İktisadi ve İdari Bilimler Fakültesi Dergisi, 5*(3). https://doi.org/10.30798/makuiibf.435845

Maria Sandi, A. (1991). Investing in the future: Setting educational priorities in the developing world. *Futures, 23*(2). https://doi.org/10.1016/0016-3287(91)90033-x

Ohiagu, O. P., & Okorie, V. O. (2014). Social media: Shaping and transmitting popular culture. *Covenant Journal of Communication, 2*(1).

Parks, R. F., Lowry, P. B., Wigand, R. T., Agarwal, N., & Williams, T. L. (2018). Why students engage in cyber-cheating through a collective movement: A case of deviance and collusion. *Computers and Education*, 125. https://doi.org/10.1016/j.compedu.2018.04.003

Paul, J. A., Baker, H. M., & Cochran, J. D. (2012). Effect of online social networking on student academic performance. *Computers in Human Behavior, 28*(6). https://doi.org/10.1016/j.chb.2012.06.016

Phillipson, C., Allan, G., & Morgan, D. (2017). Social networks and social exclusion: Sociological and policy perspectives. *Social Networks and Social Exclusion: Sociological and Policy Perspectives*. https://doi.org/10.4324/9781315242897

Psacharopoulos, G., & Patrinos, H. A. (2018). Returns to investment in education: A decennial review of the global literature. *Education Economics, 26*(5). https://doi.org/10.1080/09645292.2018.1484426

Rafique, S., Khan, M. H., & Bilal, H. (2022). A critical analysis of pop culture and media. *Global Regional Review, VII*(I). https://doi.org/10.31703/grr.2022(vii-i).17

Sahnoun, M., & Abdennadher, C. (2022). Returns to investment in education in the OECD countries: Does governance quality matter? *Journal of the Knowledge Economy, 13*(3). https://doi.org/10.1007/s13132-021-00783-0

Smith, K. P., & Christakis, N. A. (2008). Social networks and health. *Annual Review of Sociology, 34*. https://doi.org/10.1146/annurev.soc.34.040507.134601

Tandon, A., Kaur, P., Dhir, A., & Mäntymäki, M. (2020). Sleepless due to social media? Investigating problematic sleep due to social media and social media sleep hygiene. *Computers in Human Behavior, 113*. https://doi.org/10.1016/j.chb.2020.106487

Vernon, L., Barber, B. L., & Modecki, K. L. (2015). Adolescent problematic social networking and school experiences: The mediating effects of sleep disruptions and sleep quality. *Cyberpsychology, Behavior, and Social Networking, 18*(7). https://doi.org/10.1089/cyber.2015.0107

Vevere, V., & Mons, A. (2020). Applying behavioural economics in education: Study of undergraduate practices of selecting higher educational institutions. SHS Web of conferences, (p. 74). https://doi.org/10.1051/shsconf/20207401035.

Vural, O. F. (2015). Positive and negative aspects of using social networks in higher education: A focus group study. *Educational Research and Reviews, 10*(8).

Wilson, T. D., Aronson, E., & Carlsmith, K. (2010). The art of laboratory experimentation. In *Handbook of social psychology*. https://doi.org/10.1002/9780470561119.socpsy001002.

Wilson, T. D., Reinhard, D. A., Westgate, E. C., Gilbert, D. T., Ellerbeck, N., Hahn, C., Brown, C. L., & Shaked, A. (2014). Just think: The challenges of the disengaged mind. *Science, 345*(6192). https://doi.org/10.1126/science.1250830

The manufacturer's authorised representative in the EU is Springer Nature Customer Service Centre GmbH, Europaplatz 3, 69115 Heidelberg, Germany. If you have any concerns regarding our products, please contact ProductSafety@springernature.com

Printed and bound by CPI Group (UK) Ltd, Croydon, CR0 4YY
01/10/2026
02225904-0003